Via Ports

Echoes: Classics of
Hong Kong Culture and History

Series General Editor: Robert Nield

The life of Hong Kong and its region has been explored in a vast number of books. They include ground-breaking scholarly studies of great standing, and literary works that shed light on people, places and events. Many of these books unfortunately are no longer available to the general reader.

The aim of the Echoes series is once more to make available the best of those books that would otherwise be lost. The series will embrace not only history, but also memoirs, fiction, politics, natural history and other subjects. The focal point will be Hong Kong, but the series will extend to places connected with the city or sharing some of its experiences. In this way we hope to bring a growing number of classic publications to a new and wider readership.

Other titles in the Echoes series:

Anglo-China: Chinese People and British Rule in Hong Kong, 1841–1880
Christopher Munn

A Biographical Sketch-Book of Early Hong Kong
G. B. Endacott with new introduction by John M. Carroll

Chinese Christians: Elites, Middlemen, and the Church in Hong Kong
Carl T. Smith with new introduction by Christopher Munn

City of Broken Promises
Austin Coates

Edge of Empires: Chinese Elites and British Colonials in Hong Kong
John M. Carroll

Macao and the British, 1637–1842: Prelude to Hong Kong
Austin Coates

A Macao Narrative
Austin Coates

Power and Charity: A Chinese Merchant Elite in Colonial Hong Kong (with a new preface)
Elizabeth Sinn

The Road
Austin Coates

The Taking of Hong Kong: Charles and Clara Elliot in China Waters
Susanna Hoe and Derek Roebuck

Thistle and Bamboo: The Life and Times of Sir James Stewart Lockhart
Shiona Airlie

Via Ports

From Hong Kong to Hong Kong

Alexander Grantham

With a new introduction by Lord Wilson of Tillyorn

香港大學出版社
HONG KONG UNIVERSITY PRESS

Hong Kong University Press
14/F Hing Wai Centre
7 Tin Wan Praya Road
Aberdeen
Hong Kong
www.hkupress.org

First published in 1965 by Hong Kong University Press.

ISBN 978-988-8083-85-5

British Library Cataloguing-in-Publication Data
A catalogue record for this book is available from the British Library.

10   9   8   7   6   5   4   3   2   1

Printed and bound by Liang Yu Printing Factory Ltd. in Hong Kong, China

TO
MAURINE

AUTHOR'S NOTE

HONG KONG newspapers frequently contain shipping notices announcing the sailing of such and such a vessel from Hong Kong to London, or wherever it is, VIA PORTS. The voyage which this book describes starts in Hong Kong and ends there; the ports visited are those colonies in which I served: Bermuda, Jamaica, Nigeria and Fiji and the Western Pacific, as well, of course, as Hong Kong.

I did not keep a diary and I made no notes. For my story I have relied mainly on my memory which, at times, may be at fault, but only, I believe, on points of detail. I have recounted, and commented on, those happenings that remain foremost in my mind.

CONTENTS

ILLUSTRATIONS

Sir Alexander Grantham, G.C.M.G., Governor of Hong Kong, 1947–1957

1. The author and W. R. Scott at Macau 1923

2. The author and his future wife outside General Munthe's house in Peking 1925

3. General Munthe

4. The author and wife with Tags and Philip at 'La Garza'

5. 'La Garza', Bermuda

6. Tennis in Jamaica. Author second from right

7a. Government House, Lagos

7b. Chieftain with retainers at garden party, Government House, Lagos

8. The Lodge, Lagos

9a. Government House, Suva, Fiji

9b. 'Retreat', Government House, Suva

10a. Presentation of *yangona* at the Fijian ceremony welcoming a new governor

10b. A Fijian *bure*

11. Welcome by school children, Marakei, Gilbert Islands

12. *Maneaba* at Abaokoro, Tarawa

13a. With Queen Salote at Tonga, with Prince Tungi at extreme left

13b. With Prime Minister Ata of Tonga

14a. Feast at Tonga

14b. A Tongan *tapa* cloth

15a. Inspecting guard of honour on arrival in Hong Kong, 1947

15b. The author, Bishop R. O. Hall and Mr T. W. Kwok

16. Government House, Hong Kong

INTRODUCTION TO THE PAPERBACK EDITION

Hong Kong owes a great deal to Sir Alexander Grantham. He was the territory's longest serving Governor until exceeded, by the short period of one month, by another of Hong Kong's great post-War Governors, Sir Murray MacLehose (later Lord MacLehose of Beoch). Grantham took over as Governor after the brief return of Sir Mark Young, who had the great misfortune to arrive in Hong Kong in the summer of 1941 and be forced to surrender to the invading Japanese army on Christmas Day that year. Sir Alexander it was who steered Hong Kong through recovery from the depredations of the war years; through spill-over into Hong Kong of the ending of China's Civil War with the victory of the Communist Party in 1949; and into the years when Hong Kong, perforce, had to transform itself from a trading entrepôt into a manufacturer in its own right.

Grantham was well prepared for his task. He was one of the few governors who had started his career as a cadet in the Hong Kong civil service. As such he had two years of training in Cantonese in Canton (Guangzhou) and Macao, followed by over ten years in the Hong Kong administration, mostly within the central Government Secretariat. He wryly records that his most senior post was as Extra Assistant Colonial Secretary.

Grantham also had wide experience of colonies other than Hong Kong, serving in Bermuda, Jamaica and Nigeria, and as Governor of Fiji. But it is Grantham's life after he returned to Hong Kong in 1947 that is both the summit of his career and likely to be of most interest to a present-day reader of his memoir.

Grantham was a pragmatist. He brought to his governorship an unstuffy attitude to administration and an understanding of the dynamic of change taking place in modern China. As China fell apart in the last years of the Civil War and then was pulled together again after the Communist victory, he took the view, far in advance of his contemporaries, that China was bound to become the dominant power in the region. He also believed that, at some point, Hong Kong was bound to return to the control of Mainland China. This, he was sure, would mean the whole territory. He did not think it conceivable that China would ever renew the lease to the New Territories.

Meanwhile, he also saw it as crucial that the Hong Kong Government both had to be, and be seen to be in the eyes of the people of Hong Kong, in charge of what went on in the territory. Both before 1949, in dealing with the Nationalists, and after 1949, when the victorious Communist army had reached but never crossed the border, that meant a constantly balanced policy of avoiding if possible anything that might be seen by the new Government of China as a provocative use of Hong Kong's territory and, at the same time, resisting any demands from that quarter that might be seen as undermining the authority of the Hong Kong Government. Nationalist agents were quietly shipped back to Taiwan. So too, after a sufficient lapse of time to allow passions to subside, was a Nationalist aircraft which made a forced landing in Hong Kong after being shot up by the Chinese Air Force while carrying out intelligence probes along the China coast and whose surrender was demanded by the Chinese authorities.

Grantham, with the help of his advisers, both Hong Kong Chinese and expatriate civil servants, was a master of the art of how a small territory, with the anachronistic title of colony, could survive on the coast of a huge country ruled by a government with a communist ideology and both the emotion and rhetoric of anti-imperialism and anti-colonialism. The riots of 1956, with Nationalist supporters fighting Communist supporters and the police losing control, showed all too clearly what could go wrong when the right balance was lost.

Similar pragmatism determined domestic policy towards such issues as housing. Refugees poured into Hong Kong in the last stages of China's Civil War and immediately after the Communist victory. At first it was thought that the tide would flow back again as it had in the past. By 1950 it was clear that history was not going to repeat itself in this instance and the border was closed. The disastrous fire among squatter housing at Shek Kip Mei on Christmas Day 1955 showed that the Hong Kong Government had to do something about housing its now vastly expanded population. So, with the Legislative Council approving a policy that all squatters must be housed, and an estimated one in three of the population needing rehousing either as squatters or slum dwellers, the laissez-faire capitalist government of Hong Kong launched what must be one of the largest government housing project in the world. The results are recognisable prominently, over fifty years later, in the massive amount of public housing built and controlled by Hong Kong's Housing Authority.

Grantham spends little time in his memoir dealing with the issue of constitutional reform. That is probably a fair reflection of how small a part it played in his thinking compared with all the other immediate crises he faced, including the U.N. embargo on trade with Mainland China arising out of the Korean War. Sir Mark Young had floated relatively modest ideas for change in keeping with the sort of developments happening in other British colonies in the aftermath of the War. With all the turmoil swirling round Hong Kong before and after the Communist victory in 1949, Grantham thought that any attempt at substantial reform would be seriously destabilising. Those looking back from the vantage point of Hong Kong's later wrestling with the issue of improving representative government, tend to see this as a significant moment that put reform off the agenda for many years thereafter. At the time Grantham understandably regarded placing reform in cold storage as a minor issue in comparison with his larger objective of putting Hong Kong on its feet after the destruction of the Second World War and keeping it steady through all the storms that followed.

These are gentle memoirs, affectionate rather than analytical. Grantham is as inclined to record the comment of a British soldier in the New Territories, complaining that those providing the food had failed to de-bone the kippers, as he is to complain about Whitehall officials sometimes treating the Crown Colony as a sub-department of the Colonial Office. But what he writes gives a very good flavour of his time in Hong Kong and the ethos of those in the Colonial Service, both before and after the War. As for the bones in the historical fish, the historians can now pick at those, in detail and at their leisure, in the government papers now open to all in the U.K. Government's National Archives.

Grantham did an immense amount for Hong Kong. He left behind many reminders of his time in office. One was the naming of the Governor's suitably old-fashioned launch, which lived on until 1997 and in which governors, at the beginning and end of their tours of duty, made their ceremonial arrivals and departures. It was called *The Lady Maurine*, named after Sir Alexander Grantham's American wife, whom he had met when visiting Peking in 1925. *The Lady Maurine*, like the work done by Sir Alexander, lived on for many years after what was clearly an emotional departure in 1957 when he wondered whether he was "going home" or "leaving home".

David Wilson (Lord Wilson of Tillyorn)
Edinburgh
November 2011

PART ONE

Pre-war Days

CHAPTER ONE

HONG KONG, 1922–1935

O N a bright December morning in 1922, a few days before Christmas, the good ship *City of York* was steaming through the China Sea as she approached Hong Kong. On deck stood two new Cadets of the government administration, Thomas Megarry and myself, eagerly watching the approach to our destination and admiring the panorama of sea and sky and land spread out before us. Now the vessel passed Lyemun, the narrow entrance to the harbour. On one side, lay the island of Hong Kong with its chain of hills culminating in Victoria Peak 1,800 feet above the city of Victoria. On the other, stretched the mainland with the 'Nine Dragons', another range of mountains, forming a splendid backdrop to the twin city of Kowloon. We knew that the harbour, enclosed between the island and the mainland, was one of the finest in the world, but were not prepared for the beauty or the bustling activity. Ocean liners lay alongside the Kowloon wharves, ships flying the flags of many nations and coastal and river steamers from Canton and inland ports of China —their names painted in English letters and Chinese characters— strained at buoys in the stream, loading and unloading cargoes, junks with bat's-wing sails skimmed the water, ferries shuttled to and fro, while launches, whistling and tooting, darted hither and thither on their busy errands: a veritable arena of maritime commerce. It was exhilarating and, strangely enough, seemed to harmonize with the quiet majesty of the hills: nature and man not in conflict but complementing each other. The harbour is the very heart of the city and, as we learnt later, even when not visible to the eye, makes its presence felt.

But as the ship tied up at the dock side, we had to concentrate on the business of getting ourselves and our baggage ashore, for no one had come to meet us. Rival gangs of coolies disputed for the privilege of carrying our impedimenta and mulcting two innocents abroad. They spoke no English, we spoke no Chinese; however, we managed to make them understand that we wanted to cross the harbour to Hong Kong. It was indicated we should get into rickshaws, which we obediently did and started off, whilst they jog-trotted behind with our trunks and bags slung from poles. The rickshaw-pullers deposited us at the ferry terminal whence we crossed to the

Hong Kong side by a double-ended 'Star' ferryboat, a five-minute journey. From the ferry one gets a comprehensive view of Hong Kong, and as we drew nearer we saw that the city begins at the very water's edge with commercial buildings, banks and shops—many with arcaded verandahs—occupying the narrow strip of level land on the water-front, beyond which the ground rose steeply. Houses now took over, becoming fewer and more scattered on the higher slopes until on the topmost ridge we espied many elegant residences. This was the Peak district, at that time reserved for Europeans. I felt that whatever lay in store for me in my new job, I should at least be surrounded by beauty.

With some difficulty, we found our way to the Hong Kong Hotel and paid off the baggage-coolies, having been bullied into giving them double the proper amount. This was the best hotel in the Colony but we felt we could afford it with our princely salaries of £250 a year. The next step was to report ourselves at the Colonial Secretary's Office. Accordingly, the hotel porter put us in sedan-chairs and, proceeding along Queen's Road, we observed with fascination the jumble of cars, rickshaws, bicycles, coolies carrying loads and pedestrians, and caught glimpses of narrow streets that seemed to go straight up the mountain side—one being appropriately named Ladder Street. And so up Battery Path with its banyan trees and fern-covered banks above the hurly-burly of the street. Soon, all too soon, for I was feeling as nervous as on my first day at school, the chair-bearers put us down at the C.S.O. Two new boys were about to enter the headmaster's study for their first interview. But the friendliness of our reception, accompanied by apologies for the failure to have us met—the despatch from London giving the date of the ship's arrival had been overlooked—quickly put us at ease. We learnt that we should be going to Canton to study Cantonese for two years and our departure was arranged for a few days hence. This gave us time to explore Hong Kong and to do a little shopping.

Outstanding in my memory is the ride on the Peak Tram, a cable car that goes 1,200 feet above sea level and in those days the only means of reaching the Peak, unless one had the energy to walk up the very steep Peak Road on which cars were prohibited. At the upper terminus one either walked or took a rickshaw or sedan-chair. With the absence of noise it was peaceful and soothing whilst the views were superb. From one side we gazed over the city and harbour, the muffled sounds of which reached us faintly from below. On the other, we saw distant islands rising from a glass-like sea in a crimson sunset, and after dark the myriad lights of fishing junks like fairy lamps.

CANTON AND MACAU

Canton, about a hundred miles up the Pearl River, could be reached by train in four hours, but most people chose the comfortable river steamers which took eight hours, either going by the night-boat and sleeping on board, or by the day-boat. I preferred the day-boat, as the scenery was delightful, especially in the early evening when toilers in the fields and the fishermen in their boats wended their way homeward. It reminded me of eighteenth and nineteenth century engravings of oriental scenes. Those engravings may not be as accurate as a photograph but they are far more expressive of the spirit of the places they depict.

To Canton I would hardly apply the adjective 'beautiful': 'exciting' would be more appropriate. It bustles with activity, even more than Hong Kong. The river and the river-front are a perfect bedlam of noise. At all hours of the day and night, junks, tow-boats, stern-wheelers, river steamers and launches come and go with cargoes of goods and animals being loaded or unloaded and passengers getting on and off, to the accompaniment of yelling and shouting, blowing of steamers' whistles and the squealing of pigs and squawking of chickens. Away from the water-front the activity is almost as great but the noises are different.

Originally, Canton had been encircled by massive walls and had no motor roads, the principal streets being not much more than twelve feet wide and paved with large uneven granite blocks. By 1922, most of the walls had been demolished and broad thorough-fares driven through the city. Along these, cars would dash at reckless speed, their horns blowing ceaselessly, and woe betide any pedestrian or rickshaw unlucky enough to get in the way. These however were only the main avenues and most of the picturesque streets remained. Many of them consisted of shops selling the same kind of merchan-dise; a street for silk, one for ivory, another for silverware or jewellery and jade, as well as streets where more practical commodities such as rice or firewood could be bought. The gold-lettered signs of the shops and the bolts of richly coloured brocades and satins in Silk Street made a particularly gay sight.

About half a dozen of the Cadets lived in the 'Yamen', the residence in Manchu days of the military governor, consisting of two old rambling buildings and a gate-keeper's lodge in about two acres of ground surrounded by a wall, and reached by the narrow

'Flowery Pagoda Street' that led to a pagoda. Although right in the middle of the noisy city, it had an air of quiet, rather like the Temple in London. The rest of the Cadets lived on Shameen, a strip of land about three-quarters of a mile long and a third of a mile wide, separated from the city on three sides by a narrow creek, the third side being the Pearl River. In those days, Shameen was an international settlement with its own governing body which kept the place beautifully clean in contrast to the rest of Canton. Most of the consulates and foreign business firms were located here; a little bit of Europe tacked on to a Chinese city. I was glad I lived at the Yamen and not on Shameen.

To concentrate on one language to the exclusion of everything else should result at the end of two years in a high degree of fluency in speaking, reading and writing, even if the accent be not perfect. But Chinese is a very difficult language for foreigners, and of all the dialects Cantonese is the hardest. To make matters worse, few of the teachers—we had to find our own—had any idea of teaching. I suppose I am average in the matter of languages, and I worked hard and passed all my examinations; nevertheless when I had finished I could do no more than make myself understood when shopping, read the easiest parts of a Chinese newspaper and write a simple letter very ungrammatically. I was incapable of carrying on a social conversation without losing the thread after a few minutes. About twenty years later when Governor of Fiji, I thought I would try my Cantonese on a Chinese storekeeper in one of the outlying villages. He listened to me in polite bewilderment for a few minutes and then said, 'More better you speak English'. A few Europeans have a flair for Cantonese even though they have not learnt it as children, which is the easiest and best way, but they are rare. In my days, too much stress was laid on writing and reading, instead of on speaking. This fault has since been corrected.

Despite the fact that we took our studies seriously—or most of us did—we had plenty of time for play. Some of us bought ponies, which cost little. I paid 15 shillings for mine. We would ride out into the country; our favourite rendezvous being the White Cloud Mountain, on the way to which was an ancient monastery where we would hob-nob with the monks. During the hot summer months we started off as soon as it was light. We were, however, not the only early birds, for this was the time of day when the city night-soil was carried to the fields outside the city. Following a train of coolies with their buckets was a very odoriferous proceeding, but one gets used to most things, even smells. Once or twice we got into the crossfire of contending sides in a local civil war and, with bullets whistling about us, hastily withdrew.

Provided we passed our examinations at the specified six-monthly intervals, the authorities in Hong Kong did not bother us, and we never dreamed of asking for permission to absent ourselves. On one occasion a Police Cadet had gone on a British cruiser as the guest of the captain, his cousin, to Weihaiwei, whence he went to Peking. Unfortunately, the Hong Kong Commissioner of Police happened to be staying at the same hotel and asked Scott what he was doing there; was he not supposed to be studying Cantonese in Canton and not mandarin in Peking? Luckily for Scott the Commissioner was a kindly man with a sense of humour.

After I had been in Canton for about nine months the Hong Kong government decided to rebuild part of the Yamen which meant that two of us had to move elsewhere. So Scott and I chose to go to the Portuguese colony of Macau rather than to Shameen.

Macau is four hours by river steamer from Hong Kong and double that distance from Canton. Canton is the apex of the triangle of which Hong Kong and Macau are the eastern and western base points respectively. We took with us our boys, cook and coolies, our furniture, our ponies, our dog Wendy, and our cats, Gin and Bitters. We must have been quite a sight going through the streets of Canton and as it started to rain, my boy hopefully held an umbrella over the mattresses on which were crouching in utter misery Gin and Bitters.

Macau is quite different from either Hong Kong or Canton. Most of the people are Chinese as they are in Hong Kong and entirely so in Canton, but there are more Eurasians—Macanese. The climate also is much the same, hot and muggy in summer, cool or cold and sunny in winter, but there the similarity ends. The Portuguese have been in Macau for four hundred years and their imprint is distinct. Many of the narrow streets with vine-covered buildings and houses—some pink, others blue, white or green—suggest the Mediterranean rather than the Orient. Time, also, has left Macau behind, for the founding of Hong Kong with its natural deep-water harbour spelt the death knell of Macau as a commercial port. The liveliness of Hong Kong and the raucousness of Canton are absent. Instead one sees the gilded youth leaning against the Senate building or elderly Macanese languidly taking the air under the banyan trees along the graceful crescent of the Praya Grande. The impression Macau made on me then—and still did when I revisited it a quarter of a century later—was that of a once beautiful *grande dame* whose youth and vivacity had been left behind but whose grace and charm still remained. I have a very soft spot in my heart for Macau.

In my young days Macau was notorious for its gambling and its opium. The great gambling game was fantan. The croupier would have in front of him a pile of cash—a small Chinese coin about the size of a farthing—from which he would take out a handful or two and proceed to count them out in fours with a chopstick. Bets would be laid as to whether one, two or three or no cash would be left over after he had finished counting. I thought it rather a dull game. Moreover, fantan houses were not in the least romantic or glamorous. We only went when we had visitors from Hong Kong, and the sole attraction from our point of view was that drinks were on the house. Both the Macau and the Hong Kong governments operated opium monopolies, but whereas the Macau monopoly was farmed out, in Hong Kong the government itself sold the opium, the declared object being to discourage the pernicious habit of opium smoking and indirectly to raise revenue. Accordingly the price of opium was fixed at a high figure, well above that of the black market, whilst possession of non-government opium was a criminal offence. Unfortunately, this resulted in a flourishing black market, which sold below the price of government opium and which consequently was much patronized by the poorer folk, who thereby became criminals. One year the government decided to be more realistic and drastically reduced the price of its opium. Immediately the black market was killed; the sales of government opium went up and the courts were emptied of persons charged with opium offences. The quantity of opium smoked and the number of smokers remained the same. But as soon as the government's action came to the notice of well-meaning but not very practical people in England, pressure was brought to bear on the Colonial Office which peremptorily ordered the Hong Kong government to revert to the previous price. The order had, of course, to be obeyed; once again the police courts were filled with opium offenders and the black market came back to life. I always thought too little common sense was talked and written about opium. Taken in excess it is harmful, but so is alcohol. Just as the British working man likes his pint of beer at the end of a day's work, so the Chinese coolie likes his puff or two of opium. The sale of government opium has long since been abolished and to possess opium is an offence; but the evil of the drug traffic persists, with the difference that instead of opium, heroin, a derivative of opium and much more harmful, has become the habit. It would perhaps have been wiser not to have prohibited opium smoking entirely, but to have controlled the sale realistically and to have dealt severely with trafficking in heroin and similar drugs.

Scott and I enjoyed our time in Macau at our little two-storeyed semi-detached house at No. 11 Aerea Preta, or as the Chinese called it 'Hak Sha Wan' (Black Sand Beach), a rickshaw ride of about twenty minutes out of town. We worked diligently at our studies but got in a good deal of riding, going across into China for the purpose, since Macau is small—about 2½ square miles—with nowhere to hack. Passports or anything of that kind were unnecessary. We simply rode along the beach from our house; one moment we were in Portuguese territory, the next in China. Unfortunately our riding came to an untimely end when bandits started shooting at us from behind rocks. I gave my pony to a friend who soon tired of him. Failing to find anyone who, I considered, would be a kind master, I came to the reluctant conclusion that the only thing to do was to destroy him; so very early one morning I took him to a vacant square and shot him with a revolver, hurrying away as soon as the deed was done. I have often wondered what the street cleaners said when they came upon a dead pony in the middle of the town. I expect that what actually happened was that an enterprising Chinese butcher cut him up for meat. Scott was lucky enough to find a good owner for his pony in Hong Kong.

We had one very severe and unpleasant typhoon in Macau. I was patiently waiting for my teacher, wondering why he did not come. I soon knew the reason, for the sky became overcast and the wind whipped itself up to a gale—a velocity of 120 miles an hour was recorded. Our house faced on to a road on the far side of which was a low sea-wall, then the beach and the sea. Normally the sea was calm and, even half a mile or more from the shore, had a depth of less than six feet. When the typhoon was at its height, however, waves were breaking against the front of the house and we had to pile up beds and furniture against the French windows to prevent their being blown in. The ponies stabled in the backyard were almost submerged. Most uncanny was the lull as the centre of the typhoon passed over the Colony. After all was over, we discovered that our road had been washed away and for three weeks we had no electricity or water. The only other really bad storm I have experienced was in Hong Kong a few years later. In the space of eight hours, twenty inches of rain fell, accompanied by continuous thunder and lightning in terrific crashes and flashes which made the night like day. We almost thought the end of the world had come and I did not meet anyone the next day who could say he had not been frightened. Much damage was caused by the rush of water down the steep hill-sides, dislodging rocks and boulders which went hurtling down, smashing everything in their path.

PEKING

Early in 1925 I passed my final examination in Cantonese and obtained leave to visit my mother and stepfather, General Munthe, in Peking. He and my mother had married after the First World War in which my father had been killed. General Munthe, a man of character, was a striking looking person with the piercing blue eyes of a Norseman and the largest moustache I have ever seen. He came out to China in the eighties of the last century to join the Chinese Customs Service, and during the Boxer uprising in 1900 had organized the first international train that got through from Tientsin to relieve the hard-pressed foreign legations in Peking. Later he became adviser to Yüan Shih-k'ai, the first president of China, and was now head of the Legation Quarter police—all Chinese, but with their white leggings and smart appearance conspicuously different from the regular police. He spoke mandarin faultlessly and over the years had acquired a considerable knowledge of things Chinese, and had built up a large collection of pictures, porcelains and sculptures. Even now, each day after luncheon, two or three art dealers were ushered into the drawing-room to display some special treasures and often, when they left, another object would be added to the collection. Of particular fascination was a bronze bowl—I do not recollect of what dynasty—standing in the drawing-room that occasionally gave out a clear ring, even though nothing and no one had touched it. Was some spirit trying to convey a message? Part of the collection is now in the museum at Bergen, my stepfather's birth-place, and part—the General Munthe Collection—in a museum in Los Angeles.

When my ship arrived at Shanghai I learnt that the train service to Peking was disrupted owing to a civil war. In disgust I booked a passage back to Hong Kong, but at the last moment managed to secure a berth on an overcrowded Japanese steamer going by a roundabout route to Tientsin, whence I got a train that in eight hours instead of the usual three eventually reached Peking.

Peking impressed me enormously. Enclosed within the massive Tartar Wall, pierced at intervals by great gates, broad avenues run north and south and east and west, between them a labyrinth of densely crowded streets and lanes called *hutungs*. This is the Tartar City, inside which lies the Imperial City surrounded by high pinkish-red walls. Within this city again, and the centre of it all, is the Forbidden City, where in former days the Emperor and his court lived in seclusion. The magnificence of the layout, the vast golden-roofed audience halls, the palaces and the great courtyards make a truly imperial domain and vividly remind one that this was once the centre of a great empire.

My mother arranged expeditions to a number of interesting places. One day we went in rickshaws to the Summer Palace. Situated in the Western Hills a few miles out of the city, it was built by the Empress Dowager, Tz'ŭ-hsi, with funds intended for the navy after the original palace had been burnt by the Anglo-French expedition of 1860. Entering the walled precincts through elaborate gates, one sees how the buildings in clusters, or scattered over a series of low-lying hills, fit into the landscape and harmonize with their surroundings. We followed a covered way with railings and pillars of red lacquer and ceilings painted with landscapes and birds and flowers which led past buildings and courtyards alongside the lake. Roofs of bright coloured tiles crowned pavilions, their upturned corners mounted by curious little gods or grotesque beasts of porcelain, whose purpose was to ward off evil spirits. Temples climb the hills with a wealth of stairways and balustrading. The silver sheen of the lake is broken by a graceful camel-back bridge and in the Ocean Terrace Palace, on an island, the young Emperor Kwang Hsü was for a time kept a virtual prisoner by the Empress Dowager. Beyond the Summer Palace lies the Imperial Hunting Park, once a fine forest but today few trees remain.

Another day we visited the Temple of Heaven, perhaps the finest of all Peking's temples, where every year the Emperor performed ritual sacrifices and prayed for bountiful harvests. Within the wooded park, at the head of a long marble causeway, stands the round temple with triple roofs of glazed lazuli tiles matching the blue of heaven. At the opposite end of the causeway the Altar of Heaven spreads its white marble platforms open to the sky. Standing before it on a moonlight night, as we later did, the Altar's pale loveliness seemed truly celestial.

A further expedition was to the Pei Hai or Winter Palace, a favourite resort of the Emperor Kublai Khan, in the northern part of Peking. We picnicked beneath ancient cedars and explored the vast uncared-for grounds, wandering through palaces and buildings fast falling into decay, and courtyards strewn with fallen tiles, carvings, and broken gods. Crossing the lake we admired the one thing still in its pristine glory, the great Dragon Screen of nine glazed-tile dragons, four pairs of which are in corresponding colours with the central one in imperial yellow. The temple, whose entrance the screen guarded, has disappeared.

In those days that now seem so far away, Peking's social life was stimulating and cosmopolitan, made up as it was of Chinese and Europeans; all were interesting and many, persons of distinction. Resident foreigners entertained in their Chinese-style houses, the one-storey buildings grouped around courtyards. One might meet an archæologist or a botanist, enthusiastic about a recent discovery in the Gobi desert or some other remote place, or a minister from one of the foreign legations. There were collectors of old paintings, porcelains or earthenware, men of letters and artists. Occasionally a famous war-lord would put in a brief appearance, or a painted Manchu princess in jewelled head-dress and embroidered robes would lend an exotic touch. Luncheon, dinner, and cocktail parties, a week-end in a temple in the Western hills, visits to the Great Wall and the Ming Tombs, riding in the grounds of the Temple of Heaven, kept me pleasantly occupied. It was exhilarating too, to be part of Peking's street life. Rickshaws, motor-cars, carriages and donkeys, all made as much noise as possible, while wedding processions added brilliant colour. Peking carts, innocent of springs, were drawn by gaily caparisoned mules, and caravans of shaggy camels lifted disdainful heads as they came with measured tread from the Gobi Desert and wended their way through the streets. But everyone dashed for safety when a shining Rolls Royce with screaming siren and lolling war-lord hurtled by.

We visited fairs held in temple courtyards where delightful objects could be had for a trifle—a carved jade horse, a silver box studded with agate or cornelian, a delicate painted snuff-bottle or a plum tree covered with fragile blossom. Part of the fun was haggling over the price, a pastime enjoyed both by the seller and the purchaser. At a night fair on a pavement pitched above the street, articles were spread out on the flag-stones in the flickering light of little oil lamps, their squatting owners presiding over them.

On my arrival in Peking I decided to start learning mandarin, the dialect of the North and destined to become the national language of China. A teacher was duly engaged and, in contrast to my Cantonese teacher, knew how to teach. Moreover, mandarin, apart from the script, is easier than Cantonese, having only four 'tones' as compared to the nine of Cantonese. I made good progress but as time went on my enthusiasm for mandarin gave place to enthusiasm for Maurine Samson, a young American girl who was spending a few months in

Peking. I had met her soon after my arrival at one of my mother's tea-parties. Maurine accompanied us on our sightseeing trips and we often dined and danced to a White Russian orchestra at the Hotel de Pékin where she was staying. One sunny afternoon a few days before my departure for Hong Kong, I invited her to go for a walk on the wall—the top of the Tartar Wall being a favourite place for walking—and before we reached the Hatamen Gate, I had asked her if she could bear the life of an exile and live in outposts of the British Empire—could she marry me? To my joy it appeared she could. Arrived at the Gate where our rickshaws awaited us, we reluctantly descended the ramp. Our coolies seemed to sense our elation for they dashed off at a breakneck speed, giving little yells and shouting everyone out of the way, never slackening until they pulled up abruptly at the vermilion gates of General Munthe's compound. My mother and stepfather did not appear to be greatly surprised at our news, declaring themselves delighted and giving us their blessing. Maurine returned to San Francisco to persuade her family that it was all right for her to marry an Englishman and live abroad, while I went back to Hong Kong to be posted to the Colonial Secretary's Office.

MARRIAGE

The staff of the Colonial Secretary's Office was small, consisting of only three Cadets and a couple of dozen clerks in addition to the Colonial Secretary. The advantage of a small office is that one gets to know everyone. They are not just a lot of vaguely familiar faces as is inevitable in a large office. Claude Severn, the Colonial Secretary, was a kindly man if somewhat pompous; but in that era pomposity seemed inseparable from important persons such as the Colonial Secretary and heads of firms. The machinery of the Hong Kong government was ponderous in the extreme with great attention to detail. After a few years when I had got to know its working, I was amazed and shocked at the amount of time the governor, the colonial secretary and other senior officials spent on matters of minor importance that should have been left to junior officers. In the same way the Secretariat exercised a meticulous control over the activities of the government departments that must have been, and indeed was, galling to their heads. This craving for dotting the 'i's' and crossing the 't's' would probably not have occurred if the government had been faced with serious problems. The officials would then not have had the time to devote themselves to trivia. But the Colony rarely had serious problems either in the international or local political fields. It was plain straightforward administration.

The hard core of the administration was the Cadet Service whose members not only filled the senior posts in the Secretariat and the Treasury but also the headships of the Police, Education and Post Office departments. This might have been all right in the early days of the Colony and before empire-wide colonial police, education and postal services had been established. But now the system was out of date, and one by one the headships of the specialist departments were taken over by qualified officials. The last to go was the Post-master-General, when I had the satisfaction of turning this over to a member of the Colonial Postal Service shortly after my return as Governor in 1947.

The clerks in the Secretariat, and I believe throughout the government, were excellent and very hard-working; so much so that a rule had to be made that no clerk was allowed to stay on after office hours without special permission, as overwork was affecting their health. Conscientiousness was the sole reason for their working such long hours. They received no extra pay. Dictation and stenographers were unheard of; everything was written out in longhand and typed out by a Chinese typist. But the march of progress could not be halted and, notwithstanding the protests of the Chief Clerk, one lady steno-grapher, Miss Thornhill, was appointed—quite an event in the life of the office.

Most of my service in Hong Kong until my transfer to Bermuda in 1935 was in the Secretariat, and in spite of occasional bouts of frustration when my seniors did what should have been left to me, I found the work interesting, for the C.S.O. was the centre of the government machine which enabled me to obtain a good knowledge of all that was going on in the Colony. Unfortunately it gave me no opportunity for keeping up my Cantonese. Had I been more enter-prising and not about to get married I might have done this after office hours; but I did not.

I have said that Hong Kong was rarely faced with difficult or serious problems, but a very troublesome situation did arise shortly after I joined the Secretariat. This was the general strike and boycott of the Colony by China in 1925. The origin of the trouble was the shooting of some Chinese in Shanghai by British members of the internationally controlled Shanghai Municipal Police. This led to a violent anti-British campaign throughout China, and culminated in the general strike in Hong Kong and the prohibition by the Chinese government of the importation into China of goods from Hong Kong and the export of goods from China to Hong Kong. As a junior I was not concerned with the politics of the matter, and was only inconvenienced to the extent of having to do duty as a special constable and trying to cope with my own cooking and other household chores, since all our servants had left. The strike gradually petered out but the boycott, which did considerable damage to the Colony, dragged on for several months longer.

I had feared that the strike would necessitate a postponement of my marriage but happily this did not occur, and Maurine duly set sail from San Francisco accompanied by one of her sisters. My mother also came down from Peking for the great event which had been fixed for 28th October when the weather is perfect. My best man was Walter Scott who had shared quarters with me in Canton, Macau and Hong Kong. Tall, handsome, always well-turned out and aristocratic in appearance, he was approachable and friendly. He had a high degree of integrity with a streak of stubbornness. His brain was keen, and altogether he was superior to his colleagues in the Police, but to have told him so would have embarassed him acutely. He fell in love with Maurine's sister and a few years later they married. After I had gone to Bermuda in 1935, we only met when our leaves happened to coincide. He was in Hong Kong when the Colony fell to the Japanese in 1941 and was executed by them two years later. His death was a grievous loss not only to us but also to the Colonial Police Force, for by then he had shown himself to be a man of outstanding ability.

As not infrequently happens at weddings, the bride arrived late, but the fault was not hers. She was to be given away by Sir Claude Severn. On the day of the wedding he had been attending a luncheon in his honour and when he arrived at the hotel to collect the bride, forgot to have himself announced, sank into a chair and fell asleep. Upstairs the bride and her sister, anxiously watching the clock, became alarmed and descending into the lobby, discovered Sir Claude. He was quickly awakened and a waiting car whisked them to the cathedral. After the ceremony we walked down the aisle to Lohengrin's wedding march and chiming bells. The Governor, Sir Edward Stubbs, had kindly placed at our disposal his launch to take us to Cheung Chau, an island about ten miles distant where a friend had lent us his bungalow for our honeymoon. At the conclusion of the reception at the hotel, we left amid showers of rice and confetti for Queen's Pier to board the launch, gay with fluttering flags and pennants. Waving to friends as the launch moved off, we were suddenly deafened by the noise of hundreds upon hundreds of exploding fire-crackers, the Chinese mode of wishing us happiness and long life. An hour later we landed at a little wharf at Cheung Chau, thence we walked through a fishing village up a winding path to a house perched on a rocky cliff overhanging the sea. Happy days followed as we explored the island, bathed from the white beaches and made plans. The moon was full that week, and from our terrace in the soft night air we watched its silver shimmer on the sea and the lights of Hong Kong in the distance.

Our return to Hong Kong marked the first matter-of-fact business of being married. We had the good fortune to be allotted a small bungalow on the Peak where today stands a tall block of flats. With the servants of my bachelor days I continued to do the housekeeping, as Maurine had had no experience of this kind of life, least of all in a British Colony. But after a few weeks she proposed to take over, saying the house was not kept clean and the servants were stealing most of the food. A certain amount of 'squeeze' is acceptable, but not outright robbery. I was appalled, but she was adamant and take over she did. Almost at once I noticed an improvement, but the servants became sadder and sadder until eventually they left us and went to batten on some other unsuspecting bachelor. We then secured servants who did my wife's bidding.

Social Life and Protocol

Social life was pleasant and easy for a young married couple and Maurine soon got into the way of things. Hong Kong society was cosmopolitan; besides the government and service people, there was the consular crowd and the banking and commercial community. We mixed with British, Chinese, French, Americans, Germans and others, enjoying it all with the exception of ladies' bridge-luncheons. These fearsome affairs started at one o'clock with cocktails and 'small chow' (canapés) followed by an elaborate lunch, after which the ladies settled down to bridge interspersed with gossip. Tea was served in the middle of the afternoon, then more bridge and finally cocktails before the guests went home about eight o'clock. Maurine found these parties a burden and considered them a waste of time, so she gave as few as she decently could. My salary was small, but so was the cost of living, and to entertain on a modest scale was fun. From the first we made a point of inviting people of different nationalities to our parties; we found it stimulating and have followed the practice ever since.

In those days Hong Kong was very protocol-minded and the heads of firms and senior government officials were extremely conscious of their positions and demanded proper respect from their juniors which we dutifully gave. Somerset Maugham has depicted with biting sarcasm the social snobbery of the East in his book *On a Chinese Screen*. It did not bother us, for we had no aspiration to venture into the exalted world of the 'taipans'. Getting to dinner parties was sometimes quite a business. We did not possess a car and even if we had, frequently could not have used it, for some of the houses were accessible only by chair or rickshaw; whilst if the party were in Kowloon and it happened to be raining we would start off in chairs, transfer to the Peak Tram, then chairs again to the ferry, across the harbour by the ferry and finally arrive at our destination by rickshaw—five modes of conveyance. But being young we did not mind.

What we enjoyed most was the bathing and swimming during the summer. Best of all were the launch picnics. We would set out in the afternoon, having tea as the launch steamed to some beautiful bay or to an island. Bathing suits were donned and we would take it in turns aqua-planing. After an hour of this, we dropped anchor to dive and swim from the launch, or go ashore in a dinghy when energetic members of the party walked. At dusk supper was served, and if there happened to be a moon, we swam again before returning home. From the harbour at night Hong Kong presents one of the fairest spectacles in the world, the hundreds of lights, dotted or strung like necklaces over the Peak, make it impossible to tell where the lights leave off and the stars begin. Our favourite beach was Big Wave Bay—a misnomer except in the monsoon season or when a typhoon is about. The curving beach of little more than a quarter of a mile is enfolded by two arms of hills with a backdrop of other hills. We would put on our bathing suits behind some rocks, for bathing tents had not yet invaded the privacy of the beach.

During the winter, walking was our main week-end recreation, and happily Maurine liked it every bit as much as I did. The best walks were in the New Territories. The New Territories on the mainland have an area of 355 square miles and were leased to Britain by China in 1898 for a period of ninety-nine years. At the time of which I write they were entirely rural with the exception of the built-up part which is a continuation of urban Kowloon. One or two villages only were of any size and much of the country was wild and untamed. The Territories also include more than two hundred islands and islets, the largest of which, Lantau, being almost twice the size of Hong Kong island. Cheung Chau was the only island with a large village or small town. The others were either sparsely inhabited or completely uninhabited because of lack of water. The island of Hong

Kong, thirty square miles in extent, was ceded—as distinct from leased—in 1842. To it was added in 1860 the four square miles of Kowloon peninsula.

On a Sunday morning or a holiday, starting before dawn, we would cross to Kowloon and take a train or country bus to some distant point and there strike off into the hills. All day, up hill and down dale, we would go, climbing mountains from whose tops we had sweeping views of the countryside, or going down steep hill-sides into valleys patterned with terraced paddy fields, but devoid of crops at this time of year. We passed through tiny villages where I would chat with the farmers. We followed ancient paths paved with heavy granite slabs, old as the hills themselves. We came on miniature temples far away from any habitation where travellers might rest or offer incense to one of the gods. At these we would leave some sticks of incense burning on the altar. Occasionally we espied a very small shrine in an old gnarled tree, indicating the abode of a tree-spirit.

Home Leaves

Ten years elapsed between our marriage and our departure for Bermuda. During this time we had two home leaves, one of eighteen months and one of twelve months. Such long periods were not normal, but on the first occasion I read for the Bar and on the second attended the year-long course at the Imperial Defence College. Prior to the establishment of the Colonial Legal Service in the early thirties, the posts of magistrates were filled by members of the administrative service. If they had a liking for judicial work, they would be called to the Bar and in due course promoted to a colonial judgeship. But when the Colonial Legal Service came into being, judgeships were confined to members of that Service, and no one was eligible for appointment to it unless he had practised at the Bar for a specified number of years. Magistrates, too, were supposed to be members of the Legal Service. So far as judgeships were concerned, this was a wise rule for some of the administrative-judges were weak on knowledge of the law, and few had had experience as counsel. On the other hand, I thought that administrative officers made better magistrates than young barristers. What they lacked in theory they made up in common sense and understanding of human nature—the prime requisite for a magistrate. On my return to Hong Kong after passing my Bar examination, I was appointed junior magistrate at the Hong Kong court. Apart from the fact that the work was interesting and human— for my district covered the most densely populated part of Hong

Kong—I had the satisfaction of being my own master, since once on the bench the magistrate is monarch of all he surveys. This was a pleasant change from being a junior in an office. However, the legal side was not to be my destiny. Lacking the qualifications for membership of the Legal Service and in any case preferring the administrative side, I reverted to the Secretariat after eighteen months. On my second leave the Colonial Office offered me two years on secondment to the Colonial Office or one year at the Imperial Defence College. I chose the latter. The College is a combined services staff college for selected officers who have already been through the staff college of their own particular service. In addition, a limited number of civil servants and officers of the Dominions are admitted. The course, which lasts for a year, is wide and interesting and something out of the ordinary for a colonial civil servant—I was the first to attend—and I have never regretted the twelve months I spent on it.

Whilst on this second leave I applied for a transfer, explaining to a sympathetic Colonial Office official that while I was happy in Hong Kong the two men immediately senior to me were able, and I envisaged myself being blocked for promotion if I remained there. My request was noted and I returned to Hong Kong. A few months later the colonial secretaryship of Bermuda was offered me. This was exciting but there were drawbacks. I should drop about a third in salary and would have to pay my passage and that of my wife from Hong Kong to Bermuda. But looking up the careers of previous colonial secretaries in Bermuda, I observed that none had remained there for more than three years before being promoted to a higher post elsewhere. Maurine and I talked it over and decided on the more interesting though somewhat precarious course. Accordingly, in October 1935 we set sail for New York on the twelve-passenger ship, the M.S. *Tricolor* with ports of call at Shanghai, Kobe, Nagoya, Yokohama, across the Pacific to San Francisco and thence through the Panama Canal to New York—a journey lasting six and a half weeks. Never have I enjoyed a sea trip so much. My preference for ocean travel is either first class on one of the 'Queens' or a twelve-passenger freighter.

In New York we had a happy ten days seeing friends and going to theatres before embarking on the *Queen of Bermuda*, on which we received the treatment of minor V.I.P's—our first experience of this delectable dish.

CHAPTER TWO

BERMUDA, 1935–1938

ERMUDA has the distinction of being mentioned by
Shakespeare, when in *The Tempest* Ariel says to Prospero:
'. . . thou call'dst me up at midnight to fetch dew from
the still vexed Bermoothes. . . '. The islands were discovered by
the Spaniard, Juan de Bermudez—hence the name—but Spain never
claimed or occupied them, probably because the submerged coral
reefs surrounding them made the islands exceedingly hazardous to
sailing ships, and possibly because they had an evil reputation as
the home of devils and spirits—one of the islands is named Devil's
Island. It was on the reefs that the *Sea Venture* was wrecked when
taking a shipload of colonists from England to Virginia in 1612.
These 'sea venturers' were the first human beings on Bermuda and
are the original ancestors of the present-day white Bermudians. The
coloured Bermudians, comprising two-thirds of the population, are
descendants of slaves brought from Africa.

Since its founding three hundred and sixty years ago Bermuda
has had a chequered career. Seafaring was the main occupation for
the first two centuries of the Colony's existence; seafaring not being
confined to fishing and the carrying of cargoes between the West
Indies, the Americas and England, but extending to privateering, a
legalized form of piracy. When that came to an end, the resourceful
Bermudians turned their attention to 'wrecking'. Ships would be
lured to their doom by lights so placed as to lead them on to the
reefs. They would then be 'saved'—at a price—by the islanders.
Can it be wondered that the twentieth century Bermudians, whose
forebears were these red-blooded, enterprising men, jealously guard
their independence and individualism? I found them a most admirable
people and, once they got to know you, very friendly. I liked and
respected them enormously. In more modern times many Bermudians
have married Americans and Canadians, but the Bermuda character
remains much the same, I am glad to say.

After wrecking had to be given up, the colonists had a hard time.
They did not much care for farming and, when in later years Bermuda
onions, potatoes and lilies found a ready market in New York, much
of the work was done by Portuguese who had come from the Azores.
The outbreak of the American Civil War provided lucrative oppor-

tunities for blockade-running, as did prohibition in the United States after the First World War. But what has really proved the salvation of Bermuda is tourism, now the Colony's biggest industry. The pleasant and salubrious climate—it certainly is not 'vexed'—began to attract visitors from America in the latter part of the last century. Presidents of the United States found it a refuge from affairs of state and many writers have come here to work. Mark Twain, for instance, never ceased to return to this 'tranquil and contenting place'. Up to the nineteen-thirties most of the visitors were well-to-do Americans who rented houses for the winter months. These still come, but a round-the-year tourist season has been developed as well.

Bermuda has much to delight the eye: cedars—or junipers to be exact—which flourished in our time (now, alas no more, a disease having wiped them out) fiddlewood, bamboos and other trees, white beeches and some pink ones, oleanders, deep pink against the sapphire sea, hibiscus, lilies and many other flowers. The houses of coral, washed in pastel shades, have white roofs which look truly enchanting by moonlight. The islands are coral with only a shallow covering of soil, and for building material all that has to be done is to saw up blocks of coral on the site of the projected house, using the space from which the coral has been cut for a water tank. Every house is obliged to have its own water supply from rain caught on the roof, and a government regulation provides that roofs be lime-white-washed annually. It is remarkable that the water in the tanks should remain clear and fresh from one year's end to another. If the rains do not come, water has to be brought by ship from New York, an expensive business, but this seldom happens.

Bermudians are proud of the fact that their parliament is one of the oldest, if not the oldest, in the British Commonwealth outside the United Kingdom. There is a lower and an upper house. The former, the House of Assembly, is entirely elective, one of the members being the Speaker. The upper house, the Legislative Council, consists of *ex officio* members, of whom the Colonial Secretary is one, together with appointed members, and is presided over by— of all people—the Chief Justice. The respective powers of the two houses are much the same as in the case of the House of Commons and the House of Lords in Britain. The Executive Council corresponds roughly to the Cabinet in England, with the Governor as President and the members either *ex officio*—the Colonial Secretary again being one—or appointed. Some of the members are also members of the House of Assembly which provides a useful link between the executive and legislative branches of government. Bermuda has no political parties and I doubt if such a development would be a good thing for the Colony. She is also fortunate in not having an income tax. This is a deliberate act of policy, as the absence of such a tax encourages foreign business concerns to register themselves in the Colony. They have to pay a registration fee, but this is a trifle compared with the tax they would have to pay in their own countries. The income from the fees is a not inconsiderable item in the government's budget.

As the *Queen* made her way slowly along the North Shore, we stood on deck watching the approach to our new abode, now through a narrow passage between two small islands and into Hamilton Harbour, past the Princess Hotel and the Royal Bermuda Yacht Club, to the wharf at Hamilton, the capital, alongside the principal street, Front Street. Those on shore waved and shouted to their friends on the ship. This December scene of sunshine, blue sea and sky, people in white or light-coloured clothes, streets crowded with bicycles, horses and carriages presented a decided contrast to the one we had left in New York three days previously.

GENERAL SIR THOMAS ASTLEY-CUBITT

The acting Colonial Secretary and the Governor's A.D.C. came on board to welcome us, then going ashore we drove in the Governor's victoria through the town and along a cedar-lined avenue, up a steep hill to Government House. The exterior of the house of grey concrete has little to commend it, but the site is fine, overlooking spacious gardens, the town on one side and the sea on the other. At the door to greet us in the friendliest possible manner were the Governor, General Sir Thomas Astley-Cubitt, and his wife, Olive. After chatting a few minutes, the Governor said the first thing I must do was to take five official oaths and led the way into his study. 'My boy', he said, 'I think we should have a gin'. We had a gin and another before each oath. This was nine o'clock in the morning! In those days a good deal of heavy drinking took place in Bermuda which was the downfall of more than one good man. Habits have since changed.

During our stay at Government House we got to know our hosts and became devoted to them. Tom Cubitt was a most colourful character. Tall and distinguished looking, he was the beau ideal of the general. His flow of language was often lurid and he delighted in making outrageous remarks and scandalizing people. At the dinner table on one occasion he called across to the Bishop who was sitting next to Lady Cubitt, 'Bishop, did you know that the Chief Justice gets his corsets at the same shop as my wife gets hers?' He knew everyone in the Colony and all the ins-and-outs of what was going on, and was immensely popular in the best sense. When I visited Bermuda more than twenty years later he was still remembered with affection. Apart from the fact that I had a great liking for him, I found him a very good chief to work for. His wife, too, was most attractive, both in looks and personality.

The Colonial Secretary was not provided with quarters and to find a house was difficult as the most suitable ones had already been taken for the winter by American visitors. The House of Assembly considered the question of an official residence for the Colonial Secretary, but the proposal was rejected for the reason—as I was told privately by a member—that if they gave one to the Colonial Secretary they would also have to give one to the Chief Justice, and whilst I was well enough liked, the Chief Justice was unpopular. However, we managed to get something that would do for the few months until the Cubitts left, when we moved into Government House pending the arrival of the new Governor. Then once again we had to go house hunting. Luckily an American friend came to our rescue and lent us her house whilst she was away for the summer. This gave us time to continue our search. At last we found a really charming house, 'La Garza', in Paget parish. We came to love 'La Garza' almost more than any other house we have occupied. Powder-blue, except for the white roof and balustrades, it had probably been built in the eighteenth century by a privateer—the later ones had elegant taste. The long drawing-room had a tray ceiling, french windows and a white marble fire-place brought from Europe. The dining-room had two fire-places and windows looking out on to the Sound. The furniture that came with the house was a mixture of good and bad. We discarded the former and used the latter. To this we added what we had brought with us and had carpets specially made in Hong Kong, including an off-white one for the drawing-room.

The garden had variety—a small grove of bamboos, that speedily got out of control if not watched, cedars, fiddlewood, palms, pines, oranges and allspice, frangipani, poinciana, clumps of white and pink ginger and oleanders, both white and pink. In the spring a host of cream, white and mauve freesias suddenly appeared as if by magic; later to disappear in the same magical way. An ancient night-blooming cereus had climbed to the top of a tree and nearby was a trellis covered with *copo del oro*, whose great gold buds arranged on the dinner table would open with a 'plop' to enchant the guests. In the same way we used the night-blooming cereus which slowly opened to display their golden chalices and to breathe out a delicious perfume.

The simple life of Bermuda was very different from the sophistication and lavish entertaining of Hong Kong. With the exception of occasional large dinners and balls at Government House or Admiralty House, informality—which did, however, I am glad to say, mean black tie at dinner parties—was the key-note. The only drawback to this enjoyable gaiety was going out to dinner on bicycles. Hiring a carriage for the evening was expensive and we did not often indulge in this luxury. Maurine was the principal sufferer, for her dresses had the habit of getting caught up in the back wheel of her bicycle. On one occasion when going to a party she fell off, which did not improve the appearance of her dress. This is one of the few times I have heard her swear. However, she usually managed without losing her temper or ruining her clothes. Motor-cars were not allowed in pre-war Bermuda. And how pleasant it was cycling along the white coral roads with no honking cars covering one with dust.

When General Cubitt left on retirement we moved into Government House. In most colonies the practice is for the acting Governor, usually the Colonial Secretary, to occupy Government House when the Governor is absent for any length of time, or between the departure of one Governor and the arrival of the new one. In Bermuda this was not done for understandable reasons. The Governor, in most cases, was a general and had allocated to him soldier-servants from the regiment stationed in the Colony. A civilian acting as Governor had no such privileges. Moreover, if the soldier-servants did agree to serve him, they were inclined to take a superior attitude. In addition the Governor brought out from England at his own—considerable—expense other servants who took their holiday when he went on leave. At the same time, good servants were very difficult to find locally. The horses and all save one of the carriages were the Governor's personal property. But needs must when the devil drives. We had no house and simply had to transfer ourselves to Government House, which we duly did, taking with us our cook and fervently hoping that the soldier-servants, who held key positions, would carry on. Looking back, we have wondered how we had the courage to tackle such a situation, or how we managed to get through. We went into it in blissful ignorance and, though we soon realized how precarious was our position, I do not think that others did, for we presented a serene front to the public. One particular day will ever remain in our minds. Just before the guests were due to arrive for a large lunch party the butler and footman, both soldier-servants, said they were quitting forthwith and would not even stay to serve. I had to use all my persuasive powers to get them to agree to see us through the meal. Not only was I successful in this but they remained for the rest of our time at Government House. Whilst I was coping with the butler and footman, Maurine was in the kitchen soothing the cook who had gone temperamental. Those weeks at Government House took years off our lives, but we survived. Never again, though, did we venture to occupy Government House when I held the position of acting Governor in Bermuda. Instead, we continued to live in our own house, which meant of course that we could not entertain on the scale expected of 'His Excellency'.

In other respects being acting Governor had its compensations and the office work was even lighter than that of the Colonial Secretary. I spent one acting period drafting a new pensions ordinance, quite a complicated piece of legislation. Each Sunday I would bicycle to a different parish church and read the lessons. At one church the parson bowed to me before he bowed to the altar, which I thought was giving me undue precedence. At another time I had to attend some ceremonial function in uniform. Having no official equipage at my disposal, I drove to the side door of the building in a hired cab from which I slipped out unobtrusively before making my formal entry. No, it was not altogether easy being acting Governor in Bermuda.

Bermuda being considerably smaller than Hong Kong and the constitutional set-up completely different, the approach to my job also had to be different. Moreover I was not a junior in the Colonial Secretary's Office. I was the Colonial Secretary. In a crown colony such as Hong Kong, the Governor is the seat of power. This is not the case in Bermuda. Here the Governor is more like a constitutional monarch. If he, either of his own volition or at the behest of the Colonial Office, wishes to have any particular measure carried out he has to move with circumspection, and if it is something to which the House of Assembly has strong objections, for example the introduction of income tax, he is unlikely to win his point. Cubitt was an adept at lobbying, but his success really arose from the fact that the Bermudians knew that he had the welfare of the Colony at heart. By contrast, his successor was clumsy in his approach and did not disguise the fact that he cared little for Bermuda and the Bermudians and still less for Americans, who were the bread and butter of the Colony. The Colonial Secretary had to back up as well as he could the efforts of the Governor; his position being analagous to that of a chief of staff. Fortunately, I get on well with most people and I found the members of the House of Assembly reasonable and forthcoming, though as often as not they disagreed with me and went their own sweet way. The paper work was much less than it had been in Hong Kong, so in the office I had an easy time.

GENERAL SIR REGINALD HILDYARD

General Sir Reginald Hildyard was to be the new Governor. As was usual I sent him a copy of the arrangements for his arrival which followed well-established precedents. Much to my surprise I received a letter from him objecting to what was proposed and enclosing an alternative programme which, he said, must be followed. Accordingly I took his plan round to the Mayor of Hamilton as being the person principally concerned. The Mayor would have none of it. 'What was good enough for the Prince of Wales is good enough for Sir Reginald', so said that redoubtable old Bermudian, Sir Henry Watlington. In suitably modified language I telegraphed the gist of Sir Henry's message to Hildyard, who had by then set sail from England. He telegraphed back in still stronger terms than before, telling me to do what I was told. I again saw Watlington who would not budge. Again I telegraphed to Hildyard, and so it went on with telegrams flying back and forth. I was between the devil and the deep blue sea. I had to do my best to carry out the Governor's instructions, but I felt he was wrong, which of course I could not tell Watlington. Finally, the Mayor said that if the original programme were not adopted he and the Corporation would boycott the ceremony. At this Hildyard capitulated. He certainly did not know the Bermudians, and in fact he never did get to understand them. When I met him on his arrival he told me in no uncertain language what he thought of me, which was not a good beginning to our relationship. Matters were not improved when Tags, one of my dogs, tried to bite him.

Hildyard wanted to set aside the rules and have a motor-car, but this required the approval of the House of Assembly. After being twice rebuffed, he threatened to resign if his request were not granted. It was not granted and resign he did. Hildyard was really a kindly man, but a bad choice for the governorship of Bermuda. Finding the right man for the post was, however, not easy, since the salary was inadequate to cover the gubernatorial expenses. The Governor had to dip into his own pocket.

TAGS AND PHILIP

Tags had a brother, Philip, of the same litter but with no resemblance to him whatsoever, both undistinguished looking mongrels, albeit full of character. Cubitt had found them as puppies abandoned in a ditch and made them his constant companions. On his departure he gave them to us knowing we were fond of them. They accompanied me when I bicycled to the office and spent the day there. They followed us everywhere, even when they were not supposed to. If we happened to be at a friend's house, they would track us down and take up positions outside the front door as if they owned the place. At dinner parties at 'La Garza' we would shut them up but somehow they usually managed to escape. They would then sneak into the dining-room and get under the table, carefully keeping away from Maurine and me, for they knew they should not be there. If I did manage to get hold of one of them he would let out a piteous yelp as though he were being beaten. 'You brute', the guests seemed to say as they looked at me reproachfully. It was, of course, just an act put on by the culprit with the intention of embarrassing me. He would almost wink at me with mischievous pleasure as he was led away. The social functions that met with their highest approval were wedding receptions which they invariably gate-crashed. Avoiding us, they moved about the company enjoying the titbits that came their way. To our sorrow we had to leave them behind when we left Bermuda, as the importation of dogs into Jamaica was prohibited. I am glad to say we found a good home for them and they enjoyed lives of many happy years.

ENTERTAINING

After we had established ourselves at 'La Garza' we did a good deal of entertaining, as we liked it; also we thought the Governor, Hildyard, was not doing as much as he should, and felt it was up to us to step into the breach. Good servants were difficult to obtain so we considered ourselves lucky to have an English butler, Telfer, whose employers had recently returned to England. Telfer could turn his hand to anything, from butling to cooking and making beds. Although very conscious of his position as a 'gentleman's gentleman', he had the gift of getting on with coloured people. When we gave a party we would hire extra help from the nearby Inverurie Hotel. I recollect we paid six shillings for each helper for the evening. The charge now, I believe, is something like three pounds. They and

Telfer got on splendidly and we never had a moment's anxiety. 'You leave it to me, madam', was a favourite expression of his. Only once was there a slip-up and that had nothing to do with Telfer. We had invited to cocktails the officers of some visiting German warships. I had just finished changing when I heard the sound of marching feet. Looking out of the window, I saw the whole contingent of German officers advancing on the front door. Together with our house guests we dashed downstairs just in time to greet them. They had mistakenly come an hour early, and how long that hour seemed before the other guests commenced to arrive. Thereafter the party went with a swing. The officers were an attractive lot of men, responsive, with cultivated bearing and good manners. They stayed longer than the usual time and many departed with other guests who took them to their homes for dinner and later to dance at one of the hotels. We heard next day that they were greatly taken with the Bermuda girls, and it may be added, the girls with them.

On another occasion, when having tea at a friend's house, I sat in a window seat with a spinster and a member of one of Bermuda's oldest and most respected families. We had both been tempted with 'brownies'—small cakes of a chewy consistency— and my companion had taken her first bite of this delectable confection. As she took the remainder away from her mouth, what was my horror to see fastened in it her front false teeth which she waved before my eyes. At the moment she did not realize her loss and I quickly turned to the window, pretending to look at something outside and to stifle my wild desire to laugh. By the time I had controlled myself and turned back to her, the teeth had been restored to their place.

Nothing is more enjoyable than a Bermuda wedding. To drive in a white ribbon-bedecked victoria to a parish church decorated with flaming poinsettias, to sit in an ancient pew and sing traditional hymns, to watch through the open window the white clouds piled up in the blue sky, allowing one's mind to wander during the rather long ceremony in which the bride promises to love, honour and obey, and finally to step out into the sunny afternoon while the bells from the steeple ring out joyously, is truly romantic. Later at the home of the bride, set in terraced gardens, where the reception is held, one chats with friends, and after the bride has cut her cake and the toasts and speeches have been made, the little cedar tree that tops the bridegroom's cake is planted. The bridal bouquet is then tossed to the bridesmaids, and at last amid a shower of rice, the bride—still in her wedding gown— drives away in a flower decorated carriage to some magic spot they have chosen for their honeymoon. It is all very gay and very Bermudian.

At the Belmont Manor Hotel one evening as Maurine and I were dancing together, a summons to the telephone disclosed that I had been offered the colonial secretaryship of Jamaica. This was thrilling news, for Jamaica was a good promotion from Bermuda. Nevertheless, it was bitter-sweet: we felt sad at having to break up a home we loved and to leave Bermuda where we had spent three happy years, despite some difficult moments. But when one is a member of a world-wide service one must expect this sort of thing. Maurine made a quick trip to Jamaica to see what the house there was like, which pieces of our furniture and which carpets would fit in, for the official residence of the Colonial Secretary in Jamaica was fully furnished. Alas, most of it would not do, so we sold what we could not use. After a three-week's leave in England we sailed from Avonmouth on a banana-boat, the *Ariguani*, for Kingston. The passage of fourteen days was delightful, increasingly so as we steamed further south and the world about us assumed a tropical aspect. One forgets the thrill of seeing flying-fish and how different from the north is the deep blue of the southern sky with its incredibly white clouds, piled up like fluffy down, and the sunsets, brilliant in colour at first and imperceptibly changing to delicate shades of turquoise, lilac and salmon. We enjoyed lazy afternoons on deck reading or idly chatting, and usually indulged in a pre-dinner swim in the canvas tank put up on the after-deck, staying in the water until the last rays of sun faded and the first stars of the evening began to show. When one comes from a temperate zone, the tropic skies and nights seem remarkably clear, the moon appears larger and the stars more brilliant, and in the last few nights of our voyage that lovely constellation, the Southern Cross, rose above the horizon.

CHAPTER THREE

JAMAICA, 1938–1941

THE name 'Jamaica' comes from the Arawak 'Xaymaca', meaning 'Land of Springs', and indeed Jamaica is a land of springs. Springs are everywhere and rivers tumble through mountain gorges or emerge swiftly from the tropical forests to plunge in waterfalls to the sea. The Arawaks, a gentle friendly people, were the original inhabitants. Alas, they proved to be too gentle to withstand the Spaniards, who in the space of one generation exterminated them. In 1655, during the time of Cromwell, General Venables and Admiral Penn, whose son founded Pennsylvania, drove out the Spaniards and Jamaica became British.

As the *Ariguani* approached Kingston Harbour, we watched with keen excitement the towering Blue Mountains with depths of violet in their folds and valleys. From the entrance to the harbour a long curving sandbar runs out like the crescent of a new moon, encircling the water to form what might be called a lagoon. Here in the seventeenth century lay Port Royal, the capital of Jamaica. Palms on its creamy beaches were reflected in the water's pellucid depths, while brilliant scarlet and magenta bougainvilleas flamed out from a background of rich green. The grey stone of a girdling wall and the tower of a church could be discerned. Shops, with luxuries as well as ships' stores for sale, crowded along cobbled streets, while houses demurely hid themselves among rich foliage and trees. This was Port Royal, 'the richest and wickedest city in the world', the rendezvous of pirates and buccaneers. But the wrath of God descended on Port Royal and, one Sunday morning in 1692, smote it with earthquake and tidal wave. Nothing now remains of this once fair city save a few derelict buildings and the rampart of Fort Charles; the rest lies beneath the waves where, it is said, the tides still ring the bells of the submerged church. One of the few survivors of the disaster was the preacher who, the preceding Sunday, had warned of the impending doom.

After this calamity the capital was established at Spanish Town, originally founded as St. Jago de la Vega by the Spaniards in 1523. Although only twelve miles from the port of Kingston, Spanish Town, being inland, was found to be inconvenient as the seat of government. Accordingly, in 1871 the capital was moved to Kingston where it has been ever since. Today, Spanish Town lies sleeping in the sun with what is left of important buildings grouped round the square. On one side stands the façade and portico supported by white pillars, all that remains of old King's House. Opposite is the former House of Assembly. On another side stands the Court House, and on the fourth, Rodney's Memorial, consisting of a statue of the admiral in a classic temple flanked by pillared arcades. Near the square is the English Cathedral with its burial ground, whose ancient tombs are fast mouldering into dust. Inside, the walls and floors bear memorials, rich in sculpture and coats of arms, of the great who died here in centuries past. The vine-covered houses running out from the square, with their jalousies closed against the heat, have an aloof, withdrawn, almost secretive aspect. No shops are noticeable or signs of life.

But now we had no time to let our minds wander into the past, for the *Ariguani* had docked and the Governor's A.D.C. and other officials were waiting for us. A number of reporters and photographers had also come to interview and take pictures. We discovered that in Jamaica one's photograph is wanted almost every day of the year. Jamaica was well served by the old established *Daily Gleaner*, and by a newcomer, the *Standard*, regarded by many as too radical, though I could never understand why. It did not have a very long existence, and ceased publication shortly after I had left the Island. Some of the weekly and monthly periodicals also were good, for Jamaica had a tradition of culture and art which the present generation has maintained. After the reporters and photographers had finished with us, we drove to King's House to be the guests of the Governor, Sir Arthur Richards (now Lord Milverton), and Lady Richards. King's House seems to me a much nicer name for the Governor's residence than 'Government House', which suggests a block of government offices.

After several pleasant days at King's House, discovering the various interests and traits of our hosts, we went to the Manor House, an hotel near the mountains in the Constant Spring district, some six miles out of Kingston. Around the main building, cottages were scattered over several acres of gardens. One of these, with a delightful awning-protected verandah, became our home for three months while Vale Royal, the Colonial Secretary's house, was being put in order. Breakfast was served on our verandah, and at the appointed hour each morning we would watch a dusky maid in a freshly starched blue dress, stepping over the dew-covered grass, balancing on her head a tray piled with fruits, iced and prepared for eating, papaw, pineapple,

grape-fruit, peeled oranges with a fork firmly thrust into the centre
to be used as a handle, mangoes and star-apples.

Sir Arthur Richards

Richards had arrived to take up his appointment only ten days
earlier. This most unusual procedure of the new Governor and the
new Colonial Secretary coming at the same time would not have
arisen but for the sudden death of the previous Governor, Sir Edward
Denham, whose coffin was stoned by the crowd as it was being carried
through the streets. Jamaica had had strikes and riots on a serious
scale and the Colonial Office had wisely decided to send out without
delay the best man they could to succeed Denham. They selected
Richards, and could not have made a better choice. Liberal in sentiment, he nevertheless believed that the first duty of a Governor was
to govern, and govern he did. Firm, sympathetic to the under-privi-
leged, and progressive in his political outlook, he was neither a
reactionary nor a sentimentalist, whilst his moral courage was greater
than that of anyone else under whom I have served. He did not suffer
fools gladly and as he had a biting tongue if he chose to use it, he
made more than one enemy and was sometimes accused of being
cynical. He was not; he was a realist. He had the devotion of the civil
service, for though an exacting taskmaster, he gave praise where
praise was due and invariably stood up for his officers whenever the
press or members of the Legislative Council attacked them, and in
Jamaica some of the attacks were vicious. If the official was at fault,
he would be dealt with by the Governor, which is as it should be, but
his chief stood behind him so far as the outside world was concerned.
I have always thought that Richards should have been made Permanent Under-Secretary of State at the Colonial Office. He would have
transformed and put new life into it. Perhaps the officials there realized
this and did not relish the prospect. At any rate he was not appointed.
From there he should have been sent at the end of the war to Malaya.
If he had, I do not believe the communist rebellion in that country
would have broken out. I say this not because he had served in Malaya,
but because of his far-seeing and imaginative mind. Furthermore, he
was a strong governor,who could be tough if the situation demanded it.

He knew all about procedure and protocol but this did not prevent him from addressing a large assembly of workers at the invitation
of their leader, Bustamante, within a few days of his arrival. That the
Governor should so 'demean' himself, particularly at such a troublous
time, filled with horror the more staid members of the community.

I must confess that I was somewhat surprised myself, but I had not yet come to know my Governor as I did later. He was an excellent speaker, whether extempore or prepared. Occasionally he would make a sarcastic or cutting remark that did not endear him to the victim, but I never heard him say anything harsh that was not merited.

The root cause of the strikes and riots was the economic situation. Jamaica's economy, before the commercial discovery of bananas, had been based on sugar and reached its zenith at the beginning of the nineteenth century when the number of slaves exceeded 300,000. The planters thought the abolition of slavery, which occurred in 1833, spelled their ruin as well as that of the industry. But they and the now-freed slaves gradually adjusted themselves to their new relationship, and probably all would have been well if the United Kingdom had not adopted a free-trade policy and withdrawn the tariff protection, hitherto granted to the British West Indian colonies. The development of bananas at the turn of the century provided a second mainstay to the economy; but the growth of the population was outstripping the means of supporting it, for though the production of both sugar and bananas could have been considerably increased, the sale of them could not be. Britain now gave tariff and quota preferences up to a certain amount, but there were limits beyond which she could not go, whilst in world markets Jamaica had difficulty in competing. Things got steadily worse and unemployment continually increased. The riots in Denham's time were the culmination of a series of crises. Other West Indian islands were suffering from the same malaise and also had riots. The British government realized that something drastic had to be done and—apart from appointing a commission under the chairmanship of Lord Moyne to go into the whole question of the economic and labour situations in the West Indies—became more helpful than hitherto in the way of providing funds for unemployment relief works, which the colonies themselves could not afford. Consequently the situation was not as bad as in Denham's day, but strikes, demonstrations and the burning of cane fields still occurred sporadically. Only once, however, did the military have to be called out, and that was to guard the docks.

BUSTAMANTE

Bustamante, now Sir Alexander and current Prime Minister, a very colourful individual, was the most prominent labour leader. With aquiline features and thick greying hair brushed back, his appearance was striking. His enemies said he was nothing more than a rabble-rouser, but this I rejected, and one way and another I had quite a lot to do with him during my three years in the Colony. He could harangue and sway a crowd like no one else in the Island, but this was the outward expression of his love for humanity, especially for the humble workers. He inspired great loyalty amongst his followers and they did not in the least mind his driving around in a large motor-car and indulging his taste for champagne. Despite the fact that he and I were often on the opposite sides of the fence I had considerable affection for him. When about to leave Jamaica on transfer, I went to bid him good-bye and, although at the time he was detained under the Defence Regulations for an inflammatory speech he had made, he expressed no bitterness and made no recriminations. Two friends were saying farewell.

His cousin and political rival was Norman Manley, a brilliant lawyer with a better brain—not though a 'cold intellectual'—but lacking Bustamante's warm humanity. The aims of the two men were the same: independence and raising the standard of living of the people. But temperamentally they were, I suppose, too different to work together, and each is now head of opposing political parties. In recent years one or the other has been Prime Minister, the one not in office being leader of the opposition. Manley seemed to me to have bitterness in his soul. I may have been wrong, or perhaps now the bitterness has disappeared with the attainment of Jamaica's independence. When their active political life comes to an end, I can envisage Bustamante as Governor General or constitutional President, and Manley as happily occupying himself with his cultural pursuits.

The Legislative Council

Neither Bustamante nor Manley was a member of Executive or Legislative Council. The former was more interested in labour and trade-union matters and had not yet formed his political party, whilst the latter did not wish to stand for election under the constitution as it then was. He preferred to work from the outside. The composition of Executive Council was the same as in Hong Kong and Bermuda. The Governor presided and the members were either *ex officio* or appointed. Of the latter, Sir Alfred D'Costa was outstanding. He was descended from one of the Jewish families who had been brought from Portugal by way of Holland in the time of Cromwell. Many of them had made good in the professions and business, and quite a few gave much of their time to public affairs, though they did not engage in political activities. Sir Alfred, both wise and shrewd, contributed greatly to the deliberations of Executive Council. Apart from this he was a charming man.

The fourteen unofficial members of the Legislative Council were elected, one from each of the fourteen parishes. If nine voted against a government financial measure, the measure was defeated, whilst if all fourteen voted against any measure at all it suffered the same fate, unless in either case the Governor, who presided, declared the matter to be one of paramount importance. The government side of the House had fifteen members, some *ex officio* and some appointed. Volubility was the principal characteristic of the elected members; so much so that a Standing Order had to be made limiting the length of speeches to one hour except at the budget debate when three hours were allowed. Hard hitting with no punches pulled was frequent, but rarely did the members make virulent attacks on heads of government departments. The President quickly called them to order. For this comparative harmony the tea intervals—when we all got together in a genuinely friendly way—were largely responsible. Personalities counted too. The *bête noire* of the elected members was a certain head of department, a hard working, conscientious official who somehow or other always seemed to rub the elected members up the wrong way. On the other hand Arthur Hodges, the Treasurer, got on with them splendidly. He would wag his fat forefinger at them and lecture them as though they were a lot of naughty and rather stupid school-boys, and they did not mind in the least. Tom Hallinan, the Director of Medical Services, a remarkably bad speaker, dealt with them in another way; he would give them boxes of cigars or appoint their relatives to lowly jobs in government hospitals. He once suggested to me that in order to silence one especially troublesome member, he should be made an O.B.E., to which I replied that I did not think the Governor would be prepared to make such a recommendation. Not only were the elected members fluent speakers, as most West Indians are, but they were also apt to become emotional. When government's proposal to sell the Constant Spring Hotel, which was running at a loss, to a Catholic institution was being debated, tears streamed down the face of one member as he recounted the tortures inflicted by the Inquisition in the Middle Ages.

The sessions of the Council took up the best part of six months in the course of the year; the sittings being from 11 a.m. to 5 p.m. on three days a week, if my memory serves me aright. This was a large slice out of the day of a civil servant who had his regular adminis-trative and office work to do. Moreover, the Colonial Secretary, as leader on the government side, had to be in constant attendance and could not ignore the debates to do his 'home-work' as other government members did. When the House rose at the end of the day I would have to spend an hour or more listening to the special pleadings of one or other of the elected members for their parishes or themselves: a relief work here, a land settlement project there, or a government post for a relative. All these had to be patiently listened to and in most cases turned down. To show favouritism to one member or one parish would have been fatal. On the other hand, to have refused to listen would have led to the member becoming obstructive and would have been the reverse of oiling the wheels of government; besides it would have been unkind, for the member himself was under pressure either from his constituents or his relatives, and even if he did come away empty-handed, he could at least say he had had a talk with the Colonial Secretary. Budget time, which went on for four months, first in Finance Committee and then all over again in open Council, was particularly gruelling. By an odd custom the Colonial Secretary and not the Treasurer was in charge of the Colony's budget. The burden was a heavy one and I have never worked so hard before or since. The Secretariat staff was mixed in quality, some good, some not so good, but one and all were nice people and the *esprit de corps* of the office was high. Although the office was understaffed, the hope of getting an increase authorized by the legislature was remote. For the same reason I paid out of my own pocket for the installation in my office of an air-conditioner. The expenditure was well worth-while, for previously the temperature in my office in the morning would be touching the ninety mark. Another helpful factor was the consideration, unspoken but present nonetheless, shown me by the Governor.

Vale Royal and Other Beauty Spots

About five miles out of Kingston at Half Way Tree was Vale Royal—a charming name for a charming house—an old 'great house' where Nelson once stayed. Maurine redecorated the house in her usual style with white and pale colours which are so much pleasanter in a tropical climate than the government browns. Originally the grounds had been extensive; now only seven acres remained, half of which had been allowed to revert to bush, but within a year we had made them into smooth lawns. As the bush was cleared, we came upon surprises; a lovely cinnamon tree, a dainty pomegranate with clumps of mistletoe in its branches; and this later rewarded us with delicious fruit. About the lawns were old tamarind trees and great guangoes, lignum-vitae whose symmetrical shape made them into blue French bouquets when blossoming, poincianas like huge scarlet umbrellas, while the flowers of the golden-shower hung like clusters of grapes, and ebony trees burst into a mass of brilliant orange two or three days before rain. Lime and grape-fruit trees scented the garden and provided us with fruit, as did a Bombay mango-tree and the coconuts. Nor must I forget the exotic achee tree with shiny light-green foliage and scarlet pear-shaped fruit, whose yellow flesh when cooked tastes like scrambled eggs.

At the end of the garden a shrubbery made a resting place for the eye, with hibiscus, alamanda and other flowering shrubs giving colour. A little formal garden, somewhat higher than the rest, was reached by a short flight of steps and encircled by a stone-wall covered with plumbago which at times was a solid mass of blue. White eucharist lilies and maiden-hair fern flourished here and the finest poinsettias I have ever seen. A shrub, commonly called 'Chinese Hat' because its red and yellow flowers are in the shape of a Chinese coolie hat, grew luxuriantly on either side of the verandah steps, and was a favourite haunt of humming birds, tiny red and green ones and others with long tails like birds of paradise feathers. A blue heron came to stand for hours on end under a pink shower-tree. Not so welcome were the red-headed vultures which sometimes perched on the roof or walked about the lawns. Spike, our dog, would run among them, barking furiously, whereupon they would lazily fly away.

Perhaps loveliest of all was the garden by moonlight when it would emerge in all its nocturnal enchantment. The trees cast great shadows and in the luminous silver light the beauty of everything— flowers, lawns, the blurred outline of the pool under the trees—was enhanced a hundredfold, even the drive became a fairy thing. The palm fronds shimmered and threw out lights, while the air, fresh and cool from the mountains, wafted the scent of datura and night-blooming jasmine, and beneath the trees dancing lights of fireflies made a phantasmagoria of 'such stuff as dreams are made on'.

Vale Royal and the gardens were a comfort and solace to my arduous work. Alone with Maurine at dinner on the wide verandah, I would momentarily put aside the cares and worries of the day and the thought of the files awaiting me on my desk. Social life in Jamaica was very pleasant and the Jamaicans were congenial, but regretfully we found that my work would permit us only two social evenings a week. I do not know which we enjoyed most, going out to dinner or giving a party ourselves. We were fortunate in our butler, Clifford. Tall and almost black, he had fine features, was most dignified and thoroughly efficient. He liked our entertaining, but sometimes disapproved of a guest, considering him insufficiently important to be invited to Vale Royal; in fact he was one of the worst snobs I have ever known.

My weekly 'getting away from it all' took the form of rising at five o'clock on Sunday mornings just as it was beginning to get light and driving up into the mountains where I would leave the car and walk. The poorly surfaced road twisted up steeply and Spike, who accompanied me, invariably became car-sick, but we worked out a drill. As soon as I saw the symptoms I would stop the car, open the door and push him out. He would be sick at the side of the road, jump back into the car and off we would go again. Once a couple of peasant women, to whom I had given a lift, were car-sick. Unable to give them the Spike treatment, I had to endure the result. Walking at that time of the day was pure delight, the early rays of the sun lighting up the clear-green of the banana leaves, wood-smoke drifting upwards from a peasant's cottage, great mahogany trees, the grass by the side of the path sparkling with dew and the mountain air cool and invigorating. I felt spiritually refreshed.

Spike was a mongrel who had been brought to the house by a wretched-looking man. We could not resist the appeal in the puppy's eyes and his evident need of a home, so for the sum of five shillings he passed into our possession. Small and light tan, the name seemed to suit him. One day a cat walked in and adopted us. The servants liked her and when we asked them what they thought she should be named, Rosamond, the cook, said in a matter of fact tone, 'She is Minnie'. Spike and Minnie became good friends. In due course Minnie produced kittens, one of which we kept. This was 'Putty', the nearest the servants could get to pussy. Minnie, who was a roamer, disappeared, but to make up for our loss, Putty gave birth to two kittens, Jeremy and Tomkins.

Our favourite place for Easter or Christmas was Shaw Park Hotel on the north coast, and we loved the drive there. After passing through Spanish Town, the road leads up a gorge known as 'Bog Walk', from the Spanish 'Boca del Agua'. Through this the Rio Cobre tumbles over steep rocky places, or flows quietly beneath overhanging palms and trees and feathery bamboos where strange birds fly about. On the road, which closely follows the river, donkeys pull wooden carts, and bare-footed men and women in bright calicoes walk with a peculiar swaying gait, carrying on their heads baskets of fruit, stems of bananas or tins of water. The road winds past scattered mud-walled thatched houses, or, alas, corrugated iron ones, past small farmers' plantations of avocado and bread-fruit trees or limes and oranges, with bananas in sheltered places and clustered in defiles. Beyond the little town of Moneague, the descent to the north coast begins, the road diving down into Fern Gully, a narrow ravine whose steeply rising sides are a luxury of maiden-hair and other delicate ferns, while tree-ferns and tall vine-draped trees, whose trunks have become mossy-green in the still air, meet overhead to form a natural fern-house where it is always twilight, eerily green and fantastically beautiful. And so on to Shaw Park Hotel, formerly a Great House, and now somewhat transformed. Through the open-air dining-room, flowed a little mountain stream on whose edge grew a nutmeg tree, its foliage filtering the sunlight. It was relaxing to bathe in the fresh-water pool, swim in the sea or just laze on the beach. Pleasant too, was standing under a waterfall that cascaded over the rocks to a green dell before flowing into the sea. After dinner, we strolled in the garden in the soft night air, the coconut palms flashing captured moonbeams and, below, the lights of the little town of Ocho Rios twinkling through the trees.

Flamstead was another place we liked to visit for a night or two. Formerly a coffee estate, it was now run as a guest-house and whilst the accommodation and meals were simple, the situation high in the mountains was glorious. We liked almost shivering in the morning and evenings, thinking of the heat in Kingston, and being lighted to bed at night by old-fashioned oil-lamps. Spike, too, loved the walks. The manageress became fond of him, and when we left Jamaica offered him a home which we gladly accepted on his behalf.

Combining business with pleasure, we occasionally managed to tour other parts of the Island. Port Antonio, the site of an early Spanish settlement, has beautiful twin harbours separated by a promontory jutting out into the bay. In the lower hill-sides and the valleys, the peculiar light-green of the bananas—for this is banana country—gives the atmosphere a soft green haze.

In former days wealthy planters in the sugar lands lived in state in their Great Houses. The ruins of some of these, with overgrown gardens and stately palms, may still be seen; the most notable being Rose Hall, the finest remaining example of Jamaica architecture. The main part of the house, built of stone with a staircase rising and branching to the right and left in eighteenth century style, stands on a promontory overlooking the sea. The two wings have been completely destroyed, as have the arcaded ways which circled out from both sides of the house and must have given the enclosed space a delightful design and seclusion. The fine woodwork has been removed and its famous mahogany staircase, almost black and glowing like satin, now graces a house at Constant Spring not far from Kingston. Traces of flagging are all that remain of the garden. About a hundred and fifty years ago this great estate belonged to John Palmer whose beautiful second wife was versed in voodooism and was known as the 'White Witch of Rose Hall'. John Palmer was her fourth husband; the other three had met mysterious deaths and this subsequently became his fate also. She was so notoriously cruel to her slaves that they finally strangled her. The house is said to be haunted by her 'duppy' or ghost. Although illegal, voodooism or 'obeah' is still practised by the peasantry who are very superstitious, but it is gradually dying out.

Beyond Montego Bay in the western part of the Island are lush meadows with great trees, beneath which graze herds of white brahmin cattle with enormous horns. These estates are called 'pens', and like the sugar plantations also have their Great Houses. In the parish of Westmoreland sugar has been produced since the early days and from its principal town, Savannah-la-mar, sugar and rum are still shipped. Not far away is Black River, the haunt of crocodiles, their great size being remarked upon by some of the earliest writers.

The variety of the scenery of Jamaica was a source of constant joy to us; the mountains, the plains, the cane fields, the banana plantations. It is rich in trees, pimento (allspice), logwood and mahogany and fruit trees of many kinds, coconut palms, coffee and cassava; the list is endless. But apart from what the eye saw, there was the atmosphere or 'feel' of Jamaica, the sense of its romantic past, the Spanish Main, the days of the Great Houses, and the hope for its future. Once when driving home from Montego Bay, along the north coast on a moonlight night, the sea close on one side and the trees crowding in on the other, I felt the past strong upon me and almost believed in duppies. My chauffeur, Brown, in a rum-sodden stupor in the back of the car felt nothing.

High above Kingston on a spur of the Liguanea range is Newcastle, a group of buildings erected at the end of the last century by the military, and still used as a hill-station for troops sent from time to time for a respite from the heat of the plains. It hangs in terraces down the mountain side and is reached by a road that goes winding up by one hairpin bend after another. At night its lights, when seen from Kingston, shine like a starry constellation. A short way beyond is Greenwich, a smaller group of houses for officers. They were unoccupied and dilapidated, but since leave in a temperate climate was not possible during war time, Lady Richards and a few others, including Maurine, decided to have some of these houses put in a

livable condition and to spend the summer months there in a temperature many degrees less than in Kingston. Our little house was
situated on the very edge of a precipice, and from the verandah we
looked over the lower ranges of the mountains to the harbour and
Port Royal, four thousand feet below, and out to sea. Maurine took
with her our cats. Spike remained with me at Vale Royal, but at week-
ends he and I would go up to Greenwich. Driving up to about the
thousand foot level, I would walk the rest of the way along a mountain
trail, the air getting cooler the higher I went. Maurine would come
part of the way to meet us, and Spike, seeing her first, would dash
ahead to tell her I was coming. The walks around Greenwich were as
varied as they were delightful. A favourite jaunt of ours was to set
out with a packet of sandwiches and walk to Cinchona, named after
the tree from the bark of which quinine comes, and where there is a
large plantation of them, passing on the way Clydesdale, an abandoned
coffee estate, the barbecues of concrete terraces for drying the beans
still remaining. Across a valley rose Blue Mountain Peak, remote and
grand, the highest in all Jamaica, glowing with the intense blue of a
gentian. The atmosphere here, high in the mountains, has a crystal
clearness that makes objects miles away appear quite close. Anthony
Trollope who visited Jamaica in 1859 says in his *West Indies and
Spanish Main:* 'Nothing can be grander either in colour or grouping
than the ravines of the Blue Mountain ranges of hills'.

It was with considerable reluctance that on Sunday evening after
supper, Spike and I got into the car to drive back to Kingston; but we
consoled ourselves with the thought that in less than a week's time
we would be trudging up to Greenwich again.

WAR

At first Jamaica was little affected by the war, but as shipping
became scarcer, economic difficulties arose, in respect both of imports
and, far more seriously, of exporting the Island's produce. Sugar was
not a difficulty, because it was an essential commodity, and ships were
always made available to lift it. Bananas, which accounted for more
than half the Colony's export trade, did not come into the same
category. Moreover they required a special type of cargo space.
Inevitably a time arrived when no ships could be provided to take
the bananas away. To avert the ruin of the growers, the government,
with funds largely contributed by the British Treasury, guaranteed
to purchase all bananas that otherwise would have been exported and,
in order to offset the cost, sold the stems for sixpence each. This,

however, was found to be more trouble than it was worth, so they were simply dumped. What a waste! But there was no alternative.

To save importing wheat-flour, a cornmeal factory was built by the government using the locally grown corn (maize). Other projects of a similar nature had also to be undertaken in the war-time emergency. To have appointed a local businessman to the new post of Director of Commerce and Industry would have created friction with the rest of the business community to the detriment of the efficient operation of the organization, whilst someone brought in from outside would have lacked local knowledge. By good fortune the government had in its service an officer, F. E. V. Smith, an agricultural chemist, who had a gift for this sort of thing unusual in a civil servant. 'F.E.V.' was a tough bargainer when it came to dealing with businessmen in Jamaica, New York or Canada and was not the kind of person to go out of his way to ingratiate himself with the members of Legislative Council, but they held him in considerable awe and usually approved his schemes, giving him the funds he asked for.

The reception of nine thousand refugees from Gibraltar was only one of many problems brought by the war, but we felt glad to be working at full stretch, indirectly helping the war effort, when others were fighting on the battlefields or undergoing the 'blitz'.

Jamaica was selected by the United States government as one of the places for a base in the bases/destroyer agreement between the British and American governments—bases in the Caribbean in exchange for fifty old destroyers. President Roosevelt came on the U.S.S. *Tuscaloosa* to have a look at the proposed base in Jamaica. The Governor, Lady Richards, my wife and myself were invited to accompany him out to the site. Accordingly, one morning, we boarded the cruiser which then steamed to the bay in question. The President could not have been more charming and friendly, and had the animation and enthusiasm of a schoolboy. The atmosphere was completely informal and as we went along he pointed out and named islands and landmarks even though he had never been there previously. Impressed with the size and facilities of the base, he laughingly teased Richards, saying: 'Why, this is splendid. I have here a better harbour than you have at Kingston. There is room for the whole American Fleet'. To which Richards banteringly retorted, 'When you take over Jamaica'. The President, holding up a protesting hand, hurriedly replied, 'Oh no, we are not looking for any of Britain's headaches'.

With the war on, we did not expect transfers or promotions. I was therefore taken aback when summoned to King's House one morning to be handed by the Governor a telegram he had received from the Colonial Office offering me the post of Chief Secretary, Nigeria. I had always said I did not want to go to West Africa, but I had also said I would go wherever I was sent, so after a discussion with my wife, I accepted. It meant, of course, another uprooting and leaving house and garden, Spike and Putty, Jeremy and Tomkins. It was harder on Maurine than on me, for the garden and the house were her creations. Furthermore, she had to see to all the packing up. However, I reminded her that, when sixteen years previously I had asked her to marry me, I had warned her that in doing so she would become a vagabond, and she had replied that she would follow me to Timbuctoo if need be, and now we were going as near there as could be. Regretfully, we said goodbye to our many friends, and the Governor and Lady Richards gave a farewell dinner party in our honour, at which Sir Arthur made a very complimentary speech which greatly moved us, especially as we thought we would never serve with the Richards again. Amongst the parting gifts Maurine received was a bouquet of flowers from Bustamante who was still under detention. On account of the war-time restrictions no one except Lady Richards and the Governor's A.D.C. was allowed on the ship to see us off. Quietly the vessel moved away from the quay and bathed in the light of a flaming sunset, we slipped out of harbour and past Port Royal, watching the Blue Mountains being enveloped in dark and yet darker veils until they were obscured from our sight.

PART TWO

War Years

CHAPTER FOUR

NIGERIA, 1942-1944

WE arrived at New York in the middle of November 1941 and at once set about getting the necessary inoculations against yellow fever, smallpox, typhoid, cholera and other tropical diseases. We also had to make arrangements for passages to Nigeria which was easier said than done in war time, but we managed to secure berths on one of the Grace Line ships going to Lagos. Unhappily, as it turned out, one of the vice-presidents of Pan American persuaded us to go by plane instead. The plane was due to leave on 9th December. The Japanese attack on Pearl Harbour took place on 7th December and with America now in the war, practically all civilian flights overseas were suspended. Meanwhile the Grace Line steamer had sailed. We were stranded in New York. After several weeks, pestering the British Consul-General and anyone who we thought might be able to assist us, we took a train to Miami— being assured that a plane was going from there to Lagos and that seats on it had been reserved for us. An hour before the train arrived I was handed a telegram announcing the cancellation of the flight. We felt crushed, but there was nothing we could do except to wander gloomily about the streets until the train left again for New York. The only bright thing about the day was an inexpensive hat which Maurine bought. We called it 'Maurine's $300 hat', for it was all we had to show for the expense of the trip to Miami.

At last we got passages on a Norwegian freighter, the *Talisman*— name of good augury—sailing from New York to West Africa. February 1942 was not a healthy time in which to cross the Altantic in an unescorted vessel, but fortune was with us and nothing unto-ward occurred, which was just as well, for on the foredeck were carboys of volatile acids and on the afterdeck drums of gasoline. Had we been torpedoed, the ship would have been blown sky-high with no chance of anyone getting away in the boats. My wife was the only woman on board. Amongst the ten other passengers was a Belgian going to the Congo to collect baboons for a zoo. I could not help saying to myself, 'Is your journey really necessary?'

After twelve days at sea, as we entered the harbour at Freetown, an astonishing sight met our eyes. For nearly two weeks we had not sighted a single ship and now the universe seemed to be full of them.

We counted eighty-five of good size besides many smaller ones, recognizing two on which we had travelled in happier days. Freetown was a point of assembly for convoys and evidently one was getting ready to sail.

Leaving Freetown the *Talisman* proceeded along Africa's low-lying lushly-green coast to Monrovia, the capital of Liberia. Never had we seen such a dilapidated place calling itself a town, let alone a capital city; the main street was a dirt road full of pot-holes, the shops were battered pieces of corrugated iron. Many of the houses were falling into ruin, others were half-finished derelicts. Most of the people were very poorly clad and looked woe-begone. As the *Talisman* was going to remain at Monrovia for several days, we accepted the British Consul's kind offer of hospitality and of assistance to get us on a plane going to Lagos. The airfield, Robertsfield, was about fifty miles from Monrovia on the Firestone Company's rubber plantation, which by contrast to Monrovia spoke of efficiency and orderliness. Roads were good, work was going on among the rubber trees, and the labourers' houses and the labourers themselves were neat and clean. We were fortunate to obtain seats on a plane, full of military personnel, going to Accra in the Gold Coast. After spending a night at Accra, we boarded a freight-plane to Lagos, the capital of Nigeria and our destination.

Nigeria takes its name from the river Niger which with the Benue, a tributary, splits the country into three. At the delta and along the coast are lagoons and mangrove swamps, mosquito-ridden and malarial, but forming a useful means of communication. Some way inland is a thick forest belt which gives way to more open land rising to form a great plateau two thousand feet above sea level. From this, rise mountains six or seven thousand feet high, while in the extreme north the country falls away to the Sahara and Lake Chad. With an area of 350,000 square miles and a population in 1942 of twenty-two millions, Nigeria was the largest colony in the British Empire.

Many different tribes and peoples make up the population. In the south-west, where Lagos is situated, live the Yorubas, believed to have come originally from Upper Egypt but now completely negroid. South of the Niger and Benue are the Ibo tribes, animists and rivals of the Yorubas. On the plateau will be found the aborigines, the most primitive of all in Nigeria. In the north also dwell the Hausa and Fulani, the former negroid, the latter fairer in complexion, suggesting an Arab strain in their blood. The religion and civilization of the Hausa and Fulani are Islamic and their rulers bear the titles of emir or sultan.

As early as 1472 Portuguese ships were visiting the coast of West Africa. The first English ships reached the Niger delta in 1553. So deadly was the climate that, of those ships' crews of one hundred and forty men, one hundred died of fever. The name 'Nigeria' did not then exist and the whole of the coast of West Africa was known as the Slave Coast, because it was from here that most of the slaves for the Americas were taken. Little was known of the interior of the country until early in the nineteenth century when the African Association in London financed expeditions to explore the course of the Niger. The history of these expeditions is one of fearful hardship and undaunted courage. Mungo Park wrote to Lord Camden in 1805; '. . . that of forty-four Europeans who left for the Gambia in perfect health five only remain alive . . . but I assure you that I am far from desponding . . . and shall set sail to the east with fixed resolution to discover the termination of the Niger or perish in the attempt. . . '. Perish he did a short time later in the rapids at Bussa.

In 1807 Parliament passed an act making it illegal for slaves to be carried in British ships or to be landed in a British colony. During the following years the slave trade was gradually suppressed, while trade in palm-oil developed. In 1861 the British occupied Lagos and in 1885 established a protectorate, the Oil Rivers Protectorate, over the coastal region. In the following year the United Africa Company was granted a charter as the Royal Niger Company, following the pattern of the old East India Company. British influence steadily extended over the whole of Nigeria, with the government taking over political control from the Company. Finally North and South Nigeria were amalgamated on 1st January 1914.

West Africa had a deservedly evil reputation for a very unhealthy climate, being known as the 'White Man's Grave'. Medical science and the government's health services have since vastly improved matters and the risk to health of Europeans is much less now than formerly. But whenever one of the Europeans said to me that he had 'got the wave-length of the country', I knew it was high time he went on leave to a temperate climate. From my general observations I came to the conclusion that two years in West Africa without a break was long enough for Europeans. A few could stand it for longer without any apparent ill effects other than a mental slowing-down. Others could not take the climate at all and had to be sent home without delay. My wife and I were in Nigeria for a little more than two years and whilst in the Colony enjoyed reasonably good health. Nonetheless it took Maurine a year after she had gone home before she was completely fit again, whilst towards the end of my time I had occasional black-outs, which made me feel foolish, but after I left, I quickly recovered. Quinine or some other prophylactic against malaria had to be taken regularly. In 1942, the drug employed was mepacrine which had the effect of giving the complexion a yellowish tinge rather like a buttercup. Away from the towns, the people and the livestock still suffer from fevers and internal parasites of one kind or another, which, whilst not necessarily fatal, are very debilitating. But here, too, the victory over ill health is slowly being won.

LAGOS

On our arrival at the airport about a dozen miles outside Lagos, we drove with the Governor's A.D.C. and the acting Chief Secretary to Government House at Lagos, which is on an island connected with the mainland by a bridge. The town sprawled over flat land hardly above the level of the sea and rows of ugly wooden houses and shops were nearly all in need of repair. Naked children playing in the streets, chickens, goats and dogs—all darted out of the way as our car approached. Streets became more crowded with langorously moving people; the men dressed in flowing robes or pyjama-like garments, blue predominating, the women in printed cottons. On the other side of the island buildings and streets were better. A macadamized road skirted a broad lagoon with ships riding at anchor, and grassy slopes down to the water's edge were dotted with trees. We drove along this road, the Marina, past an imposing group of red brick buildings, the Secretariat, my future domain, and on to Government House, a long rectangular white structure of three storeys with arcaded verandahs and green jalousies; a veritable palace, and at the same time gracious. It was protected from the road by high walls with handsome iron gates, at the entrance of which a guard of the Nigeria Regiment stood stiffly at attention as we passed. Circling round the drive, the car drew up under the *porte cochère*, canopied with thumbergia whose white orchid-like flowers swayed gently on their stems. The door of the car was opened with a flourish by a smart orderly in red and yellow uniform. On entering the lounge, Lady Burns, the wife of the acting Governor, cordially greeted us. Sir Alan was abed with malaria and I went up to see him.

Sir Alan, who had previously served in Nigeria before being Governor of British Honduras, was Governor of the Gold Coast and had been sent to act as Governor of Nigeria during the absence on sick leave of the substantive Governor, Sir Bernard Bourdillon. It having been decided, and rightly in my opinion, that for the first few months until I had learnt the ropes I should not act as Governor since I had never previously been in West Africa. Burns was one of the most charming men and serving under him was a delight. I also learnt much from him, for his knowledge of Nigeria was encyclopedic. Every day at noon I would report at his office, bringing up any problems I had. I found this especially useful in matters that had not yet reached the stage of formal submission on paper. He on his side would mention anything he had on his mind. When in due course I became a governor I adopted this practice, finding it as helpful to me as Governor as I had when Chief Secretary.

The Chief Secretary's house, The Lodge, was just beyond Government House and also faced the Marina and the lagoon. A gate in the garden wall of Government House led into the garden of The Lodge, a rambling two-storeyed structure of wood, painted black and white, with verandahs along the front and a *porte cochère* at the entrance. It boasted only two bedrooms, outside one of which, the master bedroom, was a flat roof where we slept on camp beds under the stars, dashing in when it started to rain. Between the bedrooms and over the *porte cochère* was a study with a view over the lagoon. The drawing and dining-rooms were adequate but the interior décor left much to be desired, in particular festoons of electric wires hung all over the place. Maurine speedily got to work, and work she did. The outside we had painted white. The inside was not so easy. The Public Works Department did the structural work, but most of the upholstering and making of the curtains had to be undertaken by Maurine with the assistance of a 'homes' magazine and two sewing women. Fortunately our cases from New York with hundreds of yards of materials, carpets, some furniture, paintings and porcelains from Jamaica arrived safely. Much to our relief also, the carpets from Vale Royal fitted perfectly. Entirely white, the house looked larger than before and was reminiscent of the American colonial style. The interior too was white, or rather off-white. The whole effect was pleasing and residents and visitors seemed to appreciate a house that was different, and, may I say, more attractive than the stereotyped houses of West Africa.

The garden, too, needed attention. It was not as enchanting as Vale Royal's, but after it had been put in order was quite pleasing. Trees and lawns were the main feature, eucalyptus, casuarina, sealing-wax palms, jacaranda—my favourite flowering tree, whose blue flowers lying unfaded on the grass beneath are like pieces of fallen sky. Fragrant frangipani, both pink and white, flamboyant—as the poinciana is here called—coralita, jasmine and hibiscus. A wide bed of pink cannas blossomed against the long Marina garden wall. High hedges concealed a kitchen garden where we made a great effort on account of the war-time shortages, and soon were growing all our own vegetables with enough to spare for friends. We also kept chickens, ducks and guinea fowl which supplied us with poultry and eggs.

The servants' quarters constituted quite a community, almost a small village, for the wives and children lived here as well. We made a rule, however, that each servant could have only one wife and her children staying at the place at a time. They accepted this cheerfully, for they—that is those who practised polygamy—liked to keep some of their wives at home to help with the family farm. At first we found all sorts of strange people residing in the servants' compound. We put a stop to this as we did not want any undesirable characters there. Our staff was a motley crew of different tribes and religions. Some were pagans, two were devout Catholics, two Presbyterians and some Mohammedans; yet they all got on well together and seemed very tolerant of each other. Asani, the cook, was a superior fellow with any amount of personality and full of resourcefulness, which stood us in good stead when we had to provide meals at short notice for transients. A Mohammedan, he had three wives when he came to us. Shortly afterwards he took unto himself a fourth for whom he paid her father eleven pounds. Apparently she had a temper, for one morning he appeared with his hand bandaged. His bride had nearly bitten off his thumb. He was most indignant, saying that he was going to 'return her under her father's umbrella' and would demand the refund of the eleven pounds. The father had other ideas and refused to pay back the money, so Asani had to keep her. However, after a time, the two of them seemed to settle down all right and, as far as I know, lived happily ever after.

As usual we acquired pets, a nondescript little dog whose name I have forgotten, two very nice cats, Mouchette and Pom-pom given us by the wife of the Free French Commandant, hence their French names, and George, a West African parrot who was a great character. We tried, unsuccessfully, to teach him to talk, but by different sounds he made us understand him; a cluck for pleasure, a whistle to draw our attention and an awful screech when displeased. We disliked the idea of keeping him caged or chained to a perch, so we had his wings clipped and allowed him to wander wherever his fancy took him—except in the house. We tried this once with disastrous results. He tore into tiny shreds the whole of a mail that had just arrived. His favourite place was the back verandah where the servants did some of their work, cleaning silver, sorting laundry and other things. Something was always going on here and he enjoyed the chatter. After he had been with us six months he became moody and pensive. We thought he must be sick. Then one day, 'he' laid an egg. George seemed as surprised as we were, turning it over, cocking his head on one side and then the other to regard it earnestly. Interest, though, soon subsided and he carelessly stepped on it, and that was the end of the egg. Thereafter we tried to refer to him as 'she', but habit was too strong and we gave up the attempt. We did, however, change his name from George to 'Georgie'. Georgie had a sad ending. On our departure we presented him to some friends who became as fond of him as we had been. Alas, his curiosity led him to climb up a tree to investigate a strange buzzing noise. It was a swarm of bees, and Georgie was stung to death.

On returning from a tour when I was acting Governor, my A.D.C. brought back a civet-cat. I do not favour taking wild animals from their natural habitat and trying to make pets of them, but the civet-cat was there, so she and we had to accept the situation. At first she was wild and nervous but soon became tame and friendly and was altogether a gentle creature. Grey, and striped somewhat like a badger, she was about the size of a half-grown kitten, and had a small pointed nose, rather a long neck and dainty feet. She played like a domestic cat and meowed in the same way, but also made a curious chuckle in her throat when pleased. Maurine would take her for walks in the garden, the civet-cat sitting erect on her arm. She loved being put down in a flower border, feeling safe under the foliage and sniffing the damp earth appreciatively. We fed her on bananas, milk and sweets which seemed to agree with her. Pom-pom, the cat, unable to make her out would walk away in pretended boredom.

ADMINISTRATIVE WORK

I found my work considerably easier than it had been in Jamaica; straightforward administration with no political overtones. One probably worked just as long hours but the mental pressure was usually absent. The demand for independence was still non-existent, or at any rate quiescent, and the sessions of Legislative Council were infrequent. Moreover, unofficial members of the Council did not occupy the prominent place in the eyes of the people that they did in Jamaica. The important people were the chiefs, whatever their title might be, and if they had any complaints or requests to make they took them to the District Officer, the Resident or the Chief Commissioner, as the case might be, and not to the Chief Secretary.

Nigeria in colonial days was the home of 'indirect rule', that is, rule through the local chiefs, from the lowly headman of a village to an almost-regal sultan. It will be observed that the word 'rule' is used, and in fact the administrative officers were largely the rulers of Nigeria, but they exercised their authority through the chiefs. The system generally worked to the advantage and contentment of the people. The members of the administrative service, numbering less than five hundred for a population of twenty-two millions, were a devoted band of public servants, many of them living in out of the way places with few amenities.

Nigeria is such a vast country that a good deal of decentralization was inevitable. The Chief Commissioners, one each for the Northern, Western and Eastern provinces, were really lieutenant-governors, which had at one time been their title. Within their own group of provinces they took precedence over everyone except the Governor. Outside, they ranked below the Chief Secretary. Friction between headquarters and those in the field is not unusual, but I am glad to say that the relationship between the Secretariat in Lagos and the three Chief Commissioners at Kaduna in the north, Ibadan in the west and Enugu in the east was generally harmonious. Occasionally, we in the Secretariat would be embarrassed when the Governor toured the provinces and was 'got at' by a Chief Commissioner, persuading him to agree to something that we had been strenuously resisting. Perhaps the fault was ours for having failed to forewarn the Governor. When the Governor displeased us in this manner, we had either to accept the situation or endeavour to induce him to reverse his decision. This, he was naturally reluctant to do, for it might look as though the Secretariat, and not he, was master.

Military Activities

One was more conscious of war in Nigeria than in Jamaica. Military activity was much greater with two West African divisions being trained for fighting in Burma. And our neighbour on the west was Dahomey, Vichy-French territory, against which a certain amount of 'cloak-and-dagger' activity and raids were carried out from Nigeria. These activities often annoyed the General. 'Who is responsible for the defence of the Colony, you or me?' he would say irately to the head of the organization. 'Well, I was only trying to . . .', or, 'I thought it would be a good thing if . . .' . To which the General would retort, 'If you can't think better than that you'd better stop thinking'. The General usually got the better of these arguments. After the North Africa landings, most of the French African colonies, including Dahomey, joined the Allied Cause, so I invited my opposite number from Porto Novo and his wife to stay with us for a few days. On their departure I wished to make him a present and offered him a bottle of whisky as something extra special, for I knew he liked it. 'Thank you very much', he said, but he would prefer potatoes. These, although not in such short supply as whisky, were by no means plentiful, but we managed to get hold of a few pounds to give him.

Apart from providing troops for the battlefront, West Africa was a very important source of ground-nuts and palm-oil and palm kernels, required for the manufacture of edible and non-edible fats and oils. Rubber, copra, cocoa and tin were also much needed. Consequently the civil administration in all its branches was largely engaged in increasing the production of these essential commodities, inducing the peasantry to grow more, ensuring that no bottle-necks occurred on the railways and roads to delay the transport of the larger volumes to the ports and on to the ships. All this called for co-ordination within the four West African colonies, between the different departments of government, and between the administration and the commercial firms. In Nigeria the co-ordination was good, and I have no reason to doubt that it was not equally good in the other colonies. I would have frequent informal discussions with the senior members in Nigeria of the Association of West African Merchants, AWAM, in the house of one or the other of us. We found that the informality of the venue brought us closer together and so more productive of a harmonious relationship than if the discussions had been held in my office. Co-ordination between the four colonies was just as necessary as it was within each colony, and this was not so good. The solution adopted was the appointment of a Cabinet Minister resident in West Africa, with co-ordinating authority over the four colonies. The arrangement was successful, for not only did the Minister knock together the heads of the four Governors—Gambia, Sierra Leone, Gold Coast and Nigeria—but, being a Cabinet Minister, he had direct access to the Prime Minister and was thus able to get speedier action than if the usual channels of approach by individual governors to the Colonial Office had been followed.

The Minister was Lord Swinton, whose dynamic personality and drive were productive of excellent results. The periodic conferences that he held with the governors and the commanders-in-chief were well worth-while and wasted much less time than do many conferences of this nature, though we could not help being amused when he once said, 'The eyes of the world are on us, gentlemen'. He must have forgotten for the moment that he was talking to a gathering of down-to-earth military chiefs and humdrum civil servants, and was not making a speech at a political rally. His only weakness was paying too much attention to the gossip of junior administrative officers whom he met when touring. I am all in favour of the top man talking to the lower echelons and not confining himself to the seniors, for sometimes useful pieces of information are gleaned. The fact that the 'Big Chief' is not aloof is a good morale builder, but he should not take as gospel truth all that is told him.

The meetings of the West African War Council under the chairmanship of Lord Swinton were held in Accra and I attended them when acting Governor. On one occasion, Maurine was with me and we both enjoyed seeing again Sir Alan and Lady Burns, whose guests we were at Christiansborg Castle, the Gold Coast Government House. Flying in a Blenheim bomber over Dahomey and Togoland with the jungle only a few hundred feet below, we could see how the superabundant forests crowded down to the edges of the rivers and estuaries or formed tight rings round the clusters of small villages and plantations, only waiting for the slightest relaxation to steal them back.

Christiansborg Castle is believed to have been built by the Danes in 1661 as a base from which to carry on their trade in slaves, ivory and gold, and was sold to the British in 1850. Standing on the open Atlantic, its proud bastions are pounded by the waves, and although the interior was pleasant and home-like, yet the sea dominated every nook and cranny.

SOCIAL LIFE

Social life in the accepted sense of the term was less active than it had been in Jamaica. One of the reasons was the comparative fewness of women. No wife of a government officer was permitted to go to the Colony from the United Kingdom unless she had a job. Consequently the number was small and all were doing a full day's work with no time for bridge parties and such like. What social life there was amongst the residents was pleasantly informal, with weekly dances at the Ikoyi Club and bathing parties at a rather unattractive and dangerous beach. On Saturday evenings Lagos society went to an open-air cinema at which ancient films were shown. This did not, however, detract from our enjoyment. Neither did we much mind being caught in a heavy shower on our way home, as sometimes happened. We either walked or rode bicycles from our house as my petrol ration for the month was only two gallons, which certainly did not allow for any joy-riding. The allowance for whisky, gin and beer was likewise small. Most guests were solicitous of the liquor stocks of their hosts and were correspondingly moderate in the amount they consumed.

Saturday or Sunday lunches were an institution at which the main dish was ground-nut stew in the north, the home of the ground-nut, and palm-oil chop in the south, the home of the oil-palm. Both dishes are basically curries. With palm-oil chop one drank palm-toddy, the fresh sap of the oil-palm, a very cooling drink, somewhat like dry ginger-beer in taste, colour and effervescence and with a low alcoholic content. If allowed to ferment, however, the potency is considerable. The illegal distillation of alcohol from bananas, pineapples or other fruits was common and in the market at Sapele I once saw a bottle labelled 'Illicit Gin. 3d.' Ground-nut stew and palm-oil chop were very tasty but heavy for a hot climate and conducive to a boa-constrictor-like siesta at their conclusion.

The weddings of prominent Africans in either the Anglican or Catholic cathedrals were gala events, but with the temperature at a dizzy height, to say nothing of the humidity, the wait of half an hour for the belated bride and then the long service was an endurance test. Had it not been for the fascinating and diverting fashions and vivid colours of the ladies' dresses, the function would have been more than flesh could have endured. At one of these weddings three aunts of the bride, all very substantial women and dressed exactly alike in pink chiffon gowns with trains and picture hats to match, swept majestically in with an assurance that was to be envied and sat in a pew in front of us. Other guests were gorgeous in red velvet or plush which set off their dark beauty. I suppose pride kept them cool.

A pleasant gathering was the monthly dinner with an equal number of African and European men. Often these sort of affairs are stiff and awkward, but those at Lagos were happy and relaxed—and this was not due to the quantity of alcohol consumed, which was small. The Anglican and Catholic bishops, Vining and Taylor—both charming men and true and sincere Christians—were members of the Club. When they dined with us at the Lodge, they enjoyed a quiet game of bridge as a change from their more serious occupations.

The only official dinner parties we gave were during the sessions of Legislative Council when I was acting Governor. We had two of these of about forty guests each. The guests would be received by the A.D.C. and Private Secretary and were served with cocktails. They would then be lined up, husbands and wives, according to seniority in a semi-circle round the drawing-room. As soon as all was ready the A.D.C. would come and tell us and, leading the way, would announce from the doorway: 'His Excellency and Mrs Grantham'. In we would sweep, going round shaking hands with each guest in turn. This done, I would offer my arm to the ranking lady, my wife following on the arm of the ranking gentlemen and so on, and we would process into the dining-room while the band in the garden played 'The Roast Beef of England'. The table, decorated with coralita, whose dainty flowers lent themselves to graceful arrangements in nine silver bowls, with tall silver candelabra holding white candles, made an attractive picture. Over the table a six-leafed punka swayed gently, while a score of 'boys' in white uniforms with broad red sashes stood behind chairs. Throughout dinner music floated in from the garden. At the end of dinner I rose, the rest of the company doing likewise, and raising my glass proposed the toast, 'The King'. The band played the first six bars of the national anthem at the conclusion of which we drank the toast. The ladies then left and after the men had rejoined them in the drawing-room, the A.D.C. would bring up to my wife and myself in turn groups of the guests in twos and threes so that we had an opportunity to talk with everyone. At eleven-thirty the band struck up 'The King', which was the signal for the guests to depart. My wife and I moved to the door and bade everyone good-night.

At non-official dinners there was no formality; they were much the same as in a private house, except that at Government House the King's health was always drunk and the Governor was served first, which latter practice I gave up when I became Governor.

RIDING

Riding is a favourite recreation of mine and thanks to the kindness of Brigadier Owen, an expert horseman and polo player who owned a number of horses, I was able to indulge myself. My delight in riding is not solely in the feeling of well-being that comes of the exercise and the communion between rider and horse. Part of the pleasure is the enjoyment of the countryside, whether the downs of Sussex or Wiltshire, the dried paddy-fields of China or the sandy paths of Lagos. Satisfying, too, is the creaking sound of the saddle, the feel of the reins, the view of the way ahead through the horse's ears, the rhythm of a well-balanced canter or the exhilaration of a gallop, with the thud of the hoofs on the turf and the wind whistling through one's hair.

Owen would call for me in his car before it was light and we would drive out to the stables where we mounted our steeds and rode through the bush on sandy paths bordered by sweet-smelling shrubs, palms, and trees with vines falling in cascades from their branches or interlacing overhead. Emerging from the bush we rode over grassy country and often, just as the sun rose, reached the lagoon which, in the sunlight, was a shimmering mass of gold, the shore fringed with tulip-trees flaunting scarlet blossoms. Sometimes we espied a pair of golden-crested cranes or white egrets or kingfishers. We would wade our horses into the water before returning over the dew-spangled grass in air filled with the freshness of damp earth. Maurine who had never ridden before, was taught to do so by the Brigadier, and frequently went with us. But she gave it up when the hotter weather started. With all else she had to do, she found it too exhausting.

CHRISTMAS 1942

Our first Christmas in Nigeria was one of the most pleasant and unusual we have ever spent. The Governor and Lady Bourdillon invited us to go with them on the *Valiant*, a stern-wheeler, like a small-sized version of a Mississippi steamboat. She was used, amongst other things, by the Governor and senior officials for tours up the creeks and rivers to places inaccessible by land. The Governor's suite was quite luxurious and the cabin allotted to us left nothing to be desired. Deck space was ample and the saloon did double duty as a lounge and dining-saloon. On the long upper deck, forming a sort of roof for this strange craft, a skittles-alley had been fitted up and here we spent many a pleasant hour during the ensuing five days.

The party was a small one, the Governor and Lady Bourdillon, the Governor's brother, a doctor on a visit to Lagos, the Commandant of the Free French Forces in Nigeria, Colonel Adam, the Governor's A.D.C. and our two selves. The *Valiant* came up to the landing stage in front of Government House. Supplies and luggage were taken on and we all boarded. As the *Valiant* moved off, the combined domestic staffs of Government House and The Lodge, except those going with us, waved farewell and gave us a cheer, evidently looking forward to their holiday as much as we were looking forward to ours. After a jolly lunch and that essential for the West Coast, a siesta, the ladies busied themselves with decorating the saloon, making an excellent job of it. It really looked Christmassy and festive with a Christmas tree, artificial holly, mistletoe, candles and all the things that make a Christmas atmosphere.

Meanwhile the vessel had been gliding through one quiet lagoon after another on whose dark-miasmic waters floated patches of the brilliant light-green of the Nile cabbage, crisp and fresh, with short roots hanging down in the water but attached to nothing. It is blown about with every breeze or carried hither and thither by the currents. All around the margins of the lagoons lay a selvedge of this plant, then rushes and giant papyrus over which leant tall palms and trees, Indian almond, kapok, wild banana, Persian lilac, cashew and trees never dreamed of in a temperate zone. Lianas draped the trees and flung down canopies of long pennons. It was a world of greens, from bright chartreuse to the sombre velvety dark-green of the water. Just as we dropped anchor, the sun dipped into the jungle and a sense of witchery deepened as we watched the fading light, held spell-bound by a brooding mystery—the mystery of this dark continent.

Dinner was gay; this was Christmas Eve and the dull work-a-day world seemed aeons away. And we knew that on the morrow we would wake to a day of leisure and pleasing ourselves. The Governor threw off his reserve and conversation became of the give-and-take kind with swift repartee. We planned what we would do with the comforting thought that we need not do any of it if we did not feel so inclined. Finally after dinner, the A.D.C. produced an accordion and played Christmas hymns, and so to bed. Our first Christmas in Africa had started well.

At breakfast next morning there were presents at everyone's place. Lady Bourdillon had brought something amusing for each of us which, when unwrapped, caused much laughter. The servants found this exactly to their liking and broad grins lighted up their dark faces; besides, they too, had been given presents.

Bird-watching was a hobby of Sir Bernard's and after breakfast he and Lady Bourdillon and the Commandant went ashore in one of the motor-boats to bird-watch. The rest of us decided to investigate a small village nestled on the water's edge. Here we found the people living in the same primitive fashion as, no doubt, they had a thousand years ago. As we approached, the women, clasping their babies, fled to their houses of thatch and reeds, but soon peered out and gradually came nearer in order to scrutinize us more closely. Although we could not speak to each other, the universal language of smiles and grins served well enough. We followed a path that led inland to small clearings in which guinea-corn and yams were growing. These, with the fish they caught, bananas and other wild fruits, probably comprised the entire diet of these people. Seeing lovely birds, we began to understand the fascination of bird-watching, wishing we had brought glasses with us.

That night we had a traditional Christmas dinner with turkey and ham and a flaming plum pudding, and afterwards did charades. Throughout the following days, Lagos and the rest of the world were forgotten. We lived for the moment, following our fancy, fishing, shooting or just lazing, interspersed with unhurried talk. The memory of that idyllic time is still with us. All too soon, the *Valiant* up-anchored to take us back to the work-a-day world. The only consolation was that on our return to Lagos we found the harmattan, a cool, dry wind from the Sahara, blowing away the heat and humidity.

VISITORS

There was a constant stream of visitors to Lagos. Either they came for some specific purpose or were on their way through, for during the war the only regular air route from the United Kingdom and the United States to Egypt, India and China was by way of West Africa, Accra and Lagos being the staging posts. Passengers, even some of top priority, often had to wait a few days before getting an onward plane. The hotels were quite inadequate in number, and their standard of accommodation was poor. A transit camp was set up for these transients but the more important of them stayed at Government House or with us. Hardly ever was our spare room unoccupied, while if the Governor was away on tour we would look after guests at Government House, having them over for meals and generally arranging for their comfort and pleasure. It not infrequently happened that a group of newly arrived guests would be waiting in the hall for departing guests to vacate their rooms, and if the departing plane was delayed or turned back, a troublesome situation arose. Only once did catering present a real problem. That was when four Indians stayed at Government House for two weeks when the Governor was away and we looked after them. Two were Hindus who would not eat beef, and two Mohammedans who would not eat pork, and just then mutton was unobtainable. We rang the changes on poultry, since when we have hardly been able to face up to chicken.

Whilst all this made for extra work, we did not mind, for most were interesting people, from kings and royal dukes to playwrights, authors, prime ministers, foreign ministers, admirals, generals and senior civil servants of various nationalities. With some we became good friends and have remained so since. One name, in particular, comes to mind, that of Violet Seymour, the wife of the British Ambassador to China, a most delightful person and full of fun.

Oliver Stanley visited Nigeria when I was acting Governor. I believe this was the first time a Colonial Secretary had come to the Colony, so the occasion was an important one. Nor had I previously met a Secretary of State face to face. He could not have been more charming nor his visit more successful and useful. Although well briefed on Nigeria he did not pretend to 'know all the answers'. His approach to those he met was friendly and sympathetic but he stood for no nonsense. His tour of ten days throughout Nigeria, and the two days in Lagos when he arrived, and another two before he left, gave him a first-hand knowledge of the country and was a stimulus to us in our war effort.

In order that as many people as possible should have the opportunity of meeting him socially, we gave a garden party to which we invited eight hundred guests. The day was glorious, the sun shone, and there was a cool breeze. Everyone wore their best and many of the Africans came in their native dress, looking very fine. One of the chiefs was in full regalia and, enthroned on a chair with his retainers sitting on the grass around him, made a picturesque group. I believe that everybody, including Oliver Stanley, enjoyed the party, finding it a pleasant change from the comparative drabness of war-time life.

I shall mention only one other visitor, and I do not even know her name. She was a senior officer of the W.R.N.S. on a tour of inspection of West African stations. We all thought her rather pompous and tiresome; consequently the merriment was not inconsiderable when a tumbo fly bit her in a tender spot. The tumbo fly is a nasty little creature that lays its eggs under the skin. The eggs develop into maggots which, when emerging, are mildly painful.

OFFICIAL TOURS

Touring in Nigeria was very pleasurable though sometimes rather fatiguing, and I was able to do a good deal whilst acting as Governor. The Governor must keep himself informed at first hand of what is going on in his colony and get the feel of the place. This can only be done by periodic visits and personal contacts with all and sundry. The visits also make 'His Excellency' someone real to the people and not merely a remote being living in Lagos, or whatever is the capital, and they have a tonic effect on the officials in the field. My conscience was therefore clear when I went on tour; I was doing my duty.

Some tours were entirely by car along macadamized or laterite roads with smooth grass verges or the bush cut back to keep the jungle at bay. Of the many kinds of forest trees, I thought the 'silk-cotton' the finest; it rises sixty feet from a buttress-like base before sending out its branches and towering majestically over the forest. Other tours were by train or plane or by the *Valiant*, depending on the places to be visited. Travelling by the *Valiant* was most restful and soothing as she glided quietly up the creeks, some so narrow that trees on either side almost touched overhead, at other times opening out into broad lagoons. On the swampy banks stood houses built on stills, and here children played on verandahs, with chickens, dogs and cats equally at home. On arriving at a scheduled stopping place, chiefs, accompanied by their picturesque retinues, came to pay their respects. One chief, I recollect, wore a silver crown dating from the fourteenth century, probably of Portuguese origin. Anchored at night, we were lulled to sleep by the sound of the water gently lapping the vessel's side.

Travelling by rail was the most luxurious, for the Governor had his own train, consisting of six coaches, the Governor's with a lounge and two bedrooms, one for his A.D.C. and Private Secretary, one for the servants, another comprising the dining-saloon and kitchen, and a baggage coach for the Governor's car, luggage and supplies. The six coaches would be attached to a goods train, so no speed records were broken. On our first morning just before breakfast, the train stopped in the middle of nowhere. On enquiring why, I was told: because His Excellency must not be joggled while he is eating. Air travel was by a plane provided by the R.A.F., a twin-engined biplane, a D.H. 89A, I believe. It held about half a dozen passengers. On these occasions the servants would go on in advance by train or lorry.

To whatever town we went, cheerful, laughing crowds turned out to welcome us, after which we would be greeted by the chiefs and their councils and appropriate speeches would be made. At Zaria in the Northern Provinces, where I was to present the Chief's Medal to the Emir, we witnessed a most thrilling spectacle. Up a long avenue, that stretched out before our pavilion in front of the palace, came the Emir's sub-chiefs each with his own retinue. Mounted on gaily caparisoned horses, a sub-chief with his followers in brilliant turbans and garish-coloured flowing robes galloped up the avenue at terrific speed, brandishing swords and lances. Just as it seemed as though they were going to crash into us, they sharply wheeled their horses and turned aside. A few moments and another lot came. This was repeated fifteen times.

On the same tour we also visited Kano, a large and important town on the edge of the desert. Established in A.D. 999 as a trading centre, Kano has continued as such to the present day. About four hundred years ago, travellers from Timbuctoo came bringing Moslem culture and religion and the population is now predominantly Moslem. Its mud houses are square and flat-roofed, with façades decorated in geometric designs in relief picked out in bright colours. The impression is one of sun-baked clay and merciless sunlight, of a hot, dry atmosphere, of camel caravans and donkeys, of dark people in flowing white robes moving with unhurried grace.

Our arrival at Kano had been well timed, for this was a day of great rejoicing, the end of Ramadan, the month of fasting. Escorted to seats on a canopied roof-top we watched the seething mass in the square, awaiting the arrival of the Emir. Besides those on foot there were horsemen, men mounted on camels and two court jesters doing tricks to amuse us. Then we espied in the distance a large group moving towards us. Over the centre spread a huge ceremonial umbrella, the thick gold rod being twirled, causing its gold and silver cloth to flash in the sun like burnished metal. Beneath the umbrella seated on a white horse was the Emir, clothed in robes of white and yellow and wearing an enormous turban, while a scarf covered the lower part of his face. His retinue, some mounted and wearing chain-mail, others on foot, but all clad in brilliant colours, completed the spectacle. The cavalcade halted, the Emir dismounted, I descended from the roof. We greeted each other, shook hands and exchanged courtesies. The Emir mounted again, the procession moved off, and I returned to the Residency.

That evening I gave a dinner party at the Residency, the Emir being the principal guest. Well over six feet tall and big in proportion, his robes and turban made him appear even larger, while his fine features indicated a strain of Arab. His charm was manifest, even though conversation had to be conducted through an interpreter. Maurine, somewhat unwisely perhaps, expressed admiration of a white camel with jewelled trappings which she had seen in the square that morning. 'Madam, the camel is mine, and it gives me the greatest pleasure to present it to you', said the Emir. Her polite protests were in vain; the camel was hers, and if our plane was too small to take it—as indeed it was—he would have it sent by rail. Here, the Resident came to the rescue; a war-time regulation prohibited animals travelling by rail, and this delicate pampered creature was not capable of walking the eight hundred miles to Lagos.

My wife had the good fortune whilst in Kano to be invited by the Emir to visit the harem of his four wives. She recounted that it was like something out of the Arabian Nights. Accompanied by the Resident's wife who acted as interpreter, she was received at the Palace gates by an immensely tall eunuch who escorted them inside a high-walled compound and through a maze of dazzling yellow courtyards and contrastingly dark passage-ways and dim rooms— where they had glimpses of women and children—furnished with divans, cushions and rugs. The walls and high-vaulted ceilings were ornamented with designs in high relief outlined in silver and vivid colours. Finally they were ushered into a room furnished, alas, in European style. Into this dim room came in turn each of the wives in reverse order of seniority and prettiness. The youngest, Kishiya, meaning 'She who makes jealousy', was a lovely girl of seventeen, her bare hands and feet stained with indigo and henna, producing a charming effect on her warm, brown skin. She was richly clothed, and wore gold bracelets, anklets and rings, but was so shy she could hardly raise her eyes. Last to come was the number one wife. Fat and middle-aged, she had a pleasant contented face and complete self-assurance. The situation was evidently to her liking, for she dominated it and everyone present. These women are happy in their circumscribed life, finding all they wish in the lazy, dreamy atmosphere, gossiping, quarrelling, bearing and rearing children in the traditions of this ancient civilization. They have no desire to leave the precincts of the Palace, and the suggestion of such a thing shocks them. They certainly seemed content, my wife said, and the Emir's household, consisting as it did of six hundred women, was large enough to make a community with plenty of variety and interest.

Our last visit was to Sokoto whose sultan is the senior of all Mohammedans in Nigeria. Setting out from the Residency to make our official call, our car was suddenly surrounded by galloping horsemen in flying gaudy-coloured robes, shouting and brandishing spears. Before we had recovered from our startled surprise, they had formed a guard on either side and escorted us to the Palace gates. The Sultan had only recently succeeded to the throne. Young and handsome with patrician bearing, he had a gracious manner and gave the impression of a man of considerable intelligence.

GOVERNMENT HOUSE

Sir Bernard's health gave increasing cause for concern until the doctors said it was imperative for him to retire, and in May 1943 he and Lady Bourdillon departed, leaving me as acting Governor. As it seemed likely that some months would elapse before the new Governor, whoever he might be, arrived, we moved into Government House. This needed a thorough renovation for none had been carried out since the Bourdillons had first arrived eight years previously. Now was the time and here was the person to do the necessary work, namely my wife. When we learnt that the new Governor was to be Sir Arthur Richards, my former chief in Jamaica, our joy was unbounded. Furthermore Lady Richards and my wife thought as one in matters of house decorating, so she knew she could go ahead and that it would be to Lady Richards's taste.

The servants at Government House had also to be taken in hand. Some were paid by the Governor, others by the government. The latter, especially, were inefficient, lazy and untidy. After several warnings we dismissed two of them. They could hardly believe their ears. They had been at Government House for twenty years and thought they would remain there for ever, regardless of whether or no they did any work. But off we packed them with their gratuities.

The servants' compound contained a sizable village with many outsiders who had no right to be there. Word was sent that they must leave and the compound would be inspected on a certain date. Again they could not believe that their vested interests were to be interfered with, and only after repeated warnings was the place finally cleared of the unauthorized occupants. A census was then taken which revealed that the number in the compound had been reduced by more than half.

Talking with a friend shortly afterwards, she remarked that her 'boy' had told her that the gambling room at Government House had been closed down. This was news to us, for we had not been aware of its existence. Apparently the Government House servants had been running a gambling-joint, much patronized by other servants in Lagos. Being at Government House they thought they would be safe from raids by the police. But the instigators, having seen the writing on the wall, had accepted the inevitable and decamped.

HOME LEAVE

At the end of two years we were due to go on leave, and not knowing if I would be transferred whilst in England, and consequently not returning to Nigeria, we thought it best to pack up all our belongings which could then be shipped to us at my new post, should I be transferred; whilst if we did come back to Nigeria we would simply unpack them again. Lagos was devoid of professional packers so we had to undertake the task ourselves with the assistance of our servants. They were not very good at the job with the result that my wife had to do most of it. On returning to lunch one day, and finding Maurine missing, I went to the back verandah, where I espied a tiny pair of hands projecting from the top of an enormous cask—the kind used for packing crockery—with Tom, our No. 2 boy, standing outside and languidly passing to the hands plates and cups and saucers. On closer inspection I discovered that the hands belonged to Maurine who was inside the cask. No wonder it took her a year to recover from her two years in Nigeria.

We said good-bye to our friends and arranged homes for our animals, also deciding that never again would we keep pets so long as we lived our vagabond existence. It seemed unkind to walk out on a creature who had given you his all. Maurine preceded me by a few weeks, flying to California where I shortly joined her before going to England.

It was with considerable regret that we left Nigeria, for we had enjoyed the work, the friendly, cheerful people and the life, and had been fascinated by the country. But nearly everyone has the ambition to get to the top of his particular tree and my tree was the colonial service with a governorship at the top.

CHAPTER FIVE

FIJI AND THE SOUTH PACIFIC, 1945–1947

I had always hoped that one day I would be posted to Fiji and my appetite was whetted by hearing Sir Arthur Richards, who had been Governor there before going to Jamaica, talk about the islands and the people, both of whom he loved. But the prospects at the moment seemed remote. The Governor, Sir Philip Mitchell, had been in office two years only and the normal term for a governorship was five. Then the unexpected happened; the governorship of Kenya fell vacant and Mitchell was appointed to it, whilst Fiji was offered to me. Apart from the satisfaction of getting my first governorship was the thrill of going to Fiji. Furthermore, the Governor of Fiji at that time was concurrently High Commissioner for the Western Pacific and also Consul-General for the Western Pacific with authority over the British Agent and Consul in the Kingdom of Tonga.

When the appointment was made, Maurine was in California and I still in England. I therefore rejoined her in San Francisco, thence in the absence of a civilian air service—the war still being on—we travelled by an American MATS (Military Air Transport Service) plane to Honolulu and from there by an American NATS (Naval Air Transport Service) seaplane to Suva, the capital of Fiji. On both planes we were the only passengers, the rest of the space being taken up by freight. On the leg between Honolulu and Suva, the plane stopped overnight at Canton Island, an Anglo-American condominium and a regular stopping place on the air route between the west coast of America and Australasia. This was our first glimpse of a South Sea island and I was now in my own domain, for Canton Island is part of the Gilbert and Ellice Islands Colony which comes under the jurisdiction of the High Commissioner of the Western Pacific. The island, a coral atoll about twenty miles in length but nowhere more than five hundred yards wide, encloses a pear-shaped lagoon. It is not, however, a typical South Sea island, for the vegetation is sparse and very few palm trees are to be seen.

Approaching Fiji we sat in the cockpit of the plane as we flew over Vanua Levu (approximately 2,000 square miles in area), one of the two large islands of the Fiji group, and then Viti Levu, the other large island, and twice the size, on the south side of which is Suva. The plane was flying low enough to enable us to see forest-covered mountain ranges, their jagged peaks rising three or four thousand feet from the sea or from brilliant green plains. On landing at Suva, we were greeted by the Colonial Secretary, John Nicoll (now Sir John), who had been acting as Governor since the departure of Sir Philip Mitchell, and other leading officials and members of the community, after which I inspected a guard of honour of the Fiji Military Forces, a fine looking body of men. We then drove to Government House by a road skirting the sea, through the entrance gates into park-like grounds and up a winding drive of royal palms to a knoll, where the rectangular white house with arcaded verandahs looked cool and inviting.

The original Government House had been largely destroyed by a hurricane and a new one had to be built. While plans for it were being drawn up, the Governor happened to be passing through Colombo where he was much taken with the appearance of the museum. Accordingly, he sent a picture postcard of it with instructions written on the back that the design of the new Government House was to be the same as that of the museum. The postcard has been kept at Government House as an interesting souvenir. The Governor's orders were duly carried out. Inside, the model of the museum was not followed. The main drawing-room, seventy feet long, and a smaller one beyond had french windows, opening on the verandahs. Across the hall was a well proportioned dining-room suitable for large or small parties. On the upper floor was a range of bedrooms with the Governor's suite at one end, spacious and airy and having magnificent views across the bay to the distant mountains. Here on the verandah, we often shared our breakfast with a friendly bulbul which sat on the edge of the sugar-bowl or pecked at a piece of papaw. From this verandah, too, I never tired of watching the Fiji police guard lowering the flag at sunset. Dressed in blue tunics and white *sulus*—somewhat like a kilt—they marched smartly up the drive, coming to a halt as they reached the flagstaff. Then, as the sergeant of the guard commenced to lower the flag, the guard presented arms and the bugler sounded the Retreat. At the conclusion of the ceremony the guard sloped arms and silently marched away in their bare feet—another day was over.

Although the layout of the house was good, a considerable amount of refurnishing was essential if the décor was to be worthy of Government House and ourselves. Maurine undertook the task—quite a heavy one with the lack of skilled upholsterers and decorators. Some years later she was gratified to receive a letter from the wife of the then Governor saying how much she appreciated what my wife had done.

Conveniently near was my office, reached by a path bordered by crocuses, and adjacent to it the Secretariat of the High Commission—all that remained of the original Government House.

The grounds covered about fifty acres with sweeping lawns and magnificent trees, some sprouting fountains of cymbidium orchids, while flowers in great variety grew luxuriantly in beds and borders. Walls were covered with flowering vines and, in places, that climbing lily, so well named *gloriosa*, spread its beauty. Near the tennis courts, tall trees sheltered a small tropical garden into which the sun never penetrated. Here in the dim atmosphere grew sweet-smelling crinum lilies, brilliant colia, delicate ferns and orchids, both terrestrial and epiphytic.

One of the gardeners, an Indian of diminutive stature and saint-like eyes, could not bear to see a plant discarded. If told to uproot one he would plant it in some remote part of the garden to save its life. Mohammed was a time-expired convict and one day I asked the butler what his crime had been. 'Oh', said Singh lightly, 'he killed his wife and cut her up into little pieces and put her in a sack'. But then she had been unfaithful to him.

The lower part of the garden was often flooded, for Suva has only two seasons, the wet and the rainy. We thought that by a proper system of drainage, which we devised, the swampy land could be transformed into an expanse of lawn which would enhance the beauty of the trees and palms. The Director of Public Works, a likeable but obstinate Scot, was vehement in his opposition to our scheme, but I was even more obstinate and the work was carried out. Luckily it proved successful.

The domestic staff was a mixture of Fijians and Indians. Bala, an Indian, the No. 1 cook, presided in the kitchen, a natural gentleman with a humourous twinkle in his eye and always anxious to please. The butler, Singh, also an Indian, was a capable fellow who suffered from occasional drinking bouts. Beta, the senior maid, was a delightful person, competent and friendly. She loved to tell of her visit to England where she had accompanied a previous Governor and his wife, and of how helpful everyone had been to her. Vika, my wife's personal maid, a good deal younger than Beta, was likeable and devoted, but her love-life sometimes got her into trouble.

LOYALTY

Before leaving London I had been briefed at the Colonial Office about Fijian and High Commission matters, and had seen a number of people who had been to the territories; then during the journey I had read as much as possible about them. I therefore knew something of the background when on my first day I had talks with Nicoll, the Colonial Secretary of Fiji, and Harry Vaskess, the Chief Secretary of the High Commission. John Nicoll, a very capable man, had the appearance of an eighteenth century aristocrat and, with his long dominating nose, would have looked well in the dress and peruke of that period. He would not tolerate inefficiency or incompetence, and this made him respected rather than liked by his subordinates. I considered myself fortunate to have him with me subsequently—again as Colonial Secretary—in Hong Kong for a few years. Thence he was deservedly promoted to the governorship of Singapore. Whilst there he visited North Borneo where he had started his career thirty years previously. The Governor asked him if he noticed any change in the place. 'Yes', replied Nicoll, 'the grass on the railway tracks is higher'.

When King Thakombau ceded Fiji to Queen Victoria in 1874 he presented to her his war-club—the insignia of rule—with the message, 'With this emblem of the past he sends his love to Her Majesty, saying that he fully confides in Her and Her children who, succeeding Her, shall become Kings of Fiji, to exercise a watchful control over the welfare of his children and people'. The reference to the past was the warring that used to take place between the different chiefs and their followers and the cannibalism then practised. Queen Victoria's grandson, King George V, returned the club to Fiji for use as the mace in Legislative Council. The world 'love' in Thakombau's message is no empty phrase, for the love and devotion that all Fijians have for the sovereign of Britain is intense and real. Even in the remotest villages one sees in the houses pictures of the Royal Family, who are regarded as revered parents. Had I said to a Fijian that His Majesty wished him to walk into the sea and drown himself, I am quite sure he would have done so. Where else in the Commonwealth would one find such unquestioning loyalty? Needless to say the war record of the Fijians was a fine one, notably in the Solomons where Corporal Sefania Sukanivalu won a posthumous Victoria Cross. A Fijian chief, who had taken part in both World Wars, asked me hopefully one day if I thought there was any chance of war between Britain and Russia, as he would like to be in that one too.

The manner in which the Fijians responded to an appeal made by my wife for food for Britain was amazing. Tons of sugar, tinned pineapple and other things were sent to England for distribution by the W.V.S. In one instance, the people on a small and far-from-wealthy island sent in £1,000. My wife rightly thought this far more than they could possibly afford, so returned £900 with a tactfully worded letter. The £900 came back. They said they could not bear the thought of the people in Britain being short of food and they wanted, nay they insisted, on the whole of the thousand pounds being used for the purchase of food to go to England, even though it meant that they themselves might have to go short. It made them happy to think that they, like the people in Britain, were making sacrifices.

Not only are the Fijians doughty fighters and magnificent specimens of humanity, but they are one of the most attractive, hospitable and generous people I know. They have all the kindliness and friendliness of the Polynesians with a mixture of the toughness of the Melanesians. Fiji is the meeting place of Melanesia and Polynesia, and the Fijians in the Lau islands on the eastern confines of the Colony are more Polynesian than Melanesian.

There is nothing that a Fijian likes more than a party, and nothing that he likes less than work. And what need has he to work? Nature provides him with all the food he needs: bananas, coconuts, breadfruit, dalo (taro), cassava, chickens, wild pig or fish, as the case may be. Local timber and thatching for his house is easy to come by, and the climate is such that he requires neither heavy clothing nor fires to keep him warm. He loves dancing and singing; and a *meke*, a Fijian song-and-dance party, is a treat both to the eye and the ear. Some of the dances are traditional war dances, the men wearing a type of *sulu* made of broad long leaves and armlets, anklets and coronets of leaves and flowers. With their faces smeared black, their brown torsos glistening with oil, and clubs or spears in their hands, they look extremely fierce. The women dancers are most graceful, but in both the men's and women's dances the rhythm and harmony are perfect. Some are performed in a sitting posture, the body swaying, the arms and hands gesturing gracefully to the music, mostly provided by part-time singing which is rhythmic and melodious. On occasion and depending on the nature of the dance, the words of the songs will be topical, especially in those areas where the Polynesian influence is strongest.

The Fijians are, as can be imagined, great sportsmen—rugger being their favourite game. What soccer is to England, rugger is to Fiji. Boots are not generally worn except by the top teams, and the way in which the players can kick the ball with their bare feet, and the distance, is amazing. On most Saturday afternoons I would 'root' for the Police 1st XV because my office orderly, Corporal Leki, played for them. During their time in Malaya after the war, the Fiji Regiment won the army championship every year save one.

LABOUR

Unfortunately, this lotus-like existence does not fit into the modern world and it was soon found, after the establishment in the seventies of the last century of the sugar industry—sugar being the Colony's principal export—that the Fijian was an indifferent worker on the plantations. Workers from other Pacific islands were tried with equally unsatisfactory results. Finally, indentured labour was brought in from India. Had the authorities realized at the time what the outcome of this would be, they surely would have hesitated before doing it, for the Indians now outnumber the Fijians. If the two races intermarried or if unlimited land were available, no problem would arise. But neither is the case. The two races remain separate and distinct; the Fijians resentful and suspicious of the Indians, the Indians contemptuous of the Fijians. Only by the grace of God and the good nature of the Fijians have inter-communal clashes been avoided. Meanwhile the pressure on the land grows more acute as the population increases. To protect the Fijian from himself all native, i.e. Fijian-owned, land not already alienated, is controlled by the Native Land Trust Board which adopts a conservative policy in leasing land to non-Fijians. Were it not for the existence of the Board, the Fijians, who are as feckless as they are charming, would have sold most of their land to the Indians. The Indians contend that, apart from race, they are as Fijian as the Fijians themselves, having been born in the Colony—as most of them have—that Fiji is their home and that they cultivate the land more fruitfully than do we trust and fully repose in Her (Queen Victoria) that She will rule Fiji justly and affectionately, that we may continue to live in peace and prosperity'?

On the political front, too, the Indians are much more active than the Fijians and are eager for independence, or at least internal self-government and a common electoral roll for Legislative Council, in place of the present system whereby the three races, European (including Euronesians), Fijian and Indian have equal representation. A common electoral roll would result in the swamping of the Fijians—and the Europeans, too, for that matter—by the Indians. Naturally the Fijians do not favour the idea. The situation is not altogether dissimilar to that in the Federation of Malaya with the easy-going Malays and the industrious Chinese; but the Malays still preponderate numerically and are holding their own in this respect. In both territories the aim is to bring the comparatively backward native up to the level of the immigrant race so that he can compete on equal terms. In neither case can the clock be put back and the Indians returned to India and the Chinese to China. For too long, perhaps, the inclination was to preserve Fiji as a museum piece and not enough done to bring the Fijian forward to enable him to take his place in the modern world.

TOURING

Touring was essential if I were to get to know Fiji and its people. This, of course, holds good for all countries but more so where the economy is rural and not industrial. Fiji is an agricultural country despite the fact that gold is the second largest export. I therefore travelled a good deal, sometimes basing myself on Lautoka, the centre of the largest sugar-growing area and where, outside the town, the Governor had a *bure;* that is, a Fijian house made of thatch, pleasing to look at and comfortable to live in. In the towns they have been largely replaced by houses of wood with corrugated iron roofs which are easier to build and less costly to maintain. The sugar industry was in the hands of the Colonial Sugar Refining Company, an Australian concern, which was efficient and fair in its dealings with the cane growers. Thus, with Fiji's two principal industries operated by Australian interests, her economic ties with that country were close. But in other respects Fiji looked more to New Zealand and, generally speaking, the New Zealanders were better liked than the Australians; they were more 'sympatico'.

The two most interesting tours I made were on horseback across Viti Levu and Vanua Levu, each taking about five days. Here one was miles away from any road or telegraph, right in the heart of rural Fiji. Accompanying me was the District Commissioner concerned and a few Fijian officials, but as we progressed Fijians from nearby villages would join us for part of the way, so that our calvacade was rarely less than fifty strong, with our hangers-on, many of them riding bareback, laughing and singing and enjoying themselves hugely, as indeed we all were.

On arrival at a village we would be met by the *turanga-ni-koro* (village headman) or sometimes by the *buli* (head of a *tikina* or group of villages) and conducted to the bure where the *yangona* (kava) ceremony took place. This ceremony is very ancient and, in the case of the Governor, a chief or other official, is an expression of fealty. Yangona—a refreshing non-alcoholic beverage and the equivalent on non-ceremonial occasions of the Englishman's 'cuppa'—is made from the powdered root of the plant of that name and, to the accompaniment of chanting and the clapping of cupped hands, is mixed with water in a large bowl, hewn from a section of tree trunk, and strained through hibiscus fibres. When the mixture is ready a quantity is poured into a coconut shell. The bearer of the cup, holding it in outstretched hands, then turns towards the honoured guest and proceeds slowly towards him. All is silent save the quiet rustling of the fronds of the man's sulu as he advances. As the guest takes the cup and drinks, silence is broken by clapping of hands and deep cries of *ooi* ending on a high note. The other guests are similarly honoured in descending order of importance. In smaller villages the ceremony may not be carried out quite as elaborately and the cup-bearer may be dressed in an old shirt and a pair of khaki shorts, but in spirit it is the same. The *tabu* (whale's tooth) is also presented at the same ceremony with an address of loyalty and greeting. At the conclusion of the formal part of the proceedings everyone relaxes, more yangona is drunk, if one feels so inclined, and conversation becomes general. The *buli* or senior local representative would then raise with me matters of local interest or anything else that he and I might like to discuss.

On these longer tours we would frequently be invited to partake of food that had been prepared for us of local produce. I must confess I found most of it unappetizing. I thought the yams tasteless and the chickens—often chased through the village and slaughtered only a few minutes before—tough and stringy. Once I was obliged to eat three breakfasts—in addition to the regular breakfast I had had before we started out—at different villages through which we passed. But a really delicious dish was the crayfish, about the size of a prawn, from a nearby mountain stream, cooked in coconut milk and served on a banana leaf.

We spent the nights in Fijian villages, sleeping in bures, usually on enormous beds with layers of mats which I found quite comfortable. At the end of a day's ride one felt in need of a bath or swim, which created a problem if the village was distant from the sea or a stream. In one village the shower—the only one—was in the centre of the village and surrounded by a breast-high fence of thatch. When I expressed a desire to use the shower, all other taps were turned off as I proceeded to my ablutions. The trickle of water was meagre but sufficient for my purpose and I was careful not to use too much.

To visit the Yasawa group of islands—where the film *The Blue Lagoon* was shot—to the north-west of Viti Levu, and Kandavu, to the south of Viti Levu, I used the Public Works Department workboat, *Degi*. The Yasawas contain some romantic-looking islands, with sharp green-clad peaks rising steeply from the water's edge. Here we bathed in a pool which we reached by diving down from the sea, through an underwater gap in the rock-face on one side and coming up on the other into a veritable blue grotto of crystal-clear water, with the light coming in from a hole in the rock above. It was as beautiful as it was eerie.

During this visit I was presented with a number of turtles, and when we sailed for home, we had a dozen on the foredeck, looking pathetic, lying helpless on their backs. As they were more than we could deal with at Government House, we gave most of them to the War Memorial Hospital.

My principal memory of Kandavu is our departure. As the *Degi* slowly moved off in the setting sun, the villagers, waist-high in the water with the white beach and palm trees as background, sang that haunting Fijian song *Isa Lei*. The sound of their melodious voices coming over the water was one of the most lovely things I have ever heard.

Whenever I visited any of the islands in the Lau group, I travelled by an R.N.Z.A.F. Catalina flying-boat, and was usually accompanied by Ratu (Chief) Sir Lala Sukuna. Sukuna was a Rhodes scholar when the First World War broke out and being refused a commission he joined the Foreign Legion, winning the Médaille Militaire. He harboured no resentment for the slight inflicted on him by the denial of a commission, and on his return to Fiji at the end of the war joined the administration, becoming in due course Secretary for Fijian Affairs. Whilst in every way a Fijian, he was at the same time a cultured Oxonian; altogether a most delightful individual.

His wife, Adi (Lady) Maria, was equally charming, and devoted much of her time to welfare work. She was also an adept at casting the Fijian-style fishing net. My only complaint against Sukuna was the evil-smelling cigars he insisted on smoking in the plane. 'I hope, Sir, you like the aroma of these cigars. They are locally made and are quite inexpensive', he would say. 'Sukuna', I would reply, 'you know perfectly well that they stink like a defective drain, but don't let me spoil your pleasure'. And he would go on smoking, amused smiles on both our faces.

Luki, the No. 2 cook at Government House and at one time a steward on a New Zealand ship, sometimes came with me. He was a very pleasant fellow and combined with natural aplomb the dual roles of domestic servant and a minor chief in his own right. At Government House he would bring my glass of coconut water in the early morning and, sitting cross-legged on the floor, softly clapped his hands while I drank—the Fijian way of conveying respect.

On the island of Makogai, between Viti Levu and Vanua Levu, is the leper settlement run by the Catholic Order of Mary under the supervision of a government medical officer. My wife and I paid a number of visits to Makogai, invariably being impressed by the efficient manner in which the sisters conducted the settlement and the cheerfulness of the patients, most of whom were natives of Fiji or other South Pacific islands, but including one or two Catholic fathers who had contracted the disease. Neither did they seem to be despondent, being upheld, no doubt, by their faith and the inspiring view from their little cottages across the Koro Sea on which they always commented. I asked the Mother Superior—a French woman of strong character and pronounced eyebrows—if ever she had trouble with the nuns. 'Very rarely', she said, 'and if I do, I wave my eyebrows at them'.

Australia and New Zealand we also visited several times as I had to go there on official business. The friendliness of Australians and New Zealanders to strangers is a characteristic common to both, but how different are their countries. Australia impressed me with its dynamism. It was like being in a power-house with the turbines humming and vibrating. New Zealand, by contrast, is the country of the ordinary decent fellow. Everyone has a house of the same size—this is of course a simplified exaggeration—and leads the same sort of standardized life, with no have-nots and no great wealth. Although lacking the stimulation of Australia, it is a pleasant and agreeable land with great natural beauty and marvellous facilities for fishing and other sports.

WESTERN PACIFIC HIGH COMMISSION

The territories of the Western Pacific High Commission comprise the Gilbert and Ellice Islands Colony, the British Solomon Islands Protectorate, the Anglo-French Condominium of the New Hebrides, the Kingdom of Tonga and Pitcairn Island. The headquarters of the Commission was at Suva, approximately 1,200 miles from Tarawa, the capital of the Gilberts, lying to the north, and about the same distance from Honiara, the capital of the Protectorate, lying west-north-west, with Vila the capital of the New Hebrides about half-way between Suva and Honiara. 450 miles to the south-east of Suva is Nukualofa, the capital of Tonga, whilst Pitcairn is nearly 3,000 miles away to the east. Its inhabitants, descendants of the *Bounty* mutineers, number a few hundred only and, so far as I am aware, only one High Commissioner has ever visited them and that for a brief few hours when a passenger on a United Kingdom/New Zealand mail steamer.

The posts of Governor of Fiji and High Commissioner for the Western Pacific have been separated since I left the region, and the High Commissioner now has his headquarters at Honiara. I see few advantages in the change. The Solomons and the New Hebrides are entirely different in geophysical features, people and problems from the Gilbert and Ellice Islands and Tonga. The geophysical features and the economic problems of the Gilbert and Ellice Islands and Tonga are much the same, whilst there is considerable affinity between the Ellice Islanders—the Ellice Islands being the southern part of the Colony—and the Tongans, both being Polynesian, as are the people in the Lau Islands on the eastern confines of Fiji. On the other hand, the British Solomons and the New Hebrides are an extension of the Australian Solomon Islands, the Straits of Bougainville separating the Australian island of that name from Choiseul, the northernmost island of the British Solomons. It would be logical for them to be under the same administration, and, since they are less important to Britain than to Australia—to whom in fact they would seem to be vital as the Pacific War showed—should not the British Solomons, and Britain's authority in the New Hebrides be transferred to Australia? With the Solomons and the New Hebrides thus removed from the High Commission, the headquarters of the Commission could most conveniently be situated at Suva with the Governor of Fiji once more concurrently the High Commissioner. United Kingdom members of the Solomons service, to whom I put these ideas, raised the objection that the territories would be less well administered by Australia than by Britain. In the absence of any supporting evidence for this contention, I do not accept it. Furthermore the Australian government displays considerably greater interest in, and devotes more money to, the development of her Pacific lands than Britain does to hers.

But whether the headquarters of the High Commission remains at Honiara or returns to Suva, communications between the different territories will continue to present difficulties. In pre-war days, Burns Philp ran steamers between Sydney, the Solomons and the New Hebrides, whilst the British Phosphate Commission—a consortium of the representatives of the Australian, British and New Zealand governments—had vessels going from Australia to Ocean Island (the pre-war capital of the Gilbert and Ellice Islands Colony) to load phosphate. No shipping lines operated, and none does today, between the Solomons, the New Hebrides, the Gilbert and Ellice Islands and Fiji. Occasionally cargo ships call to pick up copra, otherwise communication is maintained by one or two government owned vessels carrying in discomfort a few passengers. The *Awahou*, acquired second-hand by the Gilbert and Ellice government after the war, was such a vessel. Very aged, her funnel looking like a bundle of pencils tied together, she was most unprepossessing in appearance. Subsequently, after she had been resold, she was lost with all hands in the Tasman Sea. Mrs Maude, the cultured but practical wife of the Resident Commissioner, had a large dog-kennel made and placed on the deck. In this she slept, as the only way of getting a decent night's rest and not being pitched out of her bunk or overcome by the suffocating heat in the cabin below. And when Hard, the Director of Education of the Gilbert and Ellice Islands, and his wife were going from Suva to Funafuti, some six hundred miles away, the voyage took two weeks in one of the Colony's new sixty-footers, with no fire in the galley stove for several days after a storm had put it out of action.

Communications within the territories themselves were equally inadequate and the vessels very small, so that those travelling on them had to be good sailors. With the paucity of inter-island communications, officers stationed on small islands led a lonely existence. The islands might be only a few square miles in area with a population counted in the hundreds and no other Europeans at all. They considered themselves lucky to receive four visits a year by a schooner. To summon a doctor, or to get to one, took days. Fresh vegetables and meat were unobtainable and refrigerators had not yet come to the islands. Nor did facilities exist for the solace of listening to broadcasts from Australia, New Zealand or Fiji. It is hardly to be wondered that some officers got mixed up with native women, took to drink or committed suicide.

Mr 'X' was an administrative officer in the Gilbert and Ellice Islands. His conduct with drink and women became so notorious that something had to be done about him, and he was transferred to the Solomons in the hope that the entirely new environment would save him. Then the war came and the Japanese occupied a number of the islands. Like a few other brave men, Mr 'X' remained behind in the jungle as one of the coast-watchers, sending radio reports of the movements of enemy ships and planes. The Japanese hunted the watchers relentlessly. 'X' 's group, consisting entirely of Solomon Islanders, also hunted the Japanese, accounting for nearly two hundred. For his services, 'X' was awarded the D.S.O. and, after the Japanese had been driven out, reverted to the civil administration, being posted to headquarters in Suva. But those lonely years in the Gilberts had irretrievably ruined him for normal life. His behaviour became steadily worse, until finally he had to be removed from the service. I tried in vain to secure for him an enhanced pension, on the grounds that his mental deterioration had been caused by the conditions under which he had been compelled to live in his younger days. The Colonial Office, however, would have none of it. The regulations did not cover a case of this sort and the regulations were sacrosanct.

Life in these isolated islands is now not so remote as it used to be and kerosene-operated refrigerators are supplied. Moreover after the war an unwritten convention was established by the Colonial Office by which officers in the High Commission territories are offered a transfer after seven years; a wise and humane rule.

Although the headquarters of the colony of Fiji and the High Commission were both in Suva, the secretariats were separate. The head of the High Commission secretariat was Harry Vaskess, an Australian by birth, who at the time of my arrival had been Chief Secretary for sixteen years, so what he did not know about the territories was not worth knowing. His knowledge, however, had been acquired almost entirely at headquarters since he had rarely visited the various islands because of the difficulties and slowness of travel. His headquarters' outlook made him suspicious of the three Resident Commissioners—Gilbert and Ellice, Solomons and New Hebrides—considering that a close control should be kept on them, lest they wittingly or unwittingly do something not in order. The Resident Commissioners on their side objected to being treated like children. Nonetheless, I found Vaskess a most helpful and likeable colleague and I always felt at ease in my mind that nothing would get past him that should not.

So far as getting to and from the different territories was concerned, I was in the region at a good time. The Japanese had been driven out but the Allied military forces had not been entirely withdrawn, or air-bases closed down, and the R.N.Z.A.F. kindly flew me in a Catalina, which I also used for going from place to place both in Fiji and the Gilbert and Ellice Islands, wherever a lagoon existed for coming down. The Catalina had two 'blisters' and here Maurine (when she accompanied me) and I would instal ourselves in wicker chairs; she with a parasol tied with string to the blister as a protection against the very strong sun. She went with me on a number of trips— she was the first High Commissioner's wife to visit the territories—as her presence helped to cheer up the small European communities which now included a few wives. The R.N.Z.A.F carried me free, but were obliged to charge 6d a mile for my wife. As the distance from Suva to Tarawa or Honiara and back was 2,400 miles, this amounted to quite a considerable sum, but I did not begrudge paying, as my wife's visits were much appreciated. She also shopped for them in Suva and Sydney: hammers, nails, cosmetics, pots and pans and even kitchen stoves, all the things that we take for granted but were unobtainable at that time in Tarawa and Honiara. The Catalina was slow but reliable and rarely flew higher than six thousand feet, which gave us clear views of the coral atolls surrounded by their aquamarine water over which we passed, whilst the cloud effects were superb.

GILBERT AND ELLICE ISLANDS

The Gilbert and Ellice Islands are, as the double name suggests, two separate groups. The peoples, too, are distinct, the Gilbertese being Micronesians, with straight hair and slightly mongoloid features. The Ellice Islanders are Polynesians like the Tongans and Hawaiians. The two races differ in character as well as in appearance. The Ellice Islanders are gay extroverts, the Gilbertese more serious and independent-minded. This is not to imply that they are unfriendly or unattractive; the reverse is the case. One of the possible reasons for this difference in temperament may be the fact that many of the Gilbert Islands are infertile owing to the poor soil and uncertain rainfall, with the consequence that the struggle for existence is more severe than in the Ellice Islands.

The boundaries of the Gilbert and Ellice Islands Colony, extending over both sides of the equator, enclose an area of more than a million square miles of ocean, but the land area of all the islands put together is less than 350 square miles. These coral atolls are covered by a thin layer of soil. Taro, coconut and pandanus palm are about the only things that will grow on them. The total population in 1945 was a little under 35,000, of whom 27,000 were in the Gilberts. A South Sea island is certainly romantic looking; palms growing right down to the water's edge, the golden beach encircling a lagoon, with all the colours of a black opal and, a few hundred yards beyond the perimeter of the atoll, the swell of the ocean pounding in white cascades against the reef. On landing the picture is enhanced by the laughing and singing natives, often bedecked in skirts of fronds, with garlands of hibiscus round their heads.

To spend a few days or weeks on a South Sea island may be bliss, but to remain on one for several years with none of one's own kind would be a different matter. One can sympathise with Mr 'X'. Robert Louis Stevenson lived for a time on Abemama, one of the Gilberts, but even this romantic was unable to endure the loneliness and moved to Apia, the capital of Western Samoa, where subsequently he died and is buried. A few Europeans, usually seafaring men from schooners, married local women and settled down happily; their offspring being Euronesians. The *Bounty* mutineers on Pitcairn with their Tahitian wives are the most notable example. When visiting Funafuti in the Ellice Islands, we found that many of the five hundred inhabitants bore the name of O'Brian, descendants of a lusty sea captain. Polly O'Brian, her hips swaying as she danced and with a 'come-hither' look in her eyes, was a true South Sea belle. Now she is probably fat and matronly but, I am sure, as cheerful as ever. On one occasion at Funafuti the District Officer, Roberts, proudly produced a cake for my wife which he had made with indigestion tablets instead of baking powder which he did not have; a very good effort.

Copra is produced in all the islands—the plantations being native-owned—and, with the exception of phosphate from Ocean Island, is the mainstay of the Colony's economy. In pre-war days the purchasing and shipping was done by commercial firms which also operated trade-stores. After the war they did not consider it worth their while to reestablish themselves, and all commerce is now in the hands of native-run co-operatives under the supervision of government.

Ocean Island, 250 miles west-south-west of Tarawa and only 21 square miles in extent, with its phosphate is virtually the Colony's 'gold mine', accounting for nearly half the government's revenue.

By the end of the century the phosphate will have been worked out and the island be just a mass of inhospitable looking dirty-grey coral pinnacles on which nothing will grow. The thousand or so indigenous inhabitants were moved to the fertile island of Rambi in the Fiji group in 1946 and the workers on Ocean Island now all come from elsewhere. Consequently when the island is abandoned, it will be a simple matter to return them to their homelands, the Gilbert and Ellice Islands, Australia or Hong Kong, as the case may be.

The Gilbert and Ellice islanders are all Christians and take their religion very seriously, so much so that before the war inter-sect rivalry led to sanguinary fights and killings. The only way of stopping this was to prohibit the establishment of Catholic missions in certain Protestant islands and of Protestant missions in Catholic islands.

My first visit to the Gilberts was to Tarawa, the capital of the Colony, one and a half degrees north of the equator, a coral atoll made up of a series of islets—actually the above-water ridges of a coral reef—twenty-five miles in length but nowhere more than a third of a mile wide, with the highest point eight feet above sea level. The shape of the connected islets looks like a 'V' lying on its side, the open end being a submerged coral reef with an opening through which ships enter the lagoon. At low water one can go from one islet to another by land, but to get to the more distant parts it is quicker to cross the lagoon by launch or canoe. Strung along the islet are some half dozen villages with a total population of a few thousand.

Tarawa was the scene of a fierce battle in the Pacific War, eleven hundred American marines being killed before they had wiped out the four thousand defending Japanese. On the islet of Betio, the scene of the battle, memorials have been erected to the memory of the American dead and the twenty-two Dominion and Euronesian civilians beheaded by the Japanese.

The task of the Resident Commissioner, Vivian Fox-Strangways, was not an easy one. War requirements were still paramount but they must not be allowed to press too hardly on the natives. At the same time, the Colony had to be put on its feet again after the occupation by the enemy of several of the islands. Fox-Strangways was admirably suited for the job, and although he wore only the badges of a colonel—the Gilberts and Solomons being fighting areas, the civil officers held military rank—he was held in respect by American officers of higher rank, whilst on the purely civilian side, he was an experienced and capable administrator. Good-looking, debonair and with a sense of humour, I found him a congenial colleague and felt completely at home whenever I stayed with him at his trim little 'leaf' bungalow overlooking the lagoon at Betio.

That the natives were not downtrodden and oppressed by the British colonialists must have come as a surprise to some of the Americans. They voiced criticism, both fair and unfair, and I recollect a young District Officer telling me that an American Officer had chided him at the absence of a parliament and of substantially built schools and hospitals, and ending with the question, 'What have you done for these people?' To which the District officer replied: 'We have left them alone'—a very good answer. There is no parliament or legislative council. That may come in time, but much of the administration is in the hands of local councils and appointed native officials under the supervision of the administrative officers—a replica of the indirect rule of Nigeria. The council members, particularly in the Gilberts, are not afraid of speaking their minds, not even to the High Commissioner, as I know from experience. Whilst to erect elaborate schools and hospitals would not only be unsuitable but would be unkind as well, for they would be too far above what the islanders have in their own homes. None the less, I would agree that in pre-war days not enough was done. The main thing, however, is that the people are happy. With no minerals—other than the phosphate on Ocean Island—practically no possibilities of agricultural development, no alien-minorities problem and no nations casting covetous eyes on the Colony, they can look forward with equanimity to living much the same sort of happy, carefree existence that their forefathers enjoyed, with the added advantage that they can now get schooling and medical care. For their peace of mind, let us hope that the islands do not become tourist resorts.

On the afternoon of my second day at Betio, Fox-Strangways and I crossed the lagoon to the village of Abaokoro. What a contrast! Betio was a military camp of white soldiers; Abaokoro a South Sea village with few signs of the war. Owing to the shallowness of the water, the launch had to stop some way out. Had it not been the High Commissioner on a formal visit, we doubtless would have taken off our shoes and stockings and waded ashore. As it was, four brawny islanders carried us on garlanded chairs affixed to poles. Awaiting us on the shore was the Native Magistrate and members of the *kaubere* (island council). After being presented, they conducted us up the beach along a coral path beneath arches decorated with woven pandanus and other fibres. Little paper Union Jacks were prominent and on either side the entire population, dressed in their Sunday best, was gathered to greet us. Our destination was the *maneaba* or meeting-house; perhaps community-centre would be a better term, for the maneaba is the focus of all the social activities of the village. About sixty feet long and forty feet wide, lofty in height with the thatched roof coming down from the ridge pole to eaves at head level, the boles of palms along the side and down the centre and open on all sides, it had the serenity and coolness of a cathedral. After we had taken our seats and the villagers, sitting cross-legged, had taken theirs, the Native Magistrate made an address of welcome to which I replied. Presentations were then made to me, mats and necklets of small shells, models of catamarans and woven fibre fans. In return I presented cases of soap—a much prized commodity—and cigarettes. Thereafter a general discussion ensued, mainly on local matters and the progress of the war in which I did my best with the aid of Fox-Strangways.

The proceedings over, we adjourned to the rest-house accompanied by Miss McCarthy, a Euronesian girl training to be a nurse, who acted most competently as interpreter and whose father was one of the twenty-two civilians murdered by the Japanese on Betio. In the evening we returned to the maneaba for a *batere*, a dancing and singing display, or should I say a party at which singing and dancing were the main features and which was attended by the whole of the village. Gilbertese dancing and singing is more stylized than that of the Ellice Islands, reflecting the different characters of the Micronesians and the Polynesians. It might be likened to a combination of folk dancing and ballad singing. The musical accompaniment consists of beating on an upturned wooden box with the palms of the hands. Strange as it may seem, this is effective, giving the necessary rhythm. In many of the Polynesian islands one comes across the guitar which must have been introduced from Europe or America. I never tired of these dances whether in Melanesia, Micronesia or Polynesia, and I saw many of them.

On one of the smaller islands, I forget which, we met a French Catholic nun who had come out nearly half a century before and had remained on the island ever since. She had left France prior to the advent of motor-cars so had never seen one, but airplanes she had seen, both Japanese and American.

Solomon Islands

The Solomons are a complete contrast to the Gilbert and Ellice. The largest of the Solomon Islands has an area of 2,500 square miles; the largest of the Gilberts little more than ten. The islands of the

Solomons are mountainous and forest-covered; the Gilbert and Ellice Islands (Ocean Island excepted) are less than a dozen feet above sea level and are devoid of forest trees. The climate in the Solomons is hot, humid and oppressive. Malaria is prevalent. The climate in the Gilbert and Ellice, though hot, is equable, whilst malaria is unknown.

The British Solomon Islands Protectorate consists of a double chain of islands south of the equator and extending nine hundred miles from the north-west to the south-east. Six of the islands exceed a thousand square miles in area. The mountains are rugged and heavily wooded making access to the interior very difficult.

The natives are Melanesian—'black islanders'—but the types are various, some being very black, others a good deal lighter, suggesting Polynesian blood. Some are very primitive and fierce, real 'native savages', but their toughness and inborn intelligence leads one to believe that they have a good potential, particularly those from the island of Malaita. Their fierceness is reflected in their dances which mostly have a warlike or fighting theme. They do not, however, indulge in dancing and having a gay time to nearly the same extent as the Gilbert and Ellice Islanders.

There is no common language in the Solomons, and natives in one village will often not understand those of another village only a few miles away, but those few miles are probably mountainous with impenetrable forest. 'Pidgin' English is spoken by many who have contact with Europeans, and the Protectorate must be one of the few territories in the world where government officials are required to pass examinations in pidgin. To the uninitiated, pidgin is quite unintelligible.

Whereas the peoples of other British territories in the South Pacific are all Christians, less than half of the Solomon Islanders call themselves that. The rest are pagans. The reason for this comparative lack of success of missions is the inaccessibility of the hinterland and the independent spirit of the natives.

The Solomons have a great variety of birds, cockatoos, parrots, lories, but as often happens in tropical forests they are not easy to see, with the exception of the bright-green parakeet which has such an unattractive voice. Orchids of many kinds abound, and on one of our visits it became known that my wife would like some to put in the trees at Government House. The result was that about a ton of orchids was placed in the plane, taking up most of the space. With a little coaxing they did very well in their new home at Suva and were much admired by visitors.

The economy is based mainly on copra, the coconut plantations being owned and operated by foreign companies, the largest of which is Levers with headquarters in Sydney. During the war the plantations were either destroyed or abandoned and one of my main concerns after V.J.Day was to get Levers and other commercial firms to return to the Protectorate. This they gradually did, but a government trading scheme to bring in foodstuffs and other essential supplies also had to be established. On Guadalcanal before the war gold mining had been commenced by Australian interests—the same as those that mine the gold in Fiji. With some reluctance—for access to the area is very difficult—Mr Theodore, the head of the company, agreed to recommence operations. Unfortunately the Colonial Office insisted on conditions that he felt unable to accept, so my efforts came to nothing and the gold remains in the ground. Meanwhile, the Protectorate government is unable to balance its budget without an annual grant from the British Treasury.

The lot of the expatriate official in either the Colony (Gilberts) or the Protectorate (Solomons) is not a soft one, especially away from headquarters. Amenities are lacking and the life is lonely. Of the two territories I would say that it is harder in the Solomons, the climate is worse and more unhealthy. But if life is harder, the horizons are wider and the prospects more challenging in the Protectorate than in the Colony.

The Solomons were the scene of some of the fiercest naval and air battles in the war, amongst them the battle of the Coral Sea when the Japanese lost more than a dozen ships, including three heavy cruisers and a hundred planes, and the Allies a carrier and seventy planes, and other engagements when the losses were equally heavy. The land fighting was also bitter, notably on Guadalcanal from which the Japanese only finally withdrew after several months. This was the furthest south they reached. At one time, nearly quarter of a million American soldiers were in and around Honiara.

As was my wont, I travelled from Suva by R.N.Z.A.F. Catalina, the plane coming down at Tulagi, a small sheltered island about twenty miles across the water from Honiara, the capital, on the large island of Guadalcanal. O. C. Noel, the Resident Commissioner, met me. His task was basically the same as that of his opposite number at Tarawa; that is, to get on well with the U.S. Command and, at the same time, to rehabilitate the Protectorate. He was a pleasant fellow if not very inspiring and somewhat lacking in drive. His relations with the Americans were excellent, and at this juncture this was the most important of his duties. Later on, when the

'Marching Rule'—an anti-European movement—broke out, he was not so successful.

Tulagi, the pre-war capital, had been destroyed during the fighting but we paid a brief visit to the 'Top of Tulagi', on a hillock overlooking the town, formerly the European Club, and during the war an American officers' club. Now abandoned, it had a forlorn appearance with broken tables and chairs and torn pictures of pin-up girls on the walls. One could not help thinking that this was the last glimpse of civilization that many young Americans had before going to their death in the fighting on Guadalcanal.

Now that the war had moved away from the Solomons, a protracted argument ensued as to whether the temporary capital of Honiara should become permanent or whether a return should be made to Tulagi. The decision went in favour of Honiara, just as in the case of the Gilbert and Ellice Islands, Tarawa, the temporary capital, replaced Ocean Island as the permanent capital. Since I helped to make the decision, I naturally consider the choice to have been the correct one.

From Tulagi we crossed the channel by the American equivalent of a M.T.B.—no doubt the same type of craft in which Lieutenant (and later President) Jack Kennedy served with such gallantry—the mountains of Guadalcanal, a deep purple against the setting sun, presenting an awe-inspiring sight as we sped through the water. Landing at the jetty at Kukum, a temporary affair built by the Americans and already beginning to break up, we proceeded by jeep to the Resident Commissioner's bungalow. Subsequently when the post of High Commissioner was separated from that of Governor of Fiji, it became the Government House of the High Commissioner; surely an unusual Government House for, instead of a large and imposing building of concrete or stone, the construction was of nipa palm. My bearer—to use an Indian expression—was Corporal Sulana of the Protectorate Constabulary. His uniform consisted of a khaki *lava-lava* (sulu) with a leather belt and scabbered-bayonet. He wore no jacket or shirt and his legs and feet were bare. I was happy, twelve years later, when visiting the Solomons with Prince Philip, to meet him in the role of President of the Malaita Council. He then wore a dark-blue lava-lava, white shirt, dark-blue tie and jacket and a pair of sandals, as befitted his status.

We took our meals in the Protectorate headquarters mess, for life had not yet returned to normal and the government officials still bore military rank. One advantage of the military occupation, especially by the Americans, was the availability of imported refrigerated foodstuffs and other supplies, including such luxuries as coca-cola and limited quantities of whisky, gin and beer. I found that a poor quality of whisky or gin was more palatable if taken with coca-cola than with water or soda. A speciality of the mess was 'jungle-juice', made by pickling peppers in alcohol instead of sherry. It gave zest to the dullest of soups. The smaller the peppers, the hotter they are.

On my earlier visits, before V.J.Day, when the Americans still had a large number of troops at Honiara, the place had a purposeful air about it. Later, with the war at an end and a rapid reduction in the size of the base until finally no military personnel was left, everything took on an abandoned, dejected look. The many huts, prefabricated or of nipa palm, quickly fell into decay. One saw piles of war-time litter, stacks of rusty barbed wire, old petrol drums, lorries without their engines, broken washing machines and refrigerators; in fact all the junk that an army leaves behind when it moves away. Most of the roads fell into disrepair, as did many of the bridges. Further up the coast one came across old field-guns, burnt-out Japanese tanks, the wreck of a Japanese transport. The Protectorate government bought a good deal of the American stores for use in the construction of the capital.

When I inspected the Fiji labour battalion, how glad they were to see someone from their homeland. Their reputation as cheerful workers was excellent, for the Fijian differentiated between working in peace-time and working in furtherance of the war effort. The Solomon Islanders, too, made good workers. Men had also been brought in from the Gilberts, but they suffered from home-sickness and the climate.

Getting from one part of the Protectorate to another was not so easy as on the Gilbert and Ellice Islands. Few places were suitable for a seaplane and to go by government vessel usually took too long. I did, however, manage to get to Auki, the principal town on the island of Malaita, and a few other places. At Auki I had my first experience of listening to a speech being translated from English into 'pidgin'. I have never heard anything so strange. David Trench (now Sir David, subsequently High Commissioner for the Western Pacific and, currently, Governor of Hong Kong) acted as interpreter. Even though the facts of geography and time restricted my travelling, I met most, if not all, the administrative officers during my two years in the South Pacific, for I always asked the Resident Commissioner to bring them in to headquarters if possible, in the event of my not going to their districts. I was thus able to learn at first hand of their aspirations and frustrations.

NEW HEBRIDES

The Anglo-French Condominium, set up in 1906, has been irreverently referred to as the 'pandemonium', for it has two Resident Commissioners, one British and one French, two Police Forces and everything else in duplicate; hardly the most effective or least expensive form of administration. The French government gave more attention to the condominium and greater encouragement to French commercial interests than we did to our side. The residences of the two Commissioners stood facing each other across Vila harbour on the island of Efate. They were of approximately the same height above the sea, the tops of the flagstaffs being exactly the same height. The town of Vila was like a small French colonial town and was more attractive than the average British colonial town. I have noticed this difference in Asia and Africa as well as in the South Pacific.

Lying about half way between Fiji and the Solomons, the New Hebrides, like the Solomons, consist of a double chain of islands stretching from the north-west to the south-east for 450 miles (half the length of the Solomons), with a population also about half the size of that of the Solomons. The islands are mountainous, many of them volcanic, but the soil is better than in the Protectorate which enables a variety of agricultural products to be grown, though copra is still the principal one. The natives are Melanesian but the mixture of Polynesian is stronger than in the Solomons.

Richard Blandy, the British Resident Commissioner, was well fitted for his somewhat trying and frustrating job. Born in the Channel Islands and with police experience in India and Tangier, he knew how to get on with 'foreigners'. We always enjoyed staying at his gracious house.

The New Hebrides, like Fiji, had not been the scene of fighting in the war as had the Solomons and the Gilberts, but, again like Fiji, had been an important base for American and Commonwealth forces, the main one being on Espiritu Santo, the northernmost island. Here, I saw lying bottom upwards in the channel the American passenger liner *President Hoover* which had struck a mine. Before the war, Maurine and I had travelled on her from San Francisco to Hong Kong.

Once, when taking off at Vila on the Catalina in a rough sea and gale-force wind, we wondered if the plane would survive the terrific bumping, but after a few minutes it rose above the waves into safety.

On landing at Lauthala Bay in Fiji, an inspection showed that the under side of the fuselage had been badly dented. An aircraft, like a human being, has to be replenished from time to time and, so long as the Commonwealth or the United States retained some sort of an air-base in the Gilberts and Ellice or the Solomons, the Catalina was able to refuel herself at these places. But a time came when such facilities no longer existed. Accordingly, I arranged to travel from Suva to Honiara on the Protectorate vessel the *Kurimarau*, bought second-hand from Levers after the war, calling in at Vila on the way. I mentioned this to Lieutenant Commander Scott-Elliot, the commander of the frigate H.M.S. *Amethyst*, later of Yangtse fame, when he was lunching at Government House. 'Why not come on the *Amethyst*', he said. 'I'll signal the Commander-in-Chief and get his approval. I'm sure he will agree'. He did agree, so Maurine and I, Singh, the butler, and Luki, the No. 2 cook, duly embarked on the *Amethyst*. Scott-Elliot kindly gave up his day cabin to my wife and myself, Maurine occupying the bunk whilst I slept on the floor. But she proved to be the better sailor, so we changed places. Luki was very popular with the crew and also acquired a vast quantity of 'loot' in the way of abandoned army stores at Honiara. Singh was miserable, suffering from seasickness most of the time. Scott-Elliot had never before seen the Solomons and was much intrigued with them, so much so that when he left the Navy a few years later, he bought a coconut plantation at Gizo and settled down there.

We proceeded first to Vila and, on arrival, anchored in the roadstead, the Resident Commissioners coming out in turn to make their official calls. All went well in the case of the British Resident Commissioner. He paid his call, got into his launch, which lay off a few yards from the frigate, and stood at attention as a salute of the appropriate number of rounds was fired by the *Amethyst*. When the French Commissioner left and about half the rounds had been fired, an agonizing pause ensued; the Commissioner looking more and more harassed as he remained standing at attention with his launch pitching about in the swell. The saluting gun had jammed. Tension was relieved with a deeper boom as Scott-Elliot gave orders to fire live shells from the Bofors gun.

We also called at Auki in the Solomons and had arranged to give a cocktail party on the ship in the evening, prior to going on to Honiara. Shortly before the party was due to begin, when I was on shore carrying out various inspections, I received an urgent message to return on board immediately: a storm had suddenly blown up, the ship was dragging her anchor and must proceed to sea without delay, which she did. This was most disappointing, especially for the guests who had been looking forward to a party on one of H.M. ships, and unfortunately our programme did not permit us to return the next day.

TONGA

The native name of these islands is Tonga, but Captain Cook called them the 'Friendly Islands' because of the kindly and hospitable reception he received when he visited them in 1777. They well deserve the name, for I know of no people more friendly. A living souvenir of Captain Cook's visit still exists in the person of an aged tortoise presented by Captain Cook to one of the chiefs and which now wanders, or it did when we were there, in the grounds of the palace. Pigs are sometimes referred to as 'Captain Cook', for he is reputed to have introduced them.

The Kingdom of Tonga consists of three groups of islands numbering some two hundred all told, of which many are uninhabited. Most are low-lying coral atolls, similar to the Gilbert and Ellice Islands; a few, including Vavau, the largest, are volcanic, high and mountainous. One island subsides beneath the sea from time to time and then later reappears. The capital, Nukualofa on the coral island of Tongatabu, is about 450 miles from Suva, but a distance of 80 miles only separates the western extremity of the Kingdom from the easternmost of the Fiji islands. The total land area is about 250 square miles. Just within the Tropic of Capricorn, the islands have a climate that is sub-tropical rather than tropical. Copra is the main export with bananas taking second place.

The natives are Polynesian and all are Christian, the majority being Wesleyan; and very devout they are too, regarding Sunday as the Lord's Day on which no work should be done—an exception was made in respect of war work—and no frivolous games played.

The Kingdom is a constitutional monarchy but the monarch has considerably more authority than do most constitutional monarchs. In 1900, Britain established a protectorate over the Kingdom and exercises control through an Agent and Consul, responsible to the Consul-General for the Western Pacific, i.e. the High Commissioner. The functions of the Agent and Consul are, however, advisory and not executive, for Tonga enjoys internal self-government.

Queen Salote, the present sovereign, succeeded to the throne on the death of her husband in 1941. She can boast that she is descended from a line of reigning chiefs going back more than a thousand years. But I cannot imagine Queen Salote boasting of anything. She is the essence of modesty, whilst in wisdom, charm and graciousness she can have few equals. To say that she is 'regal' might imply that she is haughty, and she is certainly not that. Perhaps I could best describe it by saying that she is 'queenly'. No wonder the British people took her to their hearts at Queen Elizabeth's coronation. She was educated in New Zealand which she visits from time to time and, when she does so, lives quietly like an ordinary citizen. She is blessed with two sons. The elder, Tungi (a title), and heir to the throne, went to school and university in Australia and since his return has occupied ministerial posts. He has considerable musical talent.

The Prime Minister, Ata, a Tongan chief, was a man whose wisdom was only equalled by his charm. The Agent and Consul— invariably an officer seconded from the Fiji administration—was Trevor Johnson, a bachelor of sound common sense, a tolerant and amused outlook on life and an accomplished pianist. It was always a pleasure to be house-guests in his pleasant bungalow.

Tonga is a happy country under Queen Salote, and while she does not wish to preserve her kingdom as a museum piece, she realizes that not all the adjuncts of western civilization would be beneficial to her people. No doubt the islands, being reasonably accessible, could be developed as tourist resorts, but she considers—and who would disagree with her—that although this would bring in a flow of dollars and pounds, it would have a corrupting influence on the islanders. Consequently, her policy is to draw on western technology in such things as medical and agricultural science and education—schooling is compulsory up to the age of fourteen—but foreigners are not allowed to own land nor is the establishment of hotels permitted. Waikiki Beach or Tahiti is not her idea of a Tongan paradise.

Nukualofa on the island of Tongatalu is a charming little town with turf-covered streets, open green spaces, avenues of cedar-like avava trees and the palace—a European-style villa—and houses embowered in flowers. On the island too, are the stately *lagis* or burial mounds of ancient kings and the mysterious trilithon—two enormous blocks of stone with a third across the top and mortized into the others, the whole forming an arch about seventeen feet high. Who erected them and when, no one knows. An equally impressive but different sight are the blow-holes. Giant combers roll in from the ocean and, striking the reef, force their way through gaps at the top, sending spouts of water sixty feet up into the air. Not so attractive are the flying-foxes—a species of bat—which throng in their thousands a grove a few miles out of Nukualofa, hanging head downwards on limbs of dead trees by day and devouring the fruit crops by night.

We have happy memories of our visits to Tonga, the melodious singing of natural voices serenading us all night beneath our bedroom windows—most soothing to fall asleep to. This was a special occasion, the centenary celebrations in December 1945 of one of the greatest of Tonga's kings, King George Tubou I. The dancing displays were as delightful as any in Polynesian lands. The feasts were happy picnic-like affairs on the grand scale, with long lines of guests sitting crossed-legged on the ground on either side of a low table covered with banana leaves and laden with delicious barbecued meats and fish, using fingers to eat with, and, at the conclusion, listening to the speech-maker. At one feast we attended, the speech-maker recounted how he had recently been to Honolulu, where he had been shown in a museum the crown of the last monarch of Hawaii, Queen Liliuo-kalani. 'That is all that remains of Hawaii's royal line, a crown in a museum. But we, the people of Tonga, still have our Queen and our independence thanks to the protection of the King of England.'

In honour of the centenary the dignity of honorary Dame Grand Cross of the Most Excellent Order of the British Empire was con-ferred on Queen Salote, and the cruiser H.M.S. *Euryalus* was sent to attend the celebrations. The Admiralty also presented four saluting guns and at noon on 4th December a party from the cruiser fired a salute from the guns, but in their enthusiasm fired twenty-two rounds instead of the regulation twenty-one.

FAREWELL TO THE SOUTH PACIFIC

Life in the South Pacific was interesting and challenging, particularly at that time, during and immediately after the war, with the rehabilitation of the devastated areas and the first steps in imple-menting new development plans for all the territories. Having been there at the beginning I was anxious to see it through, or at any rate well started, and we looked forward to at least three more years on our return from leave. Fate, in the guise of the Colonial Office, however, decreed otherwise. Maurine had flown to San Francisco where I was to join her ten days later before going on together to England. Hardly had she left, when I received a telegram offering me the governorship of Hong Kong. Had it been anywhere else I might have declined or said 'Please, not just yet'. But Hong Kong was my first love. Furthermore, the challenge in Hong Kong was greater than in Fiji and the Western Pacific. I therefore telegraphed back, accepting. My few remaining days in Suva were hectic, not least because I had to attend to all the packing up myself without my wife, and how badly I did it, as we later discovered. Being busy, I had little time to mope and regret, but my final drive round the island to the airport at Nandi, going the long way by Tavua and Ba, was a sad one. After a farewell reception at Lautoka, I had a quiet and nostalgic dinner with Harley Nott, the District Commissioner and his wife. 'It is time we moved', he said, 'if you are not to miss your plane'. At the airport many friends had assembled to see me off, amongst them Sir Hugh and Lady Ragg; Ragg who had done so much for Fiji and who was such a sensible member of the Executive and Legislative Councils.

This was the end of our sojourn in the South Seas; the reality more enchanting than the dream and exceeding all my expectations. The memory of the islands and the charm of their peoples will ever remain with me.

Sir Alexander Grantham, G.C.M.G., Governor of Hong Kong, 1947–1957

1. The author and W. R. Scott at Macau 1923

2. The author and his future wife outside
General Munthe's house in Peking 1925

3. General Munthe

4. The author and wife with Tags and Philip at 'La Garza'

5. 'La Garza', Bermuda

6. Tennis in Jamaica. Author second from right

7 *a*. Government House, Lagos

7 *b*. Chieftain with retainers at garden party, Government House, Lagos

8. The Lodge, Lagos

9 *a*. Government House, Suva, Fiji

9 *b*. 'Retreat', Government House, Suva

10 *a*. Presentation of *yangona* at the Fijian Ceremony welcoming a new Governor

10 *b*. A Fijian *bure*

11. Welcome by school children, Marakei, Gilbert Islands

12. *Maneaba* at Abaokoro, Tarawa

13 *a*. With Queen Salote at Tonga, with Prince Tungi at extreme left

13 *b*. With Prime Minister Ata of Tonga

14 *a*. Feast at Tonga

14 *b*. A Tongan *tapa* cloth

15 *a.* Inspecting Guard of Honour on arrival in Hong Kong, 1947

15 *b.* The Author, Bishop R. O. Hall and Mr T. W. Kwok

16. Government House, Hong Kong

17. Driving Locomotive 21 on the Kowloon-Canton Railway

18. Vice-Chancellor of the University, Dr L. T. Ride, on 12th June 1952, conferring the degree of Hon. LL.D. on the Chancellor of the University, Sir Alexander Grantham, Governor of Hong Kong

19. Author and wife dancing at a Consular Corps Ball, February 1954

20. Chatting with Sir Robert Ho Tung

21. With the army at Sekong, talking with the C.O., Lt.-Col. Woollcombe

22. Sino-British frontier at Lowu. Author second from right, with
Prince Peter of Greece and Denmark, extreme right

23. With a former employee of Government House, with his wife and children, at a resettlement estate (see page 156)

24. With the Lennox-Boyds

25. Author's wife greeting Mr Nehru, Prime Minister
of India, in Hong Kong, October 1957

26 *a*. The author talking to townsfolk at Tai O, Lantau Island

26 *b*. Author and wife at the Trappist monastery, Lantau Island

27. Chai Ma Wai, open prison, Hong Kong

28. Camellia granthamiana
By courtesy of the Hong Kong Government Information Services

Camellia granthamiana was discovered in October 1955 by a Chinese forester, Mr C. P. Lau. It is a striking plant with white flowers $5\frac{1}{2}$ inches across and handsome, shining bullate leaves. See 'A new species of Camellia from Hong Kong New Territory' by J. Robert Sealy in *Jour. R.H.S.* **81**: 182 (1956).

PART THREE

Hong Kong, 1947–1957

CHAPTER SIX

RETURN TO PORT, 1947–1957

WE left England for Hong Kong in July 1947, but unlike my voyage out a quarter of a century before, the 'boat' by which we now travelled was a flying one. The five-day journey was pleasant and uneventful, but as we neared our destination I felt an inner excitement and prayed that I should be able to cope with the many problems facing the Colony.

On my arrival in 1922, the sun had been shining, the sky blue and the sea sparkling, with the Peak and the 'Nine Dragons' of the Kowloon range standing out clear and sharp. On this July day, rain fell heavily as the plane taxied to the jetty, the Peak and the 'Nine Dragons' visible only intermittently through misty vapours that swirled around them. With the dark sea and sombre colours, the scene had something of a Wagnerian atmosphere.

After disembarking on the Kowloon side of the harbour, we were greeted by David MacDougall, the Colonial Secretary and an old friend and colleague, who introduced us to the three service commanders, the General, the Commodore and the Air Commodore, after which we repaired to the V.I.P. room at the airport, where Maurine donned a suitable dress and I a morning coat and a grey top hat.

As we crossed the harbour I missed something; then realized that instead of being crowded and noisy with ships from all over the world and smart passenger liners, now only a few battered freighters in war-time paint were to be seen. The sounds of bustling activity were absent and all was silent, save the beating of the rain and the booming of the guns as they fired a salute to the new Governor.

Queen's Pier, gay with bunting and red carpet, was a more cheerful sight. Here, lined up to greet us, were all the dignitaries of the Colony; council members, judges, the Consular Corps, the Anglican and Catholic bishops and others. Many faces were familiar, people we had known in our earlier days in Hong Kong. 'Bill' (now Sir Ernest) Williams in the scarlet robes of a judge had been a junior cadet with me. Full of sound common sense and kindliness, which stood him in good stead on the bench, he would wax indignant at any behaviour that was underhand or sly. Leo D'Almada, now the leader of the Portuguese community and a Q.C., had once appeared

before me, when he was counsel for the defendant and I was magistrate, in a case which at the time attracted a good deal of attention.
I was sure his client was guilty but the prosecution failed to prove
their case and I had to acquit him. The leader of the Indian community, Mr J. H. Ruttonjee, was also there; one of the nicest and
kindest men I have ever known. After him was named the Ruttonjee
Sanatorium, founded by him in memory of his daughter who had
died of tuberculosis.

Another old friend was the Anglican bishop, Ronald Hall, whom
I had known—so far as a junior in pre-war Hong Kong could know
such an exalted person as a bishop—and who had stayed with us in
Nigeria for a week during the war. Bishop Hall was a humble and
sincere Christian with a burning concern for the poor and needy.
Unscrupulous persons would sometimes play upon his sympathies
and political naïvety and use him for their own purposes. But this
was a small price to pay for his fundamental goodness. On getting to
Government House, I found a note from him, inviting me to read
the lessons at the Cathedral on the following Sunday. I declined,
knowing that if I accepted I should virtually be committed for every
succeeding Sunday.

Not all my friends and colleagues of earlier days had risen to
positions of prominence, but continued to occupy comparatively
minor roles. I was happy to renew my friendship with them as well.
The three clerks, M. A. Cameroo, E. S. Cunningham and Li Wing
Sum had worked with me in the Secretariat in the thirties when we
had been a happy team. Chan Kwok Wing, who had been my interpreter at the Magistracy—and a very good one too—was now in the
anti-corruption branch of the police. A 'boy', a cook and a chair-
bearer, who had been in my employ in former days, soon sought me
out and I was glad to be able to find jobs for them. The first Cantonese
teacher that I had had in 1922 brought himself to my notice. He was
a nice gentle creature, but quite useless as an instructor. We had
therefore parted company after six months. When I returned as
Governor, he expected me to have him appointed to a government
school which would have set him up for life. This I was not willing
to do; so he became my pensioner until the end of his days. To return
as Governor to a place where one started one's career is gratifying,
but it also has its problems.

At the conclusion of the formalities we drove to Government
House, a brand new building put up by the Japanese on the site of
the former one, whose replacement had been long overdue. Imposing
rather than beautiful with a tall tower, it was approached through

gates, flanked by guard-houses, round a drive leading to a wide *porte cochère*. The entrance hall was spacious and ran through the house to a view over the lower part of the city and the harbour. The drawing and dining-rooms were of good proportions, the latter capable of seating forty people. Running along both these rooms was a broad arcaded verandah with a double flight of steps leading down to the garden. Also on the ground-floor were the offices of the Governor, the Private Secretaries and the A.D.C.'s, and a ballroom—the one remaining part of the old house. On the upper floor, reached by two staircases, one from the main hall, the other opposite the Governor's office, were the guest-rooms and the Governor's suite.

On the harbour side was a broad lawn where we held our garden-parties, or in the summer sat after dinner. From here a steep flight of steps lined with gardenia bushes led to a lower garden with flower beds, shrubs, trees and winding paths. On the entrance front of the house, between the guard-houses and the *porte cochère*, was an oval lawn with low sago-palms. Near the guard-houses and around the circular drive were flowering trees, but the most pleasing tree of all was a *grande flora* magnolia on the front lawn outside my office window.

The garden produced no vegetables or flowers for the house, and only several weeks after our arrival did we discover that a few miles distant was a Government House vegetable and flower garden. Hitherto we had been buying vegetables and cut flowers, when one day Maurine noticed in the butler's pantry some carrots. On enquiring where they came from, she was told, from the Government House garden at Sookunpoo. We proceeded to investigate and found that indeed there was such a garden with ten gardeners. They had been having a lovely time selling the flowers and vegetables and themselves working in other jobs as well. Quickly we put things right and soon had enough flowers and vegetables for all our needs with plenty to spare for friends and hospitals.

My predecessor had converted the bedrooms from Japanese-style to European-style, but had had insufficient time to do much else. Consequently, a great deal remained to be done and Maurine was busily engaged on this for a year. Good craftsmen were available as they had not been in Nigeria or Fiji, but materials were still in short supply, so she sent to San Francisco for damask for curtains as well as other things, and by the time she had finished Government House was something of which the people of Hong Kong were proud.

REHABILITATION

Although twelve years is not a long time in the history of a country, much had happened to Hong Kong between the time of my departure in 1935 and my return in 1947. There had been the years of tribulation during the Japanese occupation from Christmas Day 1941 to 30th August 1945, when the British civilian internees and the prisoners of war had endured untold hardship and suffering. The lot of the Chinese and others not interned had also been very grievous. On the liberation of the Colony by the British Pacific Fleet, everyone set-to to get the Colony going again in a manner that was little short of amazing, in view of the poor state of health of many as a result of the privations they had undergone.

A great deal had already been accomplished before I arrived back in Hong Kong two years later. For the first six months after the return of the British there had been a military government, the head of which was Admiral Sir Cecil Harcourt. On 1st May 1946 civil government was restored with the return of Sir Mark Young who had been Governor when the Colony fell to the Japanese in 1941. It was fitting that he should now reassume his duties. A year later I succeeded him.

The Chief Civil Affairs Officer to Admiral Harcourt was David MacDougall who, on the restoration of civil government, became Colonial Secretary. He had first come out to Hong Kong as a Cadet in 1928. On the fall of the Colony he, in company with the Chinese Admiral Chan Chak and some others, had escaped to China. Subsequently, and whilst Hong Kong was still occupied by the Japanese, he had headed the Hong Kong Planning Unit at the Colonial Office in London. The task of the Unit was to prepare plans for the rehabilitation of the Colony as soon as it was re-occupied. To plan is easy, but quickly to implement those plans, or to modify them in the light of experience, is not so easy, especially for government organizations, which tend to suffer from the ponderous slowness of the bureaucratic machine.

Hong Kong was fortunate in Harcourt, Young and MacDougall, ably assisted by other government officers and leading members of the Chinese and European communities, notably Arthur Morse (now Sir Arthur), the Chief Manager of the Hongkong and Shanghai Bank. Morse's guiding thought seemed to be 'what is good for the Colony is good for the Bank': the Colony came first. A big Irishman with a booming voice, Morse looked like the popular conception of a capitalist in his well-fitting clothes and gold watch-chain; albeit a benevolent if somewhat autocratic one. I feel sure he would shudder at having the adjective 'benevolent' applied to him, but he was known as 'Uncle Arthur'. Fully comprehending the Hong Kong situation and pragmatic in his approach, Morse had little patience with economic theorists and by one short word would dismiss their more fanciful theses. Not only did he give much of his time to public affairs in the accepted sense of the term but, by authorizing loans from the Bank on practically no security, he saved more than one humble club from disaster. No wonder he was given a tremendous send-off on his final departure from the Colony in 1953.

These men knew what wanted doing, and set about doing it, whether securing rice or placing an order for a turbine for a power station. They were a remarkable team. This, combined with the inherent resourcefulness of the Chinese, led to rehabilitation from the war being speedier in Hong Kong than in most other war-devastated areas.

The destruction in Hong Kong had been serious; to give but one example, 70% of the European-style residences and 20% of the tenements were unfit for habitation at the end of the war. This had been caused partly by Allied bombing and partly by looting. Much of the latter was by the Chinese populace who desperately needed firewood for cooking. Window sashes, floors, roof timbers, supporting beams, anything that would burn, would be torn away, with calamitous effects on the rest of the building. Factors that contributed to the rapid rehabilitation were the abundant supply of labour that came streaming back from China, and the fact that government did not involve itself directly in the business of reconstruction, which would have slowed things down to an unacceptable degree. Instead, private enterprise was given its head, and, with the profit motive to spur it on, did a magnificent job. The government had, of course, to engage in a certain amount of trading, notably in rice, for trading in essential foods was still on a government-to-government basis and not open to commercial firms or individuals. Then, too, Hong Kong, unlike most other parts of the British Commonwealth, was permitted to place orders for steel and other materials in the United States and Canada, where they could be obtained more readily than in the United Kingdom.

This freedom for a sterling colony, like Hong Kong, to buy from dollar countries was sometimes criticized and envied by those not so fortunately circumstanced. The reason for this freedom was that if the merchant, exporting produce from China through Hong Kong, had been compelled to surrender for sterling the dollars he had earned in America for his goods, he would not have shipped through Hong

Kong at all, but would have done so through Chinese ports, with the result that no dollars would have accrued to Hong Kong and hence to the sterling area pool. As it was, Hong Kong was a not inconsiderable net earner of dollars for the pool. Hong Kong's very existence had always depended on her entrepôt trade. Only within the last few years has industry become more important. As an entrepôt, she must offer the best possible facilities at the lowest possible price. If she does not, the trade will go to other eastern ports. By necessity then and by tradition, Hong Kong has been for free trade with the minimum of government interference.

INSULARITY

A marked decline in social snobbishness was one of the first things I noticed after my return. The 'taipan' and the senior government official were no longer regarded, nor did they so regard themselves, as demi-gods. They were now simply ordinary human beings who, on account of their years and seniority, attracted a degree of respect. I observed, too, a greater mixing of the races, but then Hong Kong has never had a colour problem like the African colonies, and the Chinese have as much racial pride as the Europeans. It is the mental arrogance on the part of some Europeans towards Asians that has created as much, if not more resentment than the physical aggressions like the establishment of colonies and extraterritoriality. The basis of the arrogance is the assumption that the European is inherently superior to the Asian, taking such forms as the exclusion of Asians from clubs, downright rudeness or a patronizing manner. But the age of the 'blimps' is over, though a few of them still remain, even in Hong Kong.

The insularity and provincial mindedness of some of the leading businessmen, both European and Chinese, also struck me. No doubt this had always existed, but I had not been aware of it during my earlier days in the Colony. Such a narrow outlook seemed strange in one of the great commercial centres of the world. It did not, however, prevent the persons concerned from being most efficient world-traders. The gentle contempt that the Europeans from Shanghai had for Hong Kong was amusing. Shanghai in pre-communist days was a great cosmopolitan centre; a sort of New York-Paris in an oriental setting. Hong Kong, by comparison, was a small village. The feeling of the Cantonese—and most of the Chinese in Hong Kong are Cantonese—towards the Shanghai-Chinese who had come to live and set up in business in Hong Kong was one of resentment. They regarded them as altogether too smart and slick. But it was the Shanghai-Chinese businessmen, with their capital and industrial know-how, who were largely the economic salvation of Hong Kong, after commerce with China was catastrophically reduced by the embargoes imposed against trade with that country by the United States and the United Nations in 1950. Hong Kong was the innocent sufferer from those embargoes; but more of this anon.

The Governance of Hong Kong

The fundamental political problem of the British Colony of Hong Kong is its relationship with China and not the advancement to self-government and independence as is the case with most British colonies. Hong Kong should, therefore, in my opinion, have been placed under the Foreign Office instead of the Colonial Office, but with staff seconded from the Colonial Service which, unlike the Foreign Service staff, is trained in administration. This need was not so obvious when the government of China was weak, as there were then not many occasions of serious friction between the Chinese and Hong Kong authorities. But even as long ago as 1928, when I had only a few years to my credit, I wrote a paper on the subject, probably inspired by the Chinese boycott of Hong Kong a couple of years previously. With the advent of a strong and hostile government in China, as has been the case since 1949, the need became glaring. It is, however, too late now to make the change.

Practically every major issue that arose in Hong Kong, and on which London had to be consulted, was a matter of foreign policy, but we had to deal with the Colonial Office and not the Foreign Office. Not only did this make for delay; there was also less basic understanding of the issues involved. Furthermore, we felt that in arguments with other Whitehall departments, we would have had a more redoubtable champion in the Foreign Office than we had in the Colonial Office. Rightly or wrongly we believed that the Colonial Office was brushed aside by the other departments in Whitehall.

There had been some recognition of Hong Kong's involvement in matters of foreign affairs by the secondment of a member of the Foreign Service to the staff of the Governor as Political Adviser. The first appointee had arrived only a few weeks before I did in 1947. Although I thought the scheme sound in principle, I was somewhat dubious as to how it would work in practice. I was apprehensive lest the Political Adviser should 'get into the hair' of the Secretary for Chinese Affairs—a senior official of the Hong Kong government.

The Secretary for Chinese Affairs was even more apprehensive. But our fears proved to be groundless. For one thing, the Political Adviser had no administrative or executive duties; for another, he was primarily concerned with the Colony's foreign relations and, finally, we had a succession of first rate Political Advisers who were careful not to tread on the toes of the Secretary for Chinese Affairs. I found it extremely helpful to have a trained Foreign Service officer on my staff, and I think that the British Ambassador at Nanking, and subsequently after the capital was moved to Peking, the *Chargé d'Affaires* at Peking were glad that the Governor of Hong Kong had someone on his staff who spoke their language. In pre-communist days, the Political Adviser would visit the Embassy at Nanking regularly, or whenever something had blown up of mutual concern to the ambassador and the governor. When the communists came into power, the visits had to be stopped, but towards the end of my time it was possible to renew them.

What a contrast was this mutual consultation and confidence between the Ambassador and the Governor, compared with the situation in my early days, when the Consul-General at Canton and the Governor of Hong Kong were sometimes not even on speaking terms. This does not mean to imply that the ambassador or *chargé d'affaires* and the governor always saw eye to eye; although in most cases they did. At any rate, they worked in harmony and appreciated each other's point of view even when they disagreed.

The most notable difference of opinion occurred over the question of the proposed appointment by the communist Chinese government of a diplomatic representative in Hong Kong. Such a one—Special Commissioner was his title—had been appointed immediately after the war when the Nationalists were still in power. With the recognition by Britain of the new régime in China in 1950 he withdrew. Exactly what his functions and authority were was not closely defined. To have attempted to have done so might have been embarassing to all concerned. It certainly would have been to the Hong Kong government, but T. W. Kwok, the Special Commissioner, tried to be helpful in his dealings with us, save in one instance—which I recount later—when he over-reached himself to the tribulation of Hong Kong, Nanking and London. 'T.W.', a graduate of Harvard and Cambridge, was a bon-vivant and man of the world. His wife, Grace, was as beautiful as she was charming; an accomplished pianist and a keen supporter of the Y.W.C.A. A few years after the Kwoks had gone to America, I asked Mrs Kwok's sister, who was living in Hong Kong, what Grace and T.W. were doing. 'Oh, Grace is doing the washing-up and T.W. is drinking his way into society', she replied. Actually, I believe, he was teaching at a university.

'Certainly, Your Excellency!'

When I had left Hong Kong in 1935 for Bermuda I had been a junior in the Secretariat, 'Extra Assistant Colonial Secretary' was my title, I believe. I had now returned as Governor. In a crown colony the Governor is next to the Almighty. Everyone stands up when he enters a room. He is deferred to on all occasions. It is always 'Yes, Sir', 'Certainly, Your Excellency'; heady wine that is bad for the constitution if taken too long at a time. That is why it is good for a governor when on leave to have to take his place in a queue and to have his toes trodden on in a crowded railway carriage. It brings home to him that he is but an ordinary mortal like anyone else, and that the dignity attaches to the office and not to the individual. As the Queen's representative, the Governor has to behave and be treated as such. He should be dignified without being pompous, approachable and friendly without being intimate, because if he is intimate with any one individual or any particular group, he will be accused, rightly or wrongly, of favouritism. He should not confine his associations to the 'upper crust' for he belongs to everyone in the colony, from the highest to the lowest. He must be discriminating, but not exclusive, in the social entertainment that he offers and accepts. Many governors, and I was one of them, made it a rule not to accept private invitations of hospitality, but to confine himself to members of Councils, heads of the Services, the Consular Corps and so on. If he were to accept an invitation to dinner from Mr and Mrs A who held no particular position in the colony, he would then have to accept invitations from Mr and Mrs B and the whole way through the alphabet. This social aloofness of a governor by no means implies that he should be aloof in other ways, or that he should have no contacts with anyone except his officials and advisers. It is essential, I consider, that in seeking opinions he should cast his net as widely as possible and be available to people of all degrees. After a time, he gets to know who is worth seeing and who will merely waste his time. Thus he manages to keep his finger on the pulse of public opinion, and to know what is going on in the colony.

The position of the governor, as between the Colonial Office and his colony, in a dependency like Hong Kong with no elected ministers, is not always an easy one. If the constitution provided for an elected prime minister, then he, the prime minister, would speak for his territory and the governor would be the agent of the Colonial Office. But in a crown colony, where does the allegiance of the governor lie: to the Colonial Office or to the colony? Normally, no conflict arises, but occasionally it does, and the situation is not improved by a tendency on the part of the Colonial Office to treat a crown colony as though it were a sub-department of the Colonial Office. I know that the Colonial Office officials do a conscientious and honest job at which they work hard, but it is just a job. They have no attachment or loyalty to the colony with which they are at the moment concerned. They do their best, but their loyalty, naturally, is to Britain and, in the last resort if a clash of interests occurs, the colony is sacrificed. Nor do I think that people in Britain fully appreciate the fact that Britain acquired, and remains in, Hong Kong for her own purposes—principally trade. She therefore became, and is, responsible for the welfare and protection of the people. Undeniably, the residents should play their part, but there is too much of an assumption in Britain that the people of Hong Kong are fortunate to be there—which is true enough—and that therefore it is they who owe a duty to Britain, which is also true up to a point. Fundamentally, though, it is Britain that owes the duty to the Colony.

THE EXECUTIVE COUNCIL

Executive Council is composed of six official and six unofficial members and Legislative Council of nine and eight (now twelve and thirteen) respectively. The unofficial members—leading citizens, Chinese and non-Chinese—are appointed by the Secretary of State on the nomination of the Governor. The official members must vote as directed by the Governor who presides at both Councils. This may sound very authoritarian but it did not work so in practice. During my ten years as Governor, not a single instance occurred in Executive Council of all the officials voting one way and the unofficials the other. In Legislative Council there was only one such instance, and two of the unofficials said afterwards that they had inadvertently voted the wrong way. Voting was generally on non-party lines—to use a parliamentary expression, albeit there are no parties—though in Legislative Council the government members tended all to vote the same way even if not directed to do so.

When the unofficials objected to a course of action which the government proposed to take, they preferred to work out a compromise behind the scenes. To cite an example: Government wished to increase the Earnings and Profits Tax—the local equivalent to income tax—from 10% to 15%. The unofficial members protested vigorously, 'business would come to a standstill', 'the Colony would be ruined', etc., etc. The Council debate was adjourned, the unofficial members and the government officials concerned met together in private and agreed on 12½%. The debate was resumed and after a certain amount of shadow-boxing, unanimous approval was given to 12½%. This may be a time-saving method, but it must look strange to the outsider.

The only issue that created heat in Legislative Council in my time as Governor was the proposal to reduce the inequalities of rent control on landlords. This raised a storm of protest amongst the populace at large and also within the ranks of the unofficial members who were divided on the matter. None of them was a substantial landlord and considerations as to how the legislation would affect them financially did not enter into it. The actuating motives were in some cases principle, in others fear of loss of popularity. I was of the opinion at the time—or rather times for the matter came up twice whilst I was there—that the proposed legislation was just and fair and would have inflicted hardship on no one. I am still of that opinion. It would have been perfectly correct, constitutionally, for me to have directed the government members to vote in favour of the Bill which would then have been passed. Moreover, some of the unofficials would have voted with them. But when the public is strongly opposed to a certain course of action, one does not pursue it unless a matter of fundamental importance is involved. None was in this case, and government bowed to the public will.

For such a system to work, the government must not attempt to steam-roller legislation through the councils, lest the wrath of the unofficial members be incurred. In point of fact, government would be unlikely to introduce into Legislative Council measures to which strong opposition from the unofficials might be expected, because before bills are introduced they must, according to the constitution, receive the blessing of Executive Council on which the unofficials have an equality of numbers with the officials.

In a crown colony form of government, the danger of the colony being bureaucrat-ridden is inherent. Happily this did not occur in Hong Kong, mainly because Hong Kong had a tradition of free enterprise with the minimum of government interference. Consequently the civil servant did not dominate the scene. Occasionally one would try to throw his weight around too much, but he would be speedily called to order. People and press were vigilant as to their rights, but the best watch-dogs were the unofficial members of Executive Council.

Outstanding amongst them was Sir Man-kam Lo, whose death in 1959 was a great loss to the Colony. He had a first class brain, great moral courage and a capacity for digging down into details without getting lost in them. I can picture him at a meeting of the Council when some difficult or controversial subject was under discussion. Another member would be expounding his views. From the glint in 'M.K.'s eyes and the way his lips were moving, I knew he had something forceful to say. I could hardly wait for the previous speaker to finish and to hear 'M.K.' Then again, when a complex but dull matter was being dealt with by the circulation of papers, on which members would write their opinions, I would look to see what 'M.K.' had written and, as often as not, save myself the tedium of reading all the other minutes. He was invariably right to the point.

The unofficial members of Legislative Council did not use their right of asking questions in Council as much as would have been good for the government and heads of departments. All of us are the better for a little 'needling' from time to time. It helps to keep us up to the mark and this is certainly true of a crown colony government. I noticed a tendency amongst heads of departments, who had not experienced the rough-and-tumble of colonial legislatures elsewhere, to resent unofficial members asking questions in Council concerning their departments. This polite silence on the part of the Legislative Council members was one of the contributory reasons for the public regarding them as wooden dummies or 'yes men', neither of which they were.

Another disadvantage of the deferential politeness of the unofficial members becomes apparent when the Colonial Office wishes to do something that the unofficials regard as being detrimental to the interests of the Colony. Instead of supinely accepting the 'diktat' of the Colonial Office, of which the Governor may be the reluctant mouthpiece, they should protest in the loudest possible terms; if necessary sending a delegation to London with the maximum of publicity. They cannot, of course, say to the Governor, 'we know you are a fine fellow, and think as we do. It is the Colonial Office whose blood we are after'. They have got to attack the Governor as well. This would probably not be generally understood by the people, and the communist press would immediately enter the ring. If the Colony had elected ministers, as other colonies have, more attention would be paid in London to responsible local opinion than is the case at present but the risks that would follow—as I explain in subsequent paragraphs—from such a constitution, would be too great. Better leave things as they are; but the Colonial Office should pay more attention to the views of the unofficial members of Councils.

At a lower level than the Legislative Council is the Urban Council, which—as the name indicates—is concerned with urban affairs: markets, parks, conservancy and such like. Later the running of the resettlement estates for squatters—about which I write below—and low cost housing was entrusted to it, which added to its burdens. Hong Kong is too small a place, though, to have both a central government and a fully fledged municipal government. This was the experience of Singapore, which is roughly the same size as Hong Kong. When Singapore and Malaya were one—as they were before the war—a municipal government in Singapore was justified; but after the two territories each had their own governments, it became evident that there was not room for a municipal government in Singapore as well. It led to duplication, overlapping and an increase in the overall cost of administration. The Singapore municipality was therefore abolished. The Urban Council of Hong Kong is in effect the agent of the central government for certain urban services. It has no revenue raising powers and the salaried staff are employees of the central government. The unofficial members have a majority over the official members (civil servants). Up to the time I left, half of the unofficials were appointed by the Governor and half were elected, but the elections aroused scant interest. One reason for this electoral apathy was no doubt because little glamour attaches to the matters with which the Council deals, important as they are to the everyday life of the citizens and efficiently as the Council carries them out.

CONSTITUTIONAL REFORM

After the War, constitutional reform was one of the first things actively pursued by the Colonial Office and the Hong Kong Government, but with singularly little interest shown by the local populace. The substitution in the Legislative Council of elected for appointed members, with a majority over the official members and the institution of the ministerial system, which eventually was to lead to internal self-government either within or without the Commonwealth, was the order of the day in British colonial policy. But the problem in Hong Kong is different from that in other colonies, for Hong Kong can never become independent. Either it remains a British colony, or it is re-absorbed into China as a part of the province of Kwangtung. Hong Kong is also different in that the Chinese—and 99% of the population in Hong Kong is Chinese—are, generally speaking,

politically apathetic. Provided that the government maintains law
and order, does not tax them too much and that they can get justice
in the courts, they are content to leave the business of government to
the professionals and the comparatively small number of private citizens who, out of civic spirit or the honour and glory they get out of
it, are willing to serve on government councils and boards. The
majority of Chinese in the Colony also had little loyalty to Hong Kong.
Like the Europeans, they came to Hong Kong to work until they
retired home to China, just as the Europeans returned home to
Europe. Not inaptly Hong Kong has been likened to a railway station,
and its inhabitants to the passengers who pass in and out of the gates.
The Chinese who have lived all their lives in the Colony and intend
to leave their bones there, are a small minority; as are the Eurasians
who have no other home. They are the true citizens of Hong Kong,
but their total number is insignificant. The picture is changing since
China went communist, as few Chinese in Hong Kong now intend
to return to the country of their birth. They are becoming permanent
citizens.

Another peculiarity affecting Hong Kong's constitutional situation is the danger that, in a democratically elected legislature, the
politics of China—as distinct from those of the Colony—would be a
constant issue, which would have a most disturbing effect. Not until
1952 were the difficulties and dangers inherent in the Hong Kong
situation fully realized; and it was then decided that there should
be no major alterations in its constitutional set-up. During the
intervening years various schemes were proposed, approved or
amended. At last we thought we had found one that had a fair chance
of avoiding the dangers that we foresaw and that would, at the same
time, satisfy the Colonial Office. I was about to go on leave when,
just before I departed, the unofficial members of the two councils
requested me to induce the Colonial Office to drop the whole scheme.
'It was too dangerous.' 'Was it right to jeopardize the future of the
Colony for a theory that had application in other colonies but not to
Hong Kong?' That is what they said to me. I did not disagree, and
when I arrived in London I bearded the officials of the Colonial
Office. They did not like this back-pedalling nor, they thought, would
the Secretary of State, who had only just secured cabinet approval for
the final version of constitutional reform. The Secretary of State,
however, was quite ready to abandon constitutional reform for
Hong Kong: his reason being that the matter did not interest the
British electorate.

RURAL HONG KONG

Hong Kong is really a city state, with the greater part of its population—two and a half million out of a total population of three million—crowded into the urban areas of Victoria, on the island of Hong Kong, and Kowloon peninsula across the harbour. Only fairly recently have towns been growing up in the rural parts of the New Territories (the area leased by China to Britain in 1898 for 99 years). Consequently the Colony's internal administration is principally concerned with the same sort of things as in a conurbation like, say, Manchester; markets, roads, hospitals, schools, water supplies and so on. In this, Hong Kong differs from the great majority of British colonies—or what were colonies before they were granted independence—whose economies are based on agriculture. It should not, however, be thought that the rural or district administration in Hong Kong is unimportant, but it tended to be neglected in pre-war days. Largely under the inspiration of Dr G. A. C. Herklots, a Reader in biology at the University of Hong Kong who thought out his plans for rural development during his internment by the Japanese and who, after the war became the Colony's Secretary for Development, good progress was under way by the time I arrived. Herklots was a stimulating individual, full of enthusiasm and ideas, most of them good. Whilst interned, he grew tomatoes from seeds obtained from a tin of that vegetable. Whereas formerly, the Colony had no Director of Agriculture, it now had one with deputies in charge of forestry, fisheries and veterinary services.

Feeder roads, enabling farmers to get their produce to market more easily, and irrigation projects, both large and small, were being proceeded with. In this work of rural development, the Kadoorie Agricultural Aid Association, named after the brothers Horace and Lawrence Kadoorie, deserves an honourable mention. Like many Jews, the Kadoories combined a keen and forward-looking business sense with a genuine concern in philanthropy. The funds of the K.A.A.A. were supplied by the Kadoories and many a farmer owes his salvation or success to the help he has received from the Association. Horace, a bachelor, took the more active part in the management of the Association which interested him more, I suspect, than did his business affairs.

The farmers and the fishermen were now also helped to organize their own marketing without being 'squeezed' by money-lenders and middlemen. The aim of the Co-operative Department was to get them to stand on their own feet, to run the co-operative societies themselves and not to expect the department to do it all for them.

At the commencement, the department had of necessity to take a fairly direct part in running things. Those days are past: advice, and not orders, is now the practice.

It would amuse me to hear the Director of Agriculture saying that the Co-operative Department should be subordinate to him. The head of the Co-operative Department would say the same thing of the Department of Agriculture. Both cases are arguable, but I have always been distrustful of empire building and satisfactory results have been obtained by having the two departments separate. The District Commissioner of the New Territories—the only D.C. in the Colony—was inclined to be suspicious of the two departments. He feared that the enthusiasm of technical officers might outrun their discretion and so upset the peasantry. Happily this did not occur.

Whenever I spent a day out in the country with one or other of these departments I invariably came back physically and mentally refreshed. The keenness of their staffs and the good relationship between them and the farmers and fishermen was heartening. One of the leading members of a farmers' co-operative, and himself a farmer, intrigued me. He looked exactly like Mossadegh, the former and troublesome primè minister of Iran, of Abadan fame. I wonder what his racial origin was.

The life of the people in the New Territories was tranquil and ancient. The hand of the twentieth century had, seemingly, scarcely touched it. The villagers, whose lands had been handed down for generations, tilled their fields in exactly the same way as had their fathers, grandfathers and great-grandfathers before them, but although conservative, like farmers the world over, they are realists and if a new method of cultivation, a new seed or a new breed is demonstratively better than the old, they will adopt it. All the old rites and customs were followed, for the British have, until recently, been traditionalists in their handling of the peoples of their colonies. The Territories were almost more Chinese than China itself. But the modern world could not be kept out. The demand of the growing city for more and more land, for more factory sites, for country retreats for the town dweller, for areas covering several villages for reservoirs was insatiable. The conflict was going on all the time, and nothing creates deeper feelings than disputes over land. Clan feuds were also endemic in the Territories: feuds as ancient as the villages themselves. The District Commissioner did not have an easy row to hoe. This basic unease over their land was probably what stirred the New

Territories in the matter of the Heung Yee Kuk. The Heung Yee Kuk might be described as the central organization of the New Territories councils. It did not figure in the Colony's constitution or laws—there is now a Heung Yee Kuk ordinance—so had no official status. But it was not an unimportant body in New Territories' life and was consulted by the District Commissioner. At the time I am speaking of, a dispute had arisen over the elections, with the 'kuk' split into factions. There were also grievances against the government, some real, some imaginary. I do not recollect all the ins-and-outs, but the issue was a complicated one, requiring delicate and patient handling. Up to the time I left harmony had not been restored.

SCHOOLS AND THE UNIVERSITY

When the British returned in 1945, they found many of the school buildings either destroyed or so damaged that they could not be used. Consequently, there was a great shortage of school places, even though more schools were being built as fast as possible. The situation was made worse by the large number of Chinese coming into the Colony in search of work. All sorts of improvizations had to be adopted, for example three-sessional schools. In the same building, one school would be held in the morning, one in the afternoon and a third in the evening; each with its own set of teachers and pupils. Another improvization was the Workers' Schools set up by Bishop Hall. In theory and intention the idea was admirable, but in practice the schools soon became a worry, for they were the focus for communist penetration, some being completely communist dominated and centres of communist and anti-British indoctrination. These had to be closed down and, in the most flagrant cases, the teachers deported.

To close down a school was not something to be lightly undertaken. We did not want to throw the children out into the street, so either we had to build a new school—which put out of gear our school building programme—or we had to squeeze them into other schools. Usually we did a bit of both. We had considerable difficulty at first in convincing the Bishop as to what was going on in the Workers' Schools. Subversive activities were carried on in a few other schools as well. They also had to be dealt with. Detection was not easy, for although all schools were subject to inspection and their curricula to approval, and although parents sometimes tipped off the education authorities, the offending school would rig up a warning system, so that when the inspector came along, the communist books and paraphernalia would have been put out of sight.

The training of teachers was another necessity with the ever increasing number of schools. We already had one government teachers' training college, but this was insufficient. We therefore set about building another. I suggested to the Director of Education that it should be named after him. This, he said, would not do, for the existing one bore the name of a previous governor and if the new were not named after the present governor, it would suffer in prestige. Consequently, there is a Grantham Training College, of which I am very proud. A third college has since been built with the name of my successor.

One has to be careful not to let this business, of naming things after one, get out of hand. I do not think I did. Just as I am proud to have my name and crest on the Grantham Training College, so I am proud to have it on the Grantham Hospital, a voluntary, non-profit making tuberculosis hospital, and one of the finest in the Far East. Proud too, is my wife to have the Maurine Grantham Health Centre at Tsuen Wan to bear her name. Also named after us were the first two diesel locomotives on the Kowloon-Canton Railway. I have always liked trains and engines, and I got a great thrill out of driving a train all the way from Lowu to Kowloon, a distance of twenty-two miles. I also enjoyed driving an old type steam-roller along one of the main thoroughfares of Kowloon. But what should bring me international immortality is the *Camellia granthamiana*, a new species of camellia discovered in the New Territories.

Hong Kong has had a university since 1911. The buildings, like so many others, were severely damaged during the war. I remember the first Congregation held after the war for the conferment of degrees. It was a chilly winter's day and the Great Hall, where the proceedings took place, was still roofless. Not only had the University to be physically restored, but the future development had to be planned. All this gave us much anxious thought and, not until 1953 with the report of Sir Ivor Jennings and Mr (now Sir) Douglas Logan, did we achieve a blueprint for the University's development. Never have I seen such a sound plan produced in so short a time. I claim credit for it to the extent that it was largely on my insistence that Jennings and Logan were invited to come out.

The Governor is *ex officio* Chancellor, but this is not an executive position, nor is the University a department of government, though it relies largely on government grants. The government must therefore have some say in the policy of the university, but only in a broad way. It must not interfere in the administration as though it were a government institution. That this was the intention of Government was a constant fear of the University authorities. On this score I plead 'not guilty'. The University's apprehensions were not, however, entirely groundless, for the Financial Secretary and some of the unofficials of Legislative Council were critical of the administration and wanted tighter control on the financial side. Gradually mutual understanding was reached; since when the University has gone from strength to strength under the able guidance of the Vice-Chancellor, Dr (now Sir Lindsay) Ride.

Ride joined the University as Professor of Physiology in 1928, was a member of the Hong Kong Volunteer Defence Corps—indeed in appearance he looked more like a genial army officer than the popular conception of a university professor—took part in the battle of Hong Kong and, after the fall of the Colony, escaped to China where he was prominent in the B.A.A.G. (British Army Aid Group), for which he was awarded a military C.B.E. After the war he became Commandant of the Defence Force and in 1949 was appointed Vice-Chancellor. A most congenial person, he was in his element conducting the University choir.

AIRPORT AND RESERVOIRS

A new airport and a large new reservoir were already under discussion when I arrived and continued for some time thereafter. Finance—the local government bore the entire costs—was not the only problem. The question of sites had also to be decided. That for the reservoir was comparatively straightforward and the reservoir was duly built at a cost of upwards of ten millions sterling at Tai Lam Chung in the New Territories. Big as it was, yet another, even bigger, had to be constructed to keep pace with the growing demands of the Colony. Plans for this were well advanced before I left.

Finding a site for the new airport was more difficult on account of the hilly terrain. We thought we had discovered a good site at Ping Shan in the New Territories but then realized that this would not do, for planes coming in to land or to take off would have to circle over Chinese territory and would most probably be shot at. Finally, we adopted the familiar Hong Kong practice of cutting down a hill or two and throwing them into the sea. The result is a runway, capable of taking the largest jets now in operation or envisaged, running out into the sea at Kowloon Bay. The runway was completed shortly after my departure.

SOCIAL WELFARE

A new department, established shortly before my return to Hong Kong was that of social welfare. People and government were gradually becoming more social welfare conscious, whilst at the same time the needs were becoming greater. No longer could social welfare be left as a side line of the Secretariat for Chinese Affairs and to the unco-ordinated and frequently overlapping activities of voluntary bodies. It started out as a sub-department of the Secretariat for Chinese Affairs until, in a few years time, it became independent. Whilst necessarily engaging directly in a good deal of welfare work itself, the department was careful to avoid taking over the work of the charitable societies, or telling them exactly what they should or should not do. So far as they were concerned, it confined itself to guidance and co-ordination. The expansion of welfare activities was remarkable; boys' and girls' clubs, the care of the blind, the deaf, the dumb, crippled children and feeding of the needy. The list grew steadily. Whenever, too, a squatter fire or other disaster occurred, the Social Welfare Department immediately provided food, clothing and other forms of aid for the victims.

Not the least, and perhaps the most far-reaching of its achievements, was the establishment of *kaifongs* or neighbourhood associations. The kaifong, an ancient Chinese institution, had never taken root in Hong Kong, perhaps because the population was too fluctuating. A kaifong is in essence a self-help association of persons living in the same district. They were entirely self-run and democratically elected, with a benevolent eye kept on them by the Social Welfare Officer. Later, the Secretary for Chinese Affairs took them under his wing, since their activities were not confined to social welfare work—much as they did in that regard. Whenever a disaster of the kind I have just mentioned befell, the kaifongs would invariably be found in the forefront. On the occasion of the Shek Kip Mei fire, when more than 50,000 squatters were rendered homeless— about which I write later—I visited the scene and was introduced to one of the kaifong leaders. He was a venerable Chinese gentleman in the traditional long gown that is seldom worn today by persons of his class. Slowly and distinctly I said, 'Do you speak any English?' Equally slowly and distinctly he replied, 'I speak a little. I graduated from Columbia University'. A splendid public spirited citizen was Mr Parkin Wong, with a mischievous sense of humour.

Two dangers threaten the kaifongs; that they will be penetrated by subversive elements and that they will be used as a means of self-advertisement by seekers after public acclaim. The risks are, however, worth taking.

I was keenly interested in social welfare work, and decided that the best way in which I could help was by giving public encouragement and showing that the Governor was in favour of it; for though many of the Chinese themselves did welfare work in one form or another, or subscribed to charitable funds, many did not. I was always irritated by Chinese socialites, particularly of the female species, who said they did not care or could not be bothered. Just as I had no patience with European housewives who boasted that they never went into their kitchens. At any rate, I think I was successful in making social welfare socially acceptable, and the legislature more willing to loosen the purse strings for welfare projects than it had been in the past.

PUBLIC RELATIONS OFFICERS

The Public Relations Department was another post-war innovation. Good Public Relations Officers are hard to come by, particularly where colonial governments are concerned. I know that in Hong Kong we had more than one failure. But out of evil sometimes comes good. The evil on this occasion was the burning down of the British Consulate-General at Canton, which I recount later on. The good was that it resulted in my coming into contact with Jock Murray, at that time attached to the Consul-General, and thus a member of the Foreign and not the Colonial Service. 'Here is the man we want', I said to myself. It took me all of two years before I managed to get him. He was a good 'buy' and served Hong Kong admirably. He got on well with the press—both the local newspaper men and the representatives of the overseas agencies. Neither could be more important from the Colony's point of view. I do not think that the unofficial members appreciated how valuable this was for Hong Kong. Murray was not a good salesman for himself in this regard. Some heads of departments, too, were deeply suspicious of the whole idea of public relations but gradually, in the light of experience, they came to realize that the object of the P.R.O., so far as they were concerned, was to help them, and also that if he were to do so successfully they must co-operate. Later on it was found useful to have the P.R.O. attend meetings of the Executive Council, where decisions are taken at the highest level. This gave him the background, without which he could not properly explain to the public the why and the wherefore of government actions.

I did not myself go in for press conferences as a general rule. In internal matters there was normally little justification for the Governor to do so, whilst in foreign affairs, i.e. those touching on our relations with China, the issues would usually be too delicate for airing at a press conference. I did, however, see the editors of the English language newspapers at regular intervals and, from time to time, Mr Shum Wai Yau, the well balanced and likeable owner/editor of the *Wah Kiu Yat Po*, the leading Chinese language newspaper. I also had press conferences at irregular intervals with the representatives of the foreign news agencies. But all these were confidential discussions and, in the case of the local editors, were as much a means of informing myself of what was going on in the Colony and what was worrying people, as of my informing the editors about government's doings. Heads of departments were encouraged—some of them needed a good deal of prodding at first—to hold press conferences on matters of public interest within their spheres. I believe that the press appreciated these.

Under the Public Relations Officer was Radio Hong Kong, the government radio station which had been established several years before the war. Friction was constant between the head of the station and the P,R.O., the former alleging interference in the running of the programmes, the latter that he was responsible for all news and announcements going out over the air—both were right. So in due course Radio Hong Kong was made into a separate department, but did not write the news bulletins or government announcements, merely broadcasting these as received from the Public Relations Department. The arrangement worked well. A competitor to Radio Hong Kong was the commercial Rediffusion, a wired service dependent for its income on advertising, which commenced operations a year or two after my arrival. The rivalry between the two was keen, similar to the BBC and ITV. Just as the Governor of the BBC disagreed with me that the competition of a commercial station was good for it, so the Director of Broadcasting in Hong Kong would not agree that the competition of Rediffusion did it good. Monopolies, especially government ones, are apt to get complacent and to think that they know best.

Using hind-sight, I wonder if it would not have been better to have subsidized wired broadcasting right from the start, and made it available at such low cost that the majority of the population would have paid their six pence a month, or whatever was the fee, and not bought a radio receiver and listened to propaganda broadcasts from China; New Territories villages being provided with communal loudspeakers. But I do not know if such a scheme would have been practicable.

Drug Traffic and Corruption

The drug traffic had always been a matter of concern in the Colony and it was now more difficult to cope with, since heroin had replaced opium; heroin being both more pernicious and easier to smuggle. The problem had two aspects; one, the effect on those in the Colony who became addicts; the other, the traffic that was conducted through Hong Kong. Peddling, or being in possession of drugs, were criminal offences. But of what use was it to send to prison men who were addicts, as they all were, for on release they would go back to their former habits? Moreover, the pedlars, when sent to prison, usually had their families taken care of by the larger operators who employed them. Norman, the enlightened Commissioner of Prisons, conceived the idea of a rehabilitation centre-cum-prison for convicted addicts. This was opened after I had left and is proving a great success. The international traffic in drugs has big money behind it. The main source is, or was, Bangkok. We had convincing proof that some senior members of the Thai government were implicated. That government, I hasten to add, has since been replaced. We wanted to give publicity to the evidence we had collected but were told not to do so for reasons of high policy. The U.S. Narcotics Bureau frequently made charges that the communist Chinese government was exporting drugs; but of this we were never able to find proof, and we suspected that it was largely anti-Peking propaganda.

Corruption was as great a problem as ever, but we now had a special department of the police to deal with it. Most corruption is petty, but occasionally senior officials were involved. The difficulty in corruption cases is to obtain evidence that will stand up in court. A person will make a complaint to the police, but will refuse to go into open court to substantiate the charges he has made. He is afraid of retribution. We did, however, have some successes, and one head of department was sent to prison. The most difficult time was after the prohibition of the export of strategic and semi-strategic goods to China, consequent on China's entry into the Korean War. This led to a great increase in smuggling out of the Colony, and the bribery of revenue officers which was not easy to detect. A simple way was for the smuggler, usually a person of means, to suggest—with a financial inducement—to a revenue officer whose patrol was between points A and B, that at a certain time he should be at point B. The smuggler would then slip through somewhere near point A. If a revenue officer were suspected and was called upon for an explanation as to the large amount of money in his bank account, he would say that he had won it at the races, giving the date, the number of the race and the name of the horse, which was impossible to disprove. By degrees the revenue department was cleaned up. The most spectacular hauls made were of gold and narcotics and usually resulted from tip-offs, substantial sums being paid to informers if their information led to a seizure.

ENTERTAINING

For entertaining—and considerably more had to be done in Hong Kong than in any of our other posts—Government House left little to be desired. Most of the work fell on Maurine. Fortunately, we had a very good domestic staff, presided over by Ah Yau, the number 1 boy, a most admirable and kindly man. Even so, constant supervision was necessary. Because the dinner served on Monday was good, it did not follow that it would be equally good on Tuesday. The cooks—three of them—had to be kept up to the mark. In the same way, the table boys, if not watched, might appear in grubby uniforms, or during lunch or dinner, stand around daydreaming, failing to notice that the water or wine glasses needed replenishing. Periodically, Maurine would hold a post-mortem with Ah Yau, telling him what had been done correctly and what incorrectly. It took eternal vigilance to maintain a high standard.

The seating arrangements were left to me. The A.D.C. would send in to me a draft seating-plan which I would alter or approve as the case might be. This may sound petty and trivial but many people, especially wives, are very precedence-conscious, and when you invite someone to your house you do not want them to go away feeling slighted. Sometimes a ticklish question would arise as to who took precedence over whom. I got round this difficulty by giving the husband of one couple a high place, and the wife a lower one, reversing the process with another couple. At large dinner parties, after the men had rejoined the ladies, we would have a sort of general-post, and half way through this part of the evening the guests would be moved around. This made for variety. Our endeavour was to make our parties, even the formal ones, as light hearted and interesting as possible. We wanted our guests to leave Government House not only feeling honoured that they had been entertained by the Queen's representative, but also that they had had a good time. A guest has, or so I maintain, an obligation to help make a go of the party he is attending. Some people are much better than others and, since I could not remember the idiosyncracies of all who came to lunch or dinner, especially those who were invited but rarely, an appropriate note would be entered against their name in the card index kept by the A.D.C. The principal lady was expected to make the move to go home. At lunch parties no difficulty arose, for the form was that, as soon as we had all moved from the dining-room—where we had coffee at the table—into the drawing-room, the guests would, after a short interval, say their farewells. But at dinner parties there was no such obvious point of departure, and not infrequently the principal lady would go through agonies, wondering if it were time to leave. Eventually we solved the problem by I, myself, getting up and saying it was time to go to bed. If any particularly interesting people were visiting the Colony, we would arrange a small dinner party with such local residents as we considered suitable for the occasion. Then after dinner, the men would adjourn to my study, leaving the ladies to their own devices; or it might be a stag party, at which my wife might or might not appear for dinner only, leaving us directly after. We had one or two awkward or amusing incidents. When the remembrance of the Japanese occupation was still vivid, we suddenly realized about an hour only before guests were due to arrive for dinner, that the senior lady would be the wife of the Japanese Consul-General and be placed on my right. This might well have given offence to other guests. How I had failed to appreciate this previously I do not know. We had, therefore, if we could, to find a lady who would outrank the wife of the Japanese Consul-General. My wife hurriedly rang up Mrs Unwin, the wife of the Commodore, explaining our predicament and asked her if she would come to dinner and help us out. She gladly did and the day was saved. You can always rely on the Royal Navy.

Our most nerve wracking experience was in connection with the Crown Prince of Iraq who came to Hong Kong at very short notice, and we were unable to have him stay at Government House. We already had in train a farewell dinner for the British Naval Commander-in-Chief to which a number of other people had already been asked, including Michael Todd (*Around the World in 80 Days*) and his wife, Elizabeth Taylor, who were visiting Hong Kong. To this party we invited the Crown Prince and he accepted. On the morning of our dinner, I learnt that at a party the previous night, at which the Crown Prince had been present, he had created quite a scene because one of the guests was a Jew. Now Todd was a Jew—his wife was not. Todd happened to be in my office that afternoon, so I explained to him what the state of affairs was and told him that, for the ensuing evening, he was to be a Scot or anything but a Jew. He laughingly agreed. The party went off very well; the handsome Prince, in a dazzling array of decorations, could not have been more charming and agreeable. Elizabeth Taylor was breathtakingly beautiful and Todd was at his most vivacious. Nevertheless, Maurine and I heaved a sigh of relief when it was all over. Within a few months, both the Crown Prince and Todd were dead; the former by assassination, the latter in an air crash.

On the lighter side was the episode of the Cowley Father whom I invited to say grace at luncheon, as was my custom whenever a cleric was present. I made my request as he came into the drawing-room where we had foregathered for a glass of sherry. Imagine the astonishment of myself and other guests, when he stepped briskly forward and there and then said grace.

On another occasion, a clergyman of some obscure denomination from North Dakota had been to see me in my office. As I was conducting him to the door on leaving, he said 'Let us pray', and down on our knees we went.

During the racing season, which lasted about eight months of the year, we gave luncheons for thirty to forty people every three or four weeks at the Governor's box at the Jockey Club. It was exciting and gay, but the custom was for guests to remain until after tea, with the result that by the end of the afternoon we usually felt quite exhausted. The Jockey Club was a non-profit making organization and, since the Chinese are great gamblers, it had considerable sums of money to dispose of and gave very generously for the building of hospitals and schools, for the laying out of parks and other deserving causes.

The social event of the year was the garden party given at Government House on the Queen's Birthday. Anyone who had called (which was done by writing one's name in the Government House visitors' book) during the course of the year was invited. The difficulty was to remember the names of those whom we wished to invite but who, usually out of diffidence, had not called. Consequently I kept a running list of such people. Once, a young lady, whom we did not know, telephoned the A.D.C. and indignantly demanded to know why she had not been sent an invitation. 'Have you called?', the A.D.C. enquired. No, she hadn't, but she had bought a hat specially for the occasion! She received her invitation. We used to shake hands with every guest as he or she arrived, but as the population of the Colony grew, so did the number of guests, until one year we found ourselves shaking hands without stopping for an hour and a half. I do not know how many people this was. I should think about 2,000. We were not the only sufferers, for the arriving guests had to queue up for an intolerably long time. Thereafter, we shook hands no more but mingled with the guests on the lawn. We took pride in the fact that all the food was prepared, not by caterers, but on the premises by our staff. This was no mean achievement, for at our last Queen's Birthday reception the number invited had risen to 4,500.

In attendance on such occasions was the whole complement of A.D.C.'s, regular and honorary. The latter were from the three services, the three branches of the Defence Force, the regular and auxiliary police and St. John Ambulance. They were all invariably smart and alert. I considered myself fortunate in my regular A.D.C.'s, for throughout my career I have taken note of A.D.C.'s whether of governors or generals, and most of them struck me as being rather ineffective young men. In Hong Kong I chose mine from the Police Force. They had been hand-picked by the Commissioner, and woe betide them if they fell down on their job, for not only would they incur my wrath but, what they feared even more, that of the Commissioner. An A.D.C. has quite an arduous life, but it is excellent training for a young man. Two years away from police duties is, however, long enough, so I changed them at the end of that time. We made a point of letting them off whenever we could, such for instance as when we had no dinner guests—that suited us all.

We seldom lunched or dined out at private houses; only going to the service chiefs, consuls, members of councils and one or two others. Nor did we attend cocktail parties, other than those given by public bodies, the services and those already mentioned. When we did go, we had a set routine. We would arrive promptly at, say, 7 p.m.—and a governor must always arrive on time, neither a minute late nor a minute early (to arrive early is the crime of crimes)—and at 7.15 p.m. the A.D.C. would come up to me and say, 'Excuse me, Sir, but you have another engagement and it is time to leave'. This suited the host, for as long as the Governor was there, he could not feel free to attend to his other guests. The Governor had been invited to give prestige to the party. The same thing applied to charity balls which were an almost weekly feature of Hong Kong winter life. If the sponsors could say that the Governor would be present, many more tickets would sell. Since the charities were one and all worthy of support, we did not mind being used as bait. We took care not to outstay our welcome, and to remain on because we were having a good time. We knew that not only did our hosts need to be free of the duty of attending us, but many of the more elderly amongst those present were yearning to go home to bed, and would not dream of leaving until after the Governor and his lady had departed.

I did one good turn to the consuls, and also to myself, by abolishing the custom of speeches at national day parties. It was difficult, year after year, to find anything fresh to say that was not banal. One Canadian Trade Commissioner used to recite on every Dominion Day the number of miles of roads and railways in Canada: most tedious. Under the new dispensation, we contented ourselves with proposing the health of the Queen, by the consul, and of the head of state of the country concerned, by myself.

JUSTICES OF PEACE

One of the functions I always enjoyed was the annual banquet that I gave to the Chinese Justices of the Peace. To be appointed a J.P. was an honour much coveted by the Chinese. In their eyes it ranked above an O.B.E., I believe. How and when it had come to be regarded as a reward for services rendered, I do not know; certainly before my time as Governor. I took a different view of J.P.-ships, considering that appointments should be made, and only to the number required, for the performance of those duties necessary to be carried out by J.P.'s, such as visiting prisons, sitting on the magisterial bench for certain categories of cases or acting as members of tribunals of one kind or another—obviously only responsible persons would be appointed. Here was a clash of opinion between the Chinese and myself. They thought that appointments should be made for services rendered; I thought that they should be for services to be rendered. The argument never became heated or acrimonious; perhaps I did bend my principles a little. About seventy-five would attend the banquet; too large a number for the dining-room at Government House. We therefore held it in the ballroom, which was profusely decorated with flowers and music was supplied by the police band. It was a formal affair with full evening dress and decorations. Practically all the Chinese wore Chinese dress. Chinese women invariably did so on all occasions—women J.P.'s were a post-war innovation, and what heart-burning this caused. The two senior and very venerable J.P.'s sat next to me, Mr Li Po Kwai and Sir Shou Son Chow. The former was the senior. He spoke no English and my knowledge of Cantonese was slight, but he was one of those courtly gentlemen whose graciousness one cannot help feeling, even though conversation is limited.

Sir Shou Son's family had been in Hong Kong for generations, and one of his jokes was that his forebears had been pirates, which may well have been true, for, when the British first came to Hong Kong, the population of the island was only some 1,500, and piracy was the poor fishermen's side-line. Sir Shou Son was one of the first Chinese to study at a western university, having been a student at Columbia in the '70's. He and my stepfather, General Munthe, had served together in the Chinese Customs Service in Korea when that country was still part of China. Another veteran was Sir Robert Ho Tung, but his health prevented him from attending the banquets. The two were quite different. Sir Shou Son was jovial, human and everybody's friend. Sir Robert, despite the twinkle in his eye, was less approachable, more cautious and ruled his family with a rod of iron. With his acute financial sense, he had amassed a considerable fortune and was the largest individual donor to charity in the Colony. Both were over ninety when they died.

CALLS AT CANTON, MACAU AND NANKING

One of the things a governor of Hong Kong has to do soon after his arrival is to call on his opposite numbers at Canton and Macau. So far as Canton is concerned this practice ceased when in 1949 the communists came into power.

The newest arrival makes the first call, which is then returned. The first call I made was on General Chang Fa-kwei at Canton. General Chang had the reputation of being an able commander, and he was not to blame, I have been told, for Canton falling to the communists practically without a fight. He was not adequately supported and was interfered with by Generalissimo Chiang Kai-shek. He now lives quietly in retirement in Hong Kong. Be that as it may, I found him an intelligent man and a considerate host. Official and ceremonial visits are not the easiest of social occasions, but as they go, my visits to Canton and Macau were not unagreeable. We had, of course, the usual spate of speeches; more in Canton than in Macau. At Canton, Maurine's main activity was buying basketfuls of crystal prisms of eighteenth century chandeliers—relics probably of East India Company days—with which she intended to make chandeliers for Government House in Hong Kong. This she duly did with most satisfactory results; exercising much ingenuity in the process.

Only a couple of months after General Chang Fa-kwei had paid his return visit to me, Dr T. V. Soong was appointed to Canton with authority over all South China. A tactful approach was made to me through the British Consul-General that it would be embarrassing and would incur loss of face for him, Dr Soong, if he were to make the first call. It certainly would have been odd for someone with the extensive jurisdiction that Dr Soong had, and moreover a man who had at different times held the posts of Finance Minister, Foreign Minister and Prime Minister of his country, to leave cards, so to speak, on the governor of a comparatively small colonial dependency. I readily agreed, therefore, that I should make the first call. We saw a good deal of the Soongs during the time they were in Canton, which was until the latter part of 1949 when the city fell to the communists. He and his wife were fairly frequent visitors to Hong Kong.

On one of their visits, we were dining with them at the house of Mr Chen, the local manager of the Bank of China. The house was at Deep Water Bay, and just across the water from it the Yacht Club had a place where members kept their boats. During the course of conversation, Dr Soong asked Mr Chen if he often went to the Yacht Club. Mr Chen replied that he did not, because he was not allowed to be a member. I was much embarrassed, but am glad to say that a few years later the Club opened its doors to non-Europeans. By the time I left Hong Kong, the only club that did not admit non-Europeans to full membership was the Sheko Country Club. This was resented by Chinese, though the resentment was not often expressed to Europeans. An instance, though, occurred at a meeting at which I was presiding, when the question of possible sites for tenement buildings for slum dwellers was being discussed. A leading member of the Chinese community, who was present, suggested Sheko. Sheko was quite unsuitable for the purpose, and the only reason for his putting it forward was his resentment at the policy of the Club.

The new building of the Bank of China, although started by the Nationalists, was not completed until after the communists had taken over in China. My office overlooked it and one day I said to Mr Chen, who had remained on as manager, 'I suppose, Mr Chen, you will fly the communist flag from the top of your new building'. 'As I do not think you would like that, I shall not do so', was his reply, and he did not. From time to time he went to Peking and, if I happened to see him after his return, I would ask him if he had had his brain washed. But the joke became painful, so I dropped it.

Soong's visits created a security problem for our police, as he had a number of enemies who would gladly have assassinated him if there were the chance. He and I got on well together, both officially and personally. As a result, minor affairs that might have developed into unpleasant incidents were harmoniously solved. 'T.V.' is a man with a brilliant mind and one of the few Chinese I have met who, whilst remaining Chinese, are able to think like a westerner. There is much in the saying: 'East is East and West is West'—the mental processes are different. After living in the east for a long time, a westerner will come to learn the likely reaction of an easterner to a certain set of circumstances, and vice versa, but fundamentally they are different. That does not mean that we cannot like and respect each other's qualities. On the contrary, it adds fascination. A few westerners become almost oriental in their mental make-up. But whilst they cease to be European, they do not become completely Asian and are neither one thing nor the other. Neither race accepts them; but of this fact they are pathetically unaware.

We also paid a call on General and Madame Chiang Kai-shek at Nanking and the British Ambassador, Sir Ralph Stevenson, with whom we stayed. Stevenson, a handsome man who looked like a Spaniard, was a Manxman. Deservedly he had a beautiful wife who had redecorated the former consulate-general, and now embassy, with exquisite taste. We established friendly relations with both of them. At tea with the Generalissimo, Madame Chiang did the interpreting since he speaks no English. It was a pleasant occasion, if somewhat stilted, and I came away with the impression that the Generalissimo was surrounded by a court that cut him off from knowledge of the real state of affairs in China. Chiang Kai-shek is now discredited so far as the mainland of China is concerned but I should be surprised if, in the years to come after he has long disappeared from the scene, he were not restored to the Chinese pantheon for, although he had made many mistakes and eventually failed, he rendered great services to his country.

Nanking could not compare with Peking as a capital city. The new government office buildings had nothing distinguished about them, whilst even the Sun Yat-sen memorial on a fine hill-side site was not as impressive as it should have been.

Before I had exchanged calls with Canton, I had a distinguished visitor in the person of the Prime Minister of China, Mr Sun Fo, and his wife, who stayed with us for a few days. Sun Fo was the son of Sun Yat-sen, the founder of the Republic of China, which no doubt accounted for his occupying high office. The visit was a private one, but we gave a formal dinner party to which we invited leading local dignitaries. At this party I committed a 'gaffe'. In processing into dinner, I should, of course, have offered my arm to Mrs Sun, the principal lady but, by some inexplicable lapse, I led the way in with the second lady. Fortunately, T. N. Chau (now Sir Tsun Nin), the senior Chinese member of Executive Council, saw what had happened and rescued Mrs Sun. It was most embarrassing. The next day at some public function, Mr Sun made rude remarks about Hong Kong; but I do not think there was any connection between the two.

'T.N.' was a delightful person with something elfin about him. Although an Oxonian, he was not a westernized Chinese of the type that is regarded with disdain by the Chinese man-in-the-street. He was, in fact, very popular with, and implicitly trusted by them and knew instinctively what their feelings were on any particular subject, which made him a valuable member of Executive Council.

INCIDENT OF KOWLOON WALLED CITY

I have run ahead of my story and I shall now go back to 1947 when Hong Kong was rehabilitating itself with jobs a-plenty and good profits for the businessmen. In such circumstances, administration was comparatively easy and straightforward. We did not foresee the difficulties—mainly political—in store for us. The first major incident was the Kowloon Walled City affair that led to the burning down of the British Consulate-General at Canton.

By the Peking Convention of 1898, China leased to Britain for 99 years the New Territories, reserving to herself certain rights in Kowloon Walled City, an area of about six acres surrounded by a wall in the Territories. These rights had been abrogated by an Order in Council in 1899, since when the Hong Kong authorities had exercised complete jurisdiction and had treated the area as though it were just like any other part of the Colony. The Chinese government did not protest, or if it did no notice was taken. During the Pacific War, the Japanese pulled down the wall and many of the buildings enclosed within it, in order to make way for an extension to the airport. After the war the shortage of accommodation was acute owing to war damage, and many of those who poured into the Colony could find nowhere to live. They therefore built shacks for themselves on bombed sites or devastated areas, of which the old walled city was one. Although the numbers were small, about 25,000—as compared with the one million refugees with which the Colony was later saddled—they had to be moved, for not only did they create fire and health hazards, but the sites were required for rebuilding.

Accordingly the Public Works Department was engaged on a systematic campaign of clearing them out, when they went further afield.

No one had given any thought to Kowloon Walled City and its potential explosiveness. Had it not been treated like the rest of the Colony for half a century? But when the cleaning up team came to the 'city' a hostile crowd resisted; claiming that Kowloon Walled City was Chinese and not British territory. This was a direct challenge to the government. Either we gave way, in which case it would look as though we were too weak to assert our authority and we should lose the confidence of the people, or we should have to assert that authority which would probably result in bloodshed. No government can lose the confidence of its people and remain in power, and this certainly applied to Hong Kong. A fundamental issue was involved; the right of the government to exercise jurisdiction over part of its territory. There was also the likelihood of the Chinese government getting drawn in; for although the ringleaders of the crowd were private individuals acting on their own, the claim they were making was on behalf of the government of China, and already the press in China was raising the cry of 'British imperialism' and 'the sacred soil of China'.

Sir Ralph Stevenson, the British Ambassador at Nanking, was staying with me at the time. I told him I was seeking authority from London to force our way in and clear out the squatters, and that if anyone was hurt, it would blow back on him, since the Chinese government would almost certainly protest. Stevenson agreed that I had no option but to go ahead. I do not believe that the government at Nanking wanted to be difficult, but T. W. Kwok, the Chinese Special Commissioner in Hong Kong, thought he could gain kudos for himself by forcing the Governor, myself, who had only recently arrived, to give way. Instead, therefore, of discouraging the agitators, as I believe were his instructions, he encouraged them.

We had to re-assert our authority, or at any rate attempt to do so. The operation was carried out by the police. Unfortunately the Commissioner was away on leave and the acting Commissioner bungled things. The resistance was stiff; one person was killed, several were injured, and the police failed to recover the whole of the area. The press in China was now in full cry against the British authorities, with the scene shifting to Canton where mobs demonstrated against the British. Internal Chinese politics also came into play. T. V. Soong was in charge in South China and had no desire to let the mob get out of hand, but the reactionary right wing, the 'C.C.' clique (so named after the brothers Chen), was both rabidly anti-foreign and anti-Soong and wanted to create as much trouble for him as possible. This they did by inciting the rioters to attack the Consulate-General which was burnt down. The Consul-General and his staff were fortunate to escape with their lives.

The ejection of the squatters from Kowloon Walled City and the burning down of the Consulate-General had now become matters of contention between the British and Chinese governments. The Chinese government, like all weak governments, was afraid of giving way on a point that seemed to affect the national honour. They claimed jurisdiction in the Walled City, whilst we on our side were unwilling to concede the claim. Various compromises were put forward, for example, that the six acres should be made into a public garden. That broke down on the question as to which authority, British or Chinese, should be responsible for enforcing the regulations that are necessary for any public park. The issue dragged on for months. The remaining squatters did not move out, but we had no wish to exacerbate matters between H.M.G. and the Chinese government by attempting to eject them. An impasse had been reached; but so far as the Hong Kong government was concerned we had shown that we were not prepared to abrogate our rights, either by mob rule or at the behest of the Chinese government. The confidence of the people was not lost. Nonetheless, it was an unsatisfactory situation. The city became a cesspool of iniquity, with heroin divans, brothels and everything unsavoury, for whilst we regularly sent in police patrols, we did not care to prosecute malefactors in the courts, lest the controversial issue of jurisdiction be raised by the defence. We preferred to deport—an executive and not a judicial act—those who committed offences in the City. Since I left the Colony at the end of 1957, the position has improved and cases of serious crimes have been successfully taken in the courts without any repercussions.

Kowloon Walled City was our major preoccupation in 1948. Another cause of friction with Nanking was the way in which political refugees in Hong Kong from the Nationalist régime would vilify Chiang Kai-shek and his government, which was an abuse of our hospitality. One of the worst offenders was Marshal Li Chai Sum, who had occupied high posts in Chiang's government and who had been in the forefront of the boycott of Hong Kong in 1925. I reprimanded him a number of times and he invariably apologized, promising to mend his ways, but as invariably broke out again after a few weeks. Eventually, when the communists had captured Peking he went to that city, sending me on his departure a courteous letter of thanks for the kindly manner in which he had been treated whilst in the Colony. Certainly if we had expelled him and others like him, he would have received short shrift from the Nationalists. The same, of course, applies today to political refugees from communist China. Fortunately most of them behave themselves and do not castigate the Peking government, not publicly at any rate. Expulsion in their case would be to Formosa, whose authoritarian rule appeals to them almost as little as does that of mainland China. These men are in fact persons of liberal sentiment like, for instance, K. C. Wu, the former mayor of Shanghai, who went with Chiang Kai-shek to Formosa, but subsequently fell out with him and fled to America. I was able to do Wu a good turn when in the latter part of 1948 on our way through Shanghai, I arranged for the shipment of a large consignment of rice from Hong Kong which Shanghai sorely needed.

EMERGENCY IN MALAYA AND OTHER MATTERS

South of Hong Kong, in Malaya, the emergency or communist revolt had broken out. This was not of direct concern to us, but with the advance of the communists in China we could not but be interested. I myself was more directly implicated, for the Commissioner General for South East Asia commenced holding his periodic conferences which were attended by the three commanders-in-chief with head-quarters in Singapore, all the British governors, ambassadors and high commissioners from Karachi to Tokyo and Wellington. Lord Killearn had been Special Commissioner in South East Asia whilst Malcolm MacDonald had been Governor-General of the Malayan Union and British Borneo. In 1948 Killearn retired and MacDonald was in sole charge as Commissioner General. Consequently I had more to do with MacDonald than with Killearn. A genial bluff King Hal, Killearn was a big man in every sense of the word. He did a good job in South East Asia and was respected and understood by Asians. I have often noticed that what Asians resent as much as the arrogance of a blimp is the patronizing air of well meaning left-wingers. 'Poor little fellow', they seem to say, 'I'll protect you'; thus implying that they are superior. Killearn was neither a blimp nor a well meaning left-winger.

For Malcolm MacDonald I have considerable admiration and affection. His great achievement, and it was great, was to remove from the minds of Asians the image of the top British official as a pompous proconsul or as one who in any way considered himself superior to them. He did not. He felt himself as another human being like them: no better, no worse. As a former politician and cabinet minister himself he could, too, appreciate the problems and talk the same language as the Asian ministers. I am of the opinion that post-war he did more than any other Britisher to win for Britain the confidence and trust of Asians. They loved him. It was not a matter of intellect, with which he is well endowed, but of personality; an indefinable something. And the indefinables, or imponderables are just as important, if not more important, than the definables and the ponderables. Possessed of a great sense of fun and enjoyment of the ridiculous, he had the capacity of being able to laugh at himself. He was not beloved of blimps, of which Singapore had quite a number in pre-merdeka days (*merdeka* is the Malay word for freedom). Whenever I visited Singapore, I was shocked by the reactionary outlook and language of many of the leaders of the European community. Happily most of these went home after merdeka.

Although the Singapore conferences were in some respects a waste of time and paper, they enabled British representatives to get to know each other, and to see how their apparently separate problems were interrelated. The formal sessions, which took up most of the time, were tedious in the extreme. After I had attended two or three I knew it all by heart, so adjusting my dark glasses, I would indulge in a quiet nap. I would have slept more soundly if the chairs had not been so uncomfortable; but we were so crowded that only the smallest and hardest ones could be used. Even so I felt that I had more important matters to attend to in Hong Kong, and rarely stayed for the whole of the conference.

Sentimental Visit to Peking

In September of that same year, 1948, Maurine and I paid a sentimental visit to Peking. We had not been there since 1932 and we wished to see it once more before the communists marched in, which seemed likely to happen any moment. Already the sound of gun fire could be heard in the distance. My stepfather had died in Peking some years previously and my mother had returned to England before the war. We therefore stayed at the old-fashioned but comfortable Wagons-Lits Hotel. The weather was perfect and we had a happy, if somewhat nostalgic, seven days, revisiting old haunts, palaces, temples and fairs. We peered into the windows of the pavilion at the Summer Palace which my mother used to rent and where we had once stayed for a few days, enjoying particularly wandering in the Palace grounds in the evenings after they had been closed to the public. But Peking was not what it had been, the embassies had long since moved to Nanking after the Nationalists made that city their capital, and their compounds were deserted and neglected—the communists re-established the capital at Peking. The merchants, too, seemed listless, almost apprehensive, for they did not know what the future held in store. Altogether a *fin de siècle* air pervaded the place. We thought this would be our last visit to Peking, but we were wrong.

CHAPTER SEVEN

COMMUNIST CHINA

O N 1st October 1949, the Chinese communists declared themselves to be the lawful government of China. Why did China go communist? This is a question to which different answers are given. Some say, because China was betrayed. That answer in itself poses another question: betrayed by whom? By the Democratic administration in the United States? Others say the blame should be laid at the door of the Kuomintang. Perhaps we are too close to the event to be able to give an objective or conclusive answer. Nor is it easy to say with certitude whether the defeat of the Nationalists and the victory of the communists was inevitable.

The Manchu dynasty in the 19th century was steadily losing its grip and becoming more and more ineffective. China, with the longest continuing civilization in the history of mankind, had lost her inspiration and was slipping into chaos. Coincidentally, the West was striking her with violent impact. Unlike Japan, she seemed incapable of adjusting herself to the modern world, or of resisting the aggressions of the Western powers. Only jealousy prevented these powers and Japan from carving up China into colonies and spheres of influence. The European powers had ideas of dividing China into spheres of influence; they were thwarted by the United States with its Open Door policy—the object of which was equal opportunity for all to despoil China. Such a situation was galling in the extreme for the Chinese; more so than for other Asian peoples, because the Chinese, in their attitude to non-Chinese, had been more arrogant than any other nation. China was the Middle Kingdom, the centre of the universe, and now the despised barbarians were treating her with contempt—a most humiliating state of affairs. This feeling of resentment against the West is hardly to be wondered at, even though it was China's own failure that had led to her being treated with contumely. Japan, a weaker, poorer country than China, adapted herself to the modern world and stood up to the West whose respect she earned. Be that as it may, China is now having her revenge. In course of time, as China comes to occupy her rightful place in the comity of nations as a great power, and as a new generation grows up that has not experienced extraterritorial rights and other special privileges for foreigners, this feeling of resentment will no doubt abate.

Throughout history we can see instances of once great nations sinking into insignificance: Egypt, Greece, Rome. Some remain permanently in decline, others make a recovery. What did the Revolution of 1911 in China portend? Did it mean that she had merely exchanged an ineffective monarchy for an equally ineffective republic? Certainly, in the first years of the Republic it appeared so, with the country riven by civil strife. Then in 1926, with the rise to power of Chiang Kai-shek and the Kuomintang, order was gradually restored, and the country was getting on its feet. Some, though, say that already in the early thirties the Kuomintang was beginning to fail, that graft and corruption were rampant, that nothing was being done about land reform. The Japanese did not, however, take this view. They foresaw, or thought they foresaw, that China was on the way to build herself up into a powerful state. They regarded this as a threat to themselves, and were determined to nip it in the bud. Hence the series of Japanese attacks on China, commencing with the occupation of Manchuria in 1931 and only ending with the Japanese surrender at the end of the Pacific War in 1945. An interesting speculation is what would have happened if Japan, instead of trying to destroy the new China, had helped her in her endeavours to modernize herself. But she did not; she followed the path of military aggression and not that of friendly co-operation.

China was fighting an all-out war against Japan from 1937— when Japan launched her full-scale invasion—until 1945, a period of eight years. Britain and America were fighting Japan for only half that long, and they were well-disciplined and industrialized countries. China was neither. Is it therefore surprising that at the end of the war China was physically and spiritually exhausted? Her leaders seemed to be incapable of dealing with the deteriorating condition of the country and the régime slipped more and more, until finally it foundered in inefficiency and corruption. In the wings a well organized, well disciplined and dedicated group, the Chinese Communist Party was waiting, ready to give the Kuomintang the *coup de grâce* and oust it from power. China went communist by default, the default of the Kuomintang, and that need not, possibly even would not, have come to pass, but for the mistaken policy of the Japanese government. The vast majority of the people was not communist, but anything was better than the discredited Kuomintang. When the People's Liberation Army was fighting its victorious way across China in 1948 and 1949, the Central People's Government was, in the eyes of most of the people, only a new régime—but a Chinese régime—uncorrupt and just. The tragedy or the accident—

according to one's point of view—of history is that the inspiration for the rebirth of China should be communist.

But my concern as Governor of Hong Kong was how the communist take-over of China would affect the Colony. More important than that the government was communist, was the fact that it was strong. Hong Kong is 'China irredenta', and this applies whatever the complexion of the government, communist or non-communist. T. V. Soong once said to me in my office, when the Nationalists still seemed to be firmly in the saddle, 'In twenty-five years' time, I, or rather my successor, will ask for Hong Kong back and we shall expect to get it'. China would not have ceded Hong Kong to Britain in 1842 had she not been weak, and subsequent Chinese governments were not strong enough to take it back. On the contrary, China had been forced to cede a further piece of territory, Kowloon Peninsula, in 1860 and to lease the New Territories in 1898. Chiang Kai-shek, at the end of the Pacific War, probably hoped to recover Hong Kong. He pressed for the surrender of the Japanese in Hong Kong to be taken by a Chinese and not a British commander. Had this been acceded to, the next logical step would have been for the Chinese commander to have said that he was in Hong Kong to stay. And who at the end of the war, when everyone was war-weary, would have driven him out? Churchill, however, would have none of it and Hong Kong was liberated by units of the British Pacific Fleet and the surrender taken by Admiral Harcourt.

Over the years, the relations between Hong Kong and China were generally not unfriendly. Incidents, some serious, some not so serious, occurred from time to time, but our position was never directly challenged, and the frontier was devoid of barriers. Chinese from China would come and go whenever they pleased, without the necessity of passports or other documents. Equally there were no restrictions on Britons going into China. The allegiance of these Chinese was still to the land of their birth but they obeyed the Hong Kong laws and paid the Hong Kong taxes. Prior to 1949 when the communists came into power, China's national day, 10th October— the 'Double Tenth' and the anniversary of the outbreak of the revolt at Wuchang in 1911 that led to the overthrow of the Manchu dynasty —was celebrated as a public holiday in the Colony, and at many public functions the British and Chinese flags were given equal prominence. Altogether a state of affairs that pleased everyone, but China's national pride and *amour propre* had been so deeply hurt that the Chinese authorities were always endeavouring to keep alight pro-Chinese, and hence anti-British, sentiments in the breasts of their people in the Colony. The two main targets for subversive activities were the trade unions and the schools. This had an unfortunate effect on the unions for, instead of devoting their energies to the welfare of their members, they tended to devote them to political issues. After the war, when the communists in China were becoming a powerful factor in the land, this tendency became more pronounced with the unions splitting into two groups, one pro-Kuomintang, the other pro-communist. Generally, however, the subversive activities of the Kuomintang in Hong Kong were not very effective. They created trouble; sometimes considerable trouble, for example the incident of Kowloon Walled City, but they did not constitute a real threat to the safety of the Colony, for the basic reason that the Chinese government was not strong enough to challenge Britain's position.

With the coming into power of a strong government in China, this state of affairs altered completely. Moreover, the new régime was violently anti-Western, anti-British, and anti-Hong Kong. In such circumstances what were the guiding principles of our policy? On the one hand we did not want to be provocative; on the other we did not want to appease or appear to do so, to give way to unreasonable demands. The population of Hong Kong knew that the government across the border was unfriendly and strong. If we truckled to it we would lose the people's confidence and support; they might even turn against us. We had to do a balancing act all the time, especially when an incident occurred such as the closure of a communist school, the deportation of an agitator or the prosecution of a communist newspaper for a seditious article. We had to take a decision in the light (often obscure) of such facts as we had before us, and of our estimate or guess of the probable consequences of the course of action we proposed to adopt. All I can say, in retrospect, is that we managed to get by.

The general attitude of the people of Hong Kong towards the new régime in China was at first one of approval, much the same as it was in China itself; relief at the ejection of the Kuomintang, hope and expectation of a kindly and just government; a new deal in fact. Not everyone, however, saw the situation this way: a minority had grave misgivings about these 'agrarian reformers', 'leaning to the left'.

H.M.S. AMETHYST

When they reached the Yangtse in their drive southward, the communist armies halted for a while before crossing that mighty river, and it was during this phase of the civil war that the *Amethyst* incident occurred. At the request of the British Ambassador at Nanking—a hundred or more miles up river from the ocean port of Shanghai—the frigate, H.M.S. *Amethyst*, was ordered to proceed to Nanking. The Nationalist authorities—still the government of China —whose forces were on the south bank of the Yangtse were notified of the projected trip; the communists, along the north bank, were not. Before the *Amethyst* reached Nanking, she was fired on by the communists, the captain and several of the crew being killed and others wounded; the vessel herself ran aground. A relief captain, Lieutenant-Commander Kerans of the Naval Attaché's staff at Nanking, was sent to take command. For several weeks during the hottest part of the summer, this young naval officer had to sustain the morale of his crew under exceptionally trying conditions, whilst at the same time, he had to conduct interminable negotiations with the local communist commander in an endeavour to secure the release of his ship. He was hardly in a position to bargain, for he had nothing to offer. Moreover, the communists could with ease have starved him and his crew into surrender or have sunk the ship with their superior fire-power. Finally, Kerans came to the conclusion that either he must accept the humiliating terms demanded by the communists or make a dash for it, with the likelihood that he would be sunk by the communist artillery during his passage to the open sea. He decided on the latter course. The odds were heavily against him, but sometimes fortune smiles on the bold and brave. This was one of those instances. The *Amethyst* reached the sea and thence sailed to Hong Kong where Kerans and his crew received a tremendous ovation from the British community. Kerans was awarded the D.S.O. and promoted to Commander.

It was a stirring feat in the finest traditions of the Royal Navy, but one cannot help asking why the *Amethyst* was ordered to Nanking in the circumstances then prevailing, nor questioning the wisdom of the cruiser, H.M.S. *London*, being sent up the Yangtse in the face of superior shore batteries in an attempt to rescue the *Amethyst*. Inevitably she was forced to withdraw after suffering casualties. The conduct of Kerans and his men was gallant, but the episode as a whole was a slap in the face for the British, which was not displeasing to many Hong Kong Chinese, even those unsympathetic to the communists.

DEFENCE MEASURES

The communist forces reached our border in October 1949, but for months previously we had been in consultation with London, endeavouring to forecast what those forces would do when they got there. Already refugees were pouring in. Whitehall wanted us to wire the frontier and to resist by force of arms any who tried to cross into British territory. The line we in Hong Kong took was that this would be a mistake, and would almost certainly lead to bloodshed which might well incite the victorious communist army to launch an attack on the Colony. Such an attack even if unsuccessful, as it probably would have been, would be a most unhappy prelude to the relations between H.M.G. (to say nothing of Hong Kong) and the new government of China. Neither did we think that hordes of defeated Nationalist soldiers would come streaming in. I am glad to say that our view prevailed, and we were not flooded out with Nationalist soldiers, although we did get a few thousand with their camp followers. They were a nuisance, and a costly one, as well as being a source of embarrassment to us in our relations with the Chinese government, especially as some of them engaged in anti-Peking activities. Any caught at this were deported to Formosa.

It might be thought that the whole lot would have been shipped there, and even welcomed, for after all they had been fighting for Chiang Kai-shek. But his government refused to accept them on the excuse that some might be fifth-columnists. Considering that Formosa already had plenty of these gentry, I thought this pretty thin. The real reason was that by leaving them in Hong Kong the Nationalist government was spared the expense of maintaining them. George Yeh, the Nationalist Foreign Minister, admitted as much to me when I happened to meet him in New York where he was attending a session of the United Nations.

In our argument with London as to whether or not the border should be closed, we had also said that we considered that as soon as the communists had consolidated their position throughout China the refugees would go back, as they had always done on previous occasions when civil war in the neighbouring provinces of China had sent them scurrying into the Colony. But we were wrong. This time they did not go back. Instead more and more crossed the frontier so we had to close it, which was done without fuss or bother in May 1950.

With the likelihood of a permanent military threat from China, it was clear that the military forces in the Colony would have to be considerably increased. The military command was also reorganized. Instead of independent commanders for each of the three services, each responsible to his respective commander-in-chief in Singapore and with no overall commander in the Colony, the new post of General Officer Commanding-in-Chief, Hong Kong (later altered to

Commander British Forces) was created. He had overall responsibility for the land, sea, and air forces in the Colony.

Whilst I do not believe in a civilian governor interfering in purely military matters, I welcomed the change, the more so as I had lost confidence in the army commander. I thought also that he had lost confidence in himself. The new, and first, G.O. C-in-C. was General Festing, who had been in Hong Kong just after the war. He infused confidence and energy all round, but put terror into some battalion commanders who were unable to keep up with him when he went dashing up mountain sides. I am a pretty good walker myself but I had some sympathy with his officers and men, for this was in the middle of a Hong Kong summer. Festing was succeeded by General Mansergh who, when he left, was followed by General Evans, hitherto the divisional commander. I never ceased to count my blessings for having in those critical days commanders whom I fully trusted. In addition I found them pleasant and easy to work with which was important, since it is essential that the civil and the fighting services should co-operate harmoniously, and the tone for this is set by those at the top.

The Army Commander-in-Chief at Singapore also proposed that the civilian governor, myself, should be replaced by a military man. His proposal cannot have got very far in London, for I did not hear about it until some years afterwards and then only privately. A somewhat similar suggestion was made a little later; that the Commissioner General at Singapore should have executive authority over the Governor of Hong Kong in all matters appertaining to defence—a wide definition—as he had over the Governor of Singapore and the High Commissioner of Malaya, though he had never used those powers. On the face of it the arrangement was logical. The service commanders in Hong Kong were under the authority of their respective commanders-in-chief in Singapore, *ergo* the civilian governor of Hong Kong should be in the same relationship to the civilian Commissioner General; a nice tidy set-up. I thought it a bad idea, and gave my objections to the Colonial Office. In reply I was told that the matter had been decided by 'ministers'—that magic formula that is supposed to crush all argument—and that nothing more remained to be said. I persisted in saying more.

Malcolm MacDonald, the Commissioner General, held a conference with the commanders-in-chief and myself. He sided with me—he was no empire builder. Also, the matter being of considerable importance to Hong Kong, I informed the unofficial members of the Executive Council. They objected in the strongest terms. 'Malcolm MacDonald would be all right', they said; 'we know and trust him, but he is not going to remain as Commissioner General for ever. In principle we are completely opposed'. I duly reported to the Colonial Office, which sent out an official for discussions. I was not present when he and the members of the Executive Council had their meeting, but the proposal was dropped.

In June 1949 the Minister of Defence, Mr (now Lord) Alexander, visited the Colony. This heartened us all for it showed that H.M.G. was taking seriously its responsibilities to Hong Kong. And that it was not a case of mere words and polite but ambiguous phrases, soon became evident when a stream of troopships bringing reinforcements shortly started to arrive. A member of the Colonial Office, who attended the ministerial talks in London, told me later that what really actuated the government was the thought that if Hong Kong were lost it would redound to the government's disadvantage at the next election. But perhaps he was unduly cynical.

In March 1950, by which time the augmented garrison was at full strength, a parade was held of the whole of 40th Division; the largest assembly, I believe, of British forces ever held in the Far East. The setting at Sekong in the New Territories was spectacular. Encircling the Sekong plain on three sides, a range of mountains, dominated by the 3,500 feet high Tai Mo Shan, rose steeply. The parade itself was very impressive, county regiments from England, Gurkha regiments with their quick light-infantryman's step, armoured vehicles and guns. The G.O.C., General Evans, must have been proud. I know I was, as I took the salute at the march past. I had, though, a moment of panic when the stiff breeze threatened to carry away my plumed hat.

I had met General Evans a few months previously shortly after his arrival, when visiting some of the newly arrived units to see how they were settling down. Evans was a soldier's soldier; the sort of man in whom his officers and men would have implicit trust and confidence. I was, therefore, not surprised to see that he had won a triple D.S.O. Later, when he became Commander British Forces and we worked together a good deal, I found him an admirable colleague with an incisive mind, clarity of expression and ease of manner.

Most of the new army camps were in the New Territories which meant that farmers' lands had to be requisitioned. A further potential source of trouble was the damage caused to fields by army exercises and manœuvres. Thanks, however, to the close collaboration between the District Commissioner and the military, care was taken to ensure that whenever at all possible only land not being cultivated was taken, whilst in the case of damage, compensation was prompt and adequate. Generally, the villagers welcomed the presence of the troops, as they brought money into the place and created opportunities for employment. They had no cause for complaint and did not make any. In fact the boot was sometimes on the other foot, for the Army suffered considerably from thieving of corrugated iron, timber and other materials needed for the defences. And when they wished to construct a jeep-track up to Robin's Nest—an observation post in the frontier area—the number of new graves that suddenly appeared and that had not been there before, was remarkable. To remove a Chinese grave is a serious matter, calling for heavy compensation.

Most of my visits to the troops were of an informal nature and I often lunched at one or other of the officers' messes; all of which was enjoyable as well as interesting. When I visited the 7th Royal Tank Regiment, they put me in a tank and from the gun fitted with a morris tube, I shot at pegs stuck in the ground. Every time I pulled the trigger a peg fell. Jokingly, I accused the C.O. of having someone concealed in nearby bushes and, whenever I fired, pulling a string attached to the peg. At a N.A.A.F.I. canteen, I asked a young soldier if the N.A.A.F.I. did them all right. Somewhat grudgingly, he admitted that they did: his only complaint being that they did not remove the bones from the kippers!

The arrival at short notice of such a large number of troops created a variety of problems; accommodation being one of the most acute. Although many could be put under canvas, at any rate temporarily until huts or something better could be erected, a considerable number of buildings were required for hospitals, administration and one thing or another. This meant requisitioning; always an unpopular measure, especially in peace time. Generally speaking, it went smoothly with the minimum of friction. The credit for this must go both to the military and the owners of the properties affected. The civil government was the requisitioning authority; and I, as the ultimate court of appeal, as it were, had to adjudicate on a number of cases.

The sole blunder the military made was over La Salle College in Kowloon. They needed a large building for a hospital. Only two were suitable, one the Dominican Priory, the other La Salle College, both Catholic institutions. One or the other had to be taken, so I therefore asked the Catholic bishop which it should be. This was too thorny a matter for his liking, so I had to make the decision myself, and decided on La Salle. Meanwhile the Dominicans, with the threat of requisitioning over their heads, had written to the Vatican, which in turn protested to the British government. But by the time the protest reached me, the reason for it had been removed. Unfortunately, the military undertook to vacate the College by a certain date. I was surprised at the time, that they committed themselves in this manner, but they had, and never denied it. When, however, the date came round, they were unable to keep their word, which created a certain amount of ill feeling, and questions were even asked in the House of Commons.

Another problem, although of a minor nature, and I only mention it because attached to it is an amusing incident, was that of schooling for the servicemen's children. The government found what places it could for these children in suitable government schools, but the Army had to establish additional ones of its own. I asked our Director of Education what these schools were like. I quote his reply: 'The other day I was about to cross Chater Road. Also wanting to cross was a little fair-haired girl about eight years old. I offered to assist her. Looking up at me with her blue eyes, she said "and what the hell do you think you're doing, you interfering old bastard!" ' He did not think the schools were very good. That was in the early days. Later on the schools became first rate.

The welfare of the troops also engaged our attention. The officers presented little or no difficulty, since it was comparatively easy for them to meet others of their own kind, either European or English-speaking Chinese. The problem was the other ranks; young soldiers, thousands of miles from home in a strange land with, to begin with, poor accommodation and inadequate recreational and social facilities. Here the co-operative spirit characteristic of Hong Kong came into play. A committee, the Forces Civilian Entertainments Committee, of private citizens, both European and Chinese, was set up. With a subsidy from the government two excellent services clubs, the Cheero Club on Hong Kong island and the Nine Dragons Club in Kowloon, were established. In addition, concerts, bathing picnics and so on were arranged for the men.

It was about this time, I believe, that by mutual agreement the tedious business of exchanging formal calls between the Governor and the three service commanders in Hong Kong, and the three commanders-in-chief, was quietly dropped. Colonial Regulations, and presumably also the corresponding service manuals, laid down that whenever one of the seven first arrived in the Colony, he and the others should exchange calls. Meticulous instructions were given as to what the governor should wear, full dress or tropical uniform, or alternatively, on receiving a call, a morning coat. The call lasted about ten minutes. After a sufficient interval, to enable the caller to get back to headquarters, the governor would set out to return the call. Salutes were fired and altogether there was much ceremonial. We were too busy for this sort of thing. I am all in favour of formality on the right occasions, but this had ceased to be one of them. Instead of exchanging calls I would invite newly appointed Commanders-in-Chief or Commanders British Forces to dine with me quietly at Government House within a day or two of their arrival. We all found this pleasanter and a more useful way in which to get acquainted. Strictly speaking I was breaking Colonial Regulations and should have obtained the prior approval of the Colonial Office. Inevitably, if I had raised the subject with them, they would have had to consult the Admiralty, the War Office and the Air Ministry, and as likely as not one or other would have objected. In any case heavy weather would have been made out of something unimportant.

Internally, too, measures had to be taken in case the Colony were attacked. The volunteer force was reorganized. This had in fact been under study for some time previously. Instead of unco-ordinated and independent army, navy and air units, the three were combined into the Hong Kong Defence Force with its three separate arms. The Force was, in 1950, accorded the honour of the prefix 'Royal' in recognition of the distinguished part it had played in the battle of Hong Kong against the Japanese in 1941. The subordination of the three volunteer branches under an army (volunteer) 'supremo' caused a certain amount of heart burning; just as did the subordination of the regular Navy and Air Force to the G.O.C.-in-C. The resentment came from the senior service rather than the Army and the R.A.F. I have always found that, whilst the Army and the R.A.F. are willing to co-operate with the other two services, the Navy is only willing for the other two services to co-operate with it. However, the Commandant, Colonel Ride, in real life the Vice-Chancellor of the University—an odd combination of posts both of which he managed with good natured efficiency—remained unperturbed.

Compulsory service, limited to so many training periods a year, was introduced for British subjects, both European and Chinese. Those called up were directed either to the Defence Force, Auxiliary Police, or one of the branches of the Civil Aid Services. These last were called Civil Aid—not 'Defence'—for they were also used in peace-time calamities, such as fires or floods, when they proved to be of inestimable value. Their imposing chief was Charles Terry who had originally come out to Hong Kong as a police constable, had then gone into business and on retirement had decided to remain in the Colony. Other measures carried out were such things as construction of air-raid shelters, blast walls for vital buildings, an air-raid warning system, the stock piling of essential supplies. Whilst these precautions had to be taken, we did not want to alarm the populace by making them think an attack was imminent. They took it all calmly.

Stock piling was quite an expense, particularly in the case of perishable and bulky commodities like rice and soybeans, for not only did it mean the building or renting of storage space, but also the disposal of existing stocks before they had become spoiled, and their replenishment by new purchases; the whole transaction possibly resulting in a loss. This we had to regard as a sort of insurance premium. Meat posed a special problem, as insufficient cold storage was available, whilst to build enough would have been very costly, and in any case would have taken too long. The solution was dried fish, which is also protein and is well liked by the Chinese. One of the Jesuit fathers invented a process that made the fish keep almost indefinitely. The Jesuit fathers were of great help in other ways as well. One acted as Director of Agriculture after the war until we could get a professional, another perfected a new method of composting for the farmers' fields. Yet another was a leader in youth work, giving his whole time to it. On the artistic side one of the fathers adapted and produced Chinese operas for performance in English.

SUBVERSION

The defeat of the Nationalists and the establishment of the Central People's Government in China led, as we expected, to greatly increased political activity by anti-British and subversive elements of the Colony's population. They thought they could do just as they pleased and that the Hong Kong government would not dare to take action against them, lest Peking be offended. In this they made a mistake. Legislation was passed making it illegal for any society in the Colony to be affiliated with an outside organization, except with the permission of the Executive Council, which was of course given in *bona fide* cases. Hitherto a number of societies had had foreign affiliations that were detrimental to the state. The worst agitators were deported. Every state has the right to deport undesirable aliens, and in Hong Kong it had been the practice to deport Chinese aliens at the end of prison sentences for serious crimes. The duration of the ban varied according to the length of prison sentence and the nature of the crime. In addition, gangsters, against whom it was well nigh impossible to secure a conviction in the courts because they intimidated the witnesses, were deported. These gangsters were members of triad, or secret, societies, and were a constant source of worry. They operate in China and wherever there are large Chinese communities. I imagine that the ruthless and efficient régime in China today has stamped them out in that country, but they still flourish in places like Hong Kong and Singapore. Also deported, as the need arose, were political agitators. Executive Council was the authority for the issuance of deportation orders. Save in the most urgent cases, it only made an order after exhaustive and lengthy enquiries. The person concerned was also given the opportunity of stating his case, e.g. that he was innocent or that deportation would inflict an undue hardship on him or his family. If his plea were acceped, he would not be deported.

The first real showdown between the government and the subversive elements arose over an industrial dispute, the Tramways strike, which started on Christmas Day 1949. Although ostensibly a labour dispute, in which the government could not intervene other than to offer the good offices of the Labour Department, the motivation was political. The strike dragged on for several weeks, until the rank and file of the union saw that they were being duped by their leaders. This led to strife within the union. The leaders, too, committed serious breaches of the peace and were summarily deported. The reasonable offer of the Tramways Company was accepted and the strike collapsed. That, however, was not the end of the story. The deported leaders went to Canton, where the Chinese authorities gave them a big reception with speeches denouncing the Hong Kong government. But as soon as the reception was over, they were told to clear off. They had lost their jobs and could not get back to Hong Kong to their wives and families. The tramway strike and its aftermath was an eye-opener for potential trouble makers. It showed that the government was master in its own house. Of equal significance, the neglect and abandonment of the strike leaders by the authorities in Canton made the people in Hong Kong realize that the new régime in China did not portend a workers' paradise, as they had been led to believe. No propaganda from us was necessary to bring home this painful truth.

The communist newspapers in Hong Kong also became steadily more scurrilous and defamatory of the government. Many people, Chinese and non-Chinese, wondered why we did not close them down and expressed amazement at our forbearance. Was our hesitancy a sign of weakness? Were we afraid? No, we were not; but one of the most important things for which the free world stands is freedom of expression of opinion and liberty of the press. We preferred to rely on the judicial process rather than to suppress by executive act. Moreover, to secure a conviction for seditious libel, the offence had to be flagrant, and we could not risk an unsuccessful prosecution. We should then have been worse off than before. Finally, however, two of the newspapers concerned overstepped the mark and were prosecuted. The trial lasted three weeks and resulted in the defendants being convicted and fined, with an order of suspension for six months in the case of one of the newspapers. Thereafter the local communist newspapers were careful to watch their step.

FRONTIER INCIDENTS

I have already mentioned that in pre-communist days the relationship between the Chinese and Hong Kong authorities was, generally speaking, that of normal friendly states, that no barriers existed at the frontier, and that any Chinese was free to come and go as he pleased. When the communists arrived at the border all this was stopped—by them. No trains ran through from Kowloon to Canton or vice versa. The river steamer traffic was halted, and the communists prevented, or tried to prevent, people escaping to Hong Kong. It was only later, May 1950, that we imposed restrictions on people coming into the Colony. This we did, not for political reasons to keep out communists, but because we were being flooded out with refugees. The land frontier between Hong Kong and China is about 22 miles long. At the eastern extremity it runs right through the middle of the village street of Sha Tau Kok. Here the situation was bizarre, to say the least, but it worked. The communist guards and our police knew the villagers by sight, and only occasionally were they prevented —by Chinese frontier guards—from moving freely from one side to the other. Expectant mothers would sometimes come over from the Chinese side to a small clinic that we maintained. Here they would deliver their babies, then return to China with their infants, who would have been duly entered in the Hong Kong register of births as British-born subjects.

Going west from Sha Tau Kok, the boundary runs along a gully and stream which, in about six miles, becomes the Shum Chun River, the boundary for the remaining sixteen miles. For the first four miles from Sha Tau Kok steep hills rise on either side of the defile. The scenery here is grand; in the dry winter months, the grass on the hills is a pale bronze, in spring and summer, everything is green of varying shades. Perhaps the loveliest time is when the wild azaleas and lilies are in bloom. Next comes a short stretch of flat land, followed by an outcrop of hills on the British side; finally a long expanse of plain which becomes swampy towards the mouth of the Shum Chun River at Deep Bay. From Sha Tau Kok, a narrow road on the British side runs through the defile and across the flat land, until it joins the road which, in about half a mile, leads to the road bridge spanning the river at Man Kam To. A mile further down the river at Lowu is a rail cum footbridge, also leading to China. The Chinese town of Shum Chun, the garrison headquarters, is approximately half a mile inland from Man Kam To and one mile from Lowu.

The situation along the border, between Sha Tau Kok and where the Shum Chun River really becomes a river, was almost as odd as at Sha Tau Kok itself. Some farmers, living on the British side, owned land on the Chinese side. Others, living on the Chinese side, had land on the British side. Along this part of the frontier, we had erected a wire fence, provided with gates that were opened at stated times of the day to permit the farmers to pass to their fields. On strategically located hills, police block-houses had been built, so that the whole length of the frontier could be kept under observation. There were no military posts on the frontier itself. Their O.P.'s were on the hills behind.

In their early days the communists erected loudspeakers at Lowu and Man Kam To pointing towards British territory. From these speakers a stream of abuse poured forth against the British in general and the Hong Kong authorities in particular, especially when people were going from one side to the other—even when the restrictions were at their tightest there was always some movement to and fro. Knife-rest barbed wire barriers had been placed across the two bridges on the far side—the international boundary is on the north, or Chinese, side of the river. They could be moved as required to allow people or trains through. The communist guards stood on the Chinese side of the barriers; our guards on the Hong Kong side, only a few yards apart. They never spoke a word to each other, except when a communist would say to one of our policemen (Chinese)— 'We know who you are, and where your family lives. It is going to be just too bad for you, as shortly we are going to take Hong Kong, and then you will be severely dealt with'. Our men never moved a muscle. I salute their courage.

In such a situation it was inevitable that incidents should occur from time to time. The communists would shoot anyone they caught trying to escape into Hong Kong. On one occasion, at night, they had shot at, and wounded, a man who had already succeeded in reaching British soil. At that particular point the boundary fence had been set a few yards back from the actual frontier because of the configuration of the ground. The communist guards, having wounded their man, dashed over on to the British territory and dragged the poor wretch back. What could we have done? None of our police was actually on the spot. The scene had been witnessed from one of the block-houses some distance away. We had just to grin and bear it.

On another occasion a military patrol—these went along the frontier road regularly accompanied by one or more police officers—was stopped and turned back by a section of communist soldiers who had recently been making a habit of coming over on to our side of the frontier at a place which had no fencing, and spending the day there. A few days later the Commander-in-Chief, who was on a visit from Singapore, had sub-machine-guns pointed at him by the same lot of soldiers as he passed. Quite obviously we could not tolerate this violation of our territory, for if we ignored it, they would do the same thing all along the frontier and gradually nibble away our position. The G.O.C.-in-C., the Commissioner of Police and I consulted as to what should be done. At first the General wanted to throw the intruders out by force. The Chinese would have resisted, if for no other reason than that if they did not, they would probably be shot when they got back to their barracks. It was decided to play it more softly. Accordingly, the police officer in charge of the frontier area sent a note by an intermediary to his opposite number on the Chinese side, pointing out that this was British territory, that perhaps the trespassers did not realize it was, and requesting that they should desist. The letter was returned unanswered, but it had been opened, and the Chinese soldiers did not appear again. Meanwhile arrangements had been made to put up in double quick time some fencing at this particular spot. Whilst this was being done under the supervision of a Chinese P.W.D. foreman, a group of communist guards came along and reviled him. He spat on the ground and went on with his work. We all heaved a sigh of relief that another incident had ended satisfactorily. London should have been glad too, for they might have had a shooting war on their hands.

I used to visit the frontier from time to time, both because I wished to keep myself up to date with developments, and also to show our men that the Governor was interested in them. I did not, however, do it too frequently, as the visit of a V.I.P. threw an extra burden on the police in the area. I found it a relief to get away from my desk and out into the country for a few hours. I usually lunched at one of the border police-stations; happy informal occasions. I enjoy the company of policemen: perhaps because I have always, or almost always, been on the right side of the law. Whenever I went up to the barrier at Lowu bridge, one of the communist guards would photograph me. They invariably looked shamefaced about it. I do not think they knew who I was, since I was dressed like anyone else and did not have a flock of aides around me. It was simply part of their routine to photograph visitors who they supposed to be persons of some importance, since the frontier was a closed area and permission to enter it granted only sparingly. Instead, we had a 'milk run', along which we would send visiting journalists and others, and although Lowu and the actual border were not included, it was possible from certain vantage points to look into Chinese territory, and with the aid of binoculars to see what was going on. We did not want to risk an incident which might have occurred at any time.

As an example I might mention the occasion when the Duke of Kent went to the border. After he and the Duchess of Kent, his mother, had concluded their official visit, he stayed behind with us privately for a few days. He was anxious to go to the border, so arrangements were made for him to do so in company with the Commissioner of Police. At the barrier, he started to take photographs of the communist guards, who thereupon pointed their guns at him and began clicking their bolts. The Duke, at the request of the Commissioner, put his camera away. If anything had happened, the Commissioner and I would have been looking for new jobs.

A more serious incident than that concerning the Duke of Kent occurred when one of our policemen at the barrier strayed over on to the Chinese side. Although passenger trains did not go across the bridge at Lowu, goods wagons did: the procedure being for a British locomotive to push the wagons from the Hong Kong side to the Chinese side, or to pull the wagons from the Chinese side to the Hong Kong side, as the case might be. On one such occasion it was seen with dismay that one of our policemen was being led away by Chinese soldiers, with a gun at his back, on their side of the border. I imagine that during the shunting operations he had inadvertently got on to Chinese territory. This was serious, for if we failed to get back our man, the morale of the police would be shaken. Formally to request the Chinese authorities, with whom in any case we had no official contacts, would have got us nowhere, whilst to try and effect a rescue would have had extremely grave consequences. Fortunately we were blessed with a very able and astute Commissioner of Police. He said he had some contacts with, or to Canton, and he would work through them. Within less than forty-eight hours he had fixed it, and the policeman was returned to us. One of the requests that the Chinese made was that the beam of one of our searchlights should not be directed into their barracks. It disturbed the sleep of the soldiers. We considered this a small concession to make.

The debt that Hong Kong owed to Duncan MacIntosh, the Commissioner of Police, was immense and everyone knew it. Mac-Intosh began his police career in the Royal Irish Constabulary at the age of sixteen, followed by a spell in a Scottish force after which he was transferred to Singapore, where he was interned during the war and came to Hong Kong as Commissioner in 1946. He had an air of authority about him and inspired devoted awe in his officers and men. In discussions and arguments, he was a first rate tactician, knowing when to push his point and when to retreat, with the result that more often than not he got what he wanted. This, combined with his air of self-confidence, irritated some of his government colleagues, of which he was, I am sure, amusedly aware. His friendly laugh could be most disarming, especially to anyone trying to outwit him, but he could be very frank and outspoken if need be. As well as being an outstanding Commissioner of Police, he had a flair for dealing with the most delicate situations which saved the day on more than one occasion in those critical times. He did not speak a word of Cantonese; so much for the shibboleth that a man cannot do his job properly unless he knows the language of the country. If anyone deserved a knighthood it was MacIntosh. I pressed hard for him to be awarded one but without success. I consider he was treated ungenerously.

REFUGEES

Refugees were nothing new in the history of Hong Kong. Whenever there was civil war or similar commotion in South China, as not infrequently happened up to the thirties, refugees would come streaming in from the neighbouring provinces of China. Whilst in Hong Kong they would be taken care of by their relatives and friends or by charitable institutions. The government neither fed nor housed them, for it did not want to encourage any more of China's 400 millions (the pre-war population) to come begging for free lodging and free food. They invariably went back to their homes as soon as things had quietened down. An exception was in the case of the Japanese invasion of South China prior to the outbreak of the Pacific War. The refugees who, on that occasion, fled into the Colony were looked after by the government since they would not go back. The

Japanese, after they had captured Hong Kong, solved the problem by forcibly expelling them.

On the return of the British, thousands of Chinese poured into the Colony. Some had lived there before the war, most were newcomers in search of jobs, none were refugees. But even before the refugees started coming in the housing problem was serious. At the end of the war nearly three-quarters of the tenement-style buildings were, as already related, unfit for human habitation. Those who could not crowd into the congested slum dwellings established themselves in flimsy shacks in bombed-out areas in the town or on the adjacent hill-sides. It was no use their going out into the country, for what they wanted was work, and this could only be found in the urban areas. These were the first squatters. The term 'refugee' is not generally used in Hong Kong, but 'squatter'. Not all refugees are squatters, nor all squatters refugees.

In the normal course of events, and had the communists not come into power in China, no refugee problem would have arisen, and in the process of time sufficient housing would have been provided for all. Already the government was drawing up plans for the replacement of slums by decent low-cost housing estates. Then came the communist sweep down China from the north, and refugees flooded in.

The popular conception of refugees is a collection of destitute persons who have fled their own country, living in camps of dilapidated barrack-like huts and leading a confined existence inside the camps with nothing to do but drag out their days in squalid misery. This has never been the situation in Hong Kong and there are no camps. Ever since it came to be realized that the refugees had come to stay and would not go back to China and could not go elsewhere, Government's policy has been to integrate them into the rest of the community. Since they number one million out of a total population of three millions, it can well be imagined that some years will elapse before the goal is finally achieved.

The great majority of the refugees were very poor people who had abandoned their homes in China, bringing with them such scanty possessions as they could carry. In order to live, they needed money and that could only be obtained if they secured work. It is true they could collect free food at one of the centres set up for that purpose, but what they sought was a job—and independence. If they had skill, which few of them had, this would be comparatively easy. If they had not, they would be lucky if they could occasionally get casual work. How they managed to survive, I do not know, but somehow or other they did. The next thing they wanted was a place to live. Thousands slept in the streets, jealously guarding their pitches which constituted for them and their families a home. Most of them, though, built themselves a house—if a structure of a few square feet, made of beaten-out kerosene tins, old pieces of discarded match-boarding or old sacking can be called a house. Around them would be hundreds of similar shacks with little or no space between. Many of the squatter areas were as populous as a fair-sized town in England. From a distance they looked quite picturesque, especially those on the hill-sides, with their jumble of little buildings. A visit to them, however, soon dispelled sentimentality and revealed the full horror of their squalor. The Chinese by nature are a clean people, but what can one do when there is no sanitation and water has to be carried from afar, often from a polluted stream? The only redeeming feature was the squatters themselves. I never ceased to marvel at and admire their comparative cheerfulness whilst living in such appalling conditions.

To begin with, little for them was done since we predicted, wrongly as it turned out, that as soon as the new régime in China had settled down and things got back to normal, they would return to their native villages. Meanwhile, in May 1950, we imposed restrictions against any more entering, which was a reversal of Hong Kong's traditional policy. We did not wish to be inhuman, but our first care had to be for our own people. We could not let them be crowded into the sea or subjected to the risk of epidemics, to which such a large influx of people necessarily gave rise. Gradually we came to the realization that these people had come to stay. It would have been cruel to have thrust them back into China, even if that had been possible. Nor was there any other place to which they could go, for no other country would take them. The first steps that the government took were tentative. Encouragement was given to voluntary organizations, such as the Settlers' Housing Corporation, to erect inexpensive cottage-type buildings. Stand-pipes were provided in some of the squatter areas, fire lanes were driven through them. This last, in itself, aggravated the congestion, for it sterilized that amount of land. We had not, however, yet taken the plunge and gone the whole way, although plans for doing so were almost complete.

On Christmas Day 1953 occurred the disastrous fire at the Shek Kip Mei squatter area, when more than 50,000 people were rendered homeless. Fortunately only three persons lost their lives, all from heart failure. The first necessity was a crash rescue programme: feeding, clothing, accommodating; and the government organizations concerned, the kaifongs, St. John, Red Cross, Boy Scouts, the armed services and many others, were active on the scene. Each and everyone seemed to know exactly where to go, what to do, and do it. The co-ordination was remarkable. Shek Kip Mei, though, was more than just the most serious of all our squatter fires. It marked the turning point in government's policy in dealing with the refugee problem. Government now accepted the fact that the refugees had come to stay, for several years at least—and they were still managing to get in despite the restrictions. Most of these illegal immigrants came in by way of Macau. From China they entered Macau, and thence were smuggled—quite a racket grew up—across to Hong Kong by junk. This was very difficult to prevent, and once in Hong Kong they melted into the rest of the population. Accommodation was not the only problem. Medical care, education for their children, and all the amenities that the state gives to its citizens had to be provided as well.

The next thing after the crash rescue programme was to erect proper housing. Speed was of the essence. The quickest way was to put up rows of one-storey structures, but this is wasteful of land, of which Hong Kong is woefully short. To build high is the most economical in this respect, but requires more time. We compromised and decided on two-storey blocks of a temporary nature. Within seven and a half weeks of the fire, the first of these 'Bowring bungalows'—so named after Mr Bowring, the energetic and capable Director of Public Works who conceived the idea—was ready for occupation; and this was after the site had been cleared of debris, properly drained and roadways laid. Such a feat could not have been achieved without the valuable assistance of the Army with their bulldozers. The third thing was the rehousing of the rest of the squatter population. This was a long-term project and will not be finally completed for several years.

There being no government department able to deal with an entirely new activity of this magnitude, a new one had to be set up—the Resettlement Department. It was essential that the right man should be put at the head of it, a good administrator, an enthusiast with his feet firmly on the ground who would inspire his subordinates. Such a one was Holmes of the Cadet Service, who became the first Commissioner for Resettlement; and a very good one he proved to be.

The Bowring bungalows have long since been replaced by the new standard seven-storey blocks, but they served their purpose well. Each of the new style blocks houses some 2,000 persons. They are divided into rooms measuring 120 square feet, to which are allotted five adults. Substandard, it is true, but infinitely better than the congested squalor in which these pathetic people had previously been living. They are fire-proof and they are clean, and their popularity is borne out, not only by the happy smiles of the residents, but also by the fact that the amount that has to be written off for non-payment of rent is negligible. The rent is, or was, about 4s. 6d. a week. On the ground floors are shops, also for squatters. The flat roofs, which are partly covered, are used for simple schools, and for boys' and girls' clubs, both of which are a great success. A group of blocks is called a resettlement estate, which may contain as many as 60,000 souls. This creates a problem in itself, for the resident inmates cannot just be stuck in their cubicles like a lot of troglodytes in caves; schools, clinics, community centres, open spaces and other amenities have to be provided. All this we learnt by experience.

The clearance of the squatter areas and the rehousing of their occupants gradually became a routine operation: the selection of the area to be cleared, the screening and card-indexing for the inhabitants thereof, the building of the resettlement block, the removal of the squatters and their belongings into their new home, the levelling and general preparation of the vacated squatter area for another resettlement block for the reception of another lot of squatters from another area. Hard and arduous work for the staff of the Resettlement Department, but they did not seem to mind, combining practical efficiency with a humanitarian touch. The process is still going on. The squatters in the resettlement estates were now living a decent law-abiding life like other citizens; whereas in the old, or non-cleared areas, not only was the risk of fire and the outbreak of disease ever present, but lawlessness was prevalent. By degrees these old areas were brought under control, and, although the living conditions still left a great deal to be desired, in other respects they were much improved. Moreover, their inhabitants had something to look forward to, for they knew that in course of time, their turn would come to be moved into a resettlement block.

The work of the voluntary agencies, local and overseas, religious and non-religious, was amazing. They provided funds for, or built, cottage-type dwellings for refugees. They established schools, they distributed free food, they ran clinics, they opened youth clubs. In no sphere of relief work were they not actively and efficiently engaged. But the problem was so vast as to be beyond their means. The really heavy expenditure had to be assumed by the government.

When the members of the Legislative Council unanimously voted the money to succour the Shek Kip Mei victims, they also approved Government's new policy of rehousing all squatters. This was a very heavy commitment for the present and for the future. One person in every three needed rehousing, either as a squatter or a slum dweller. For a colonial dependency to undertake this out of its own resources was remarkable. Approximately one-third of the Colony's expenditure, direct and indirect, was in respect of the refugees. Here it is worth noting that the average per capita income in Hong Kong is probably only one-fifth of what it is in Britain. The refugees and their care and maintenance are not the responsibility of Hong Kong alone. They are the responsibility of the whole free world. I requested financial assistance from H.M.G. I begged, I pleaded, I wrote despatches, I wrote letters, I spoke to officials, I spoke to ministers. But all in vain, we got nothing.

Although the British government would not help us in our long term refugee programme, they did give us a contribution, and a generous one, for immediate relief after the Shek Kip Mei fire. Whether they would have done so without my urgent prompting, I do not know. The American Consul-General came to my office and said that his government wished to make a contribution, and named a substantial figure. Would it be acceptable? It certainly would. I was most sincerely grateful. How generous the Americans are. It would not have looked well had a foreign government been the first to make a contribution. Moreover, there was the distinct possibility that Peking would also donate a large sum for relief. I therefore immediately telegraphed the Colonial Office, and was very relieved to get a favourable reply with the promise of a grant.

It was not easy for the communists to cash in on the situation and to stir up trouble amongst the refugees, for the refugees had fled from the communist paradise, and had no love for the government of China. The communists, however, are adepts at exploiting every possible or even unlikely situation. Whenever, for instance, a fire occurred in a squatter area, with consequent distress for many unfortunate people, they would accuse the Hong Kong authorities of callous neglect of these citizens of China; ignoring the fact that these citizens of theirs preferred to sleep in the streets of Hong Kong rather than return to their homeland. In November 1951 a fire devastated a squatter area at Tung Tau, when some 10,000 people lost their homes. Immediate relief in the way of food and clothing was given them, but they had to move to other squatter areas, for we had at that time not yet adopted the policy of rehousing squatters in resettlement blocks. This led to a good deal of dissatisfaction and complaining, which was just what the communists wanted. Their press made bitter attacks on the government, but a more dangerous tactic was the intention they expressed of sending from Canton a 'comfort mission', the outcome of which was not difficult to foresee. The mission would have come to Hong Kong; fiery speeches would have been made against the 'imperialists', aid would have been promised from 'Mother China'; all this, be it noted, on Hong Kong soil. Rioting would have broken out with further fuel for the flames if any members of the mission had been injured or arrested.

The communists steadily increased their campaign until things came to a head. Permission for the mission to enter Hong Kong was firmly refused. Canton accepted this, but evidently co-ordination was lacking between the sponsors of the mission in Canton and those in Hong Kong, for, on 1st March 1952, a group of the latter told the crowd in Hong Kong—actually Kowloon—that the mission was coming, and that a delegation of the Hong Kong sponsors was going to the border to meet them. The sponsors did not in fact reach the border: the police turned them back before they got there. Meanwhile the crowd waiting for them had become a mob, and when the delegation returned with no comfort mission, rioting broke out. The police, advancing with Guards-like precision, quickly restored order. One rioter died of· his injuries. Further attacks by the communist press followed, but they were half-hearted affairs. They had lost the battle of the comfort mission, and did not try it again.

OTHER PROBLEMS

Other difficulties also arose from the communist take-over in China and their unfriendly attitude towards Hong Kong; for example the custody of lepers and lunatics. In pre-communist days we sent the lepers to a leprosarium run by a Catholic order at Sheklung in Kwangtung province, where we paid for their care and maintenance. Mental cases we transferred to a government asylum at Canton, paying for them also. Hong Kong had an inadequate asylum for British-Chinese and non-Chinese, though the latter were usually sent to their homeland. When the communists came into power they would not take either lepers or lunatics. In the case of the lunatics, we already had the nucleus of a mental hospital staff under the well qualified Dr Yap. The asylum had in any event to be replaced by something better, so it was only necessary to enlarge considerably the size of the proposed new hospital, which we did, and the hospital has since been opened. Dr K. C. Yeo, the very likeable Director of Medical and Health services at the time, suggested that the hospital should be named after me. I declined the honour. I have never quite decided whether he was pulling my leg or not.

As regards the lepers, we had had no experience in running a leprosarium, but a number of religious and semi-religious organizations do this kind of work in various parts of the world. We decided that the best thing would be to try to get one of these to take it on. The Mission to Lepers agreed to do so, and a great success they have made of it. But what a lot of trouble they had in finding a suitable site. We thought the best place would be out in the New Territories away from large centres of population. The District Commissioner and Dr Fraser of the Mission scoured the Territories, but all to no avail. The village elders said that the villagers would assuredly kill the lepers. Dr Fraser was at his wits' end. Reluctantly he agreed to have a look at an island between Hong Kong and Lantau. His fear was that the water supply on this small island would be insufficient for a leprosarium. (Hong Kong has practically no rainfall for six months on end.) Testings were made on the streams on the island. Thanks be to God, there was enough water, and so the leprosarium was duly established on Hayling Chau, 'Island of Happy Healing'. Willing helpers came forward, including the Royal Engineers. A vigorous local society that supports the mission has also grown up. Considering what the disease is, and how its victims are ostracized, one might expect the inmates of a leprosarium to be melancholy and depressed. On the contrary, the atmosphere of Hayling Chau was happy and the lepers were cheerful, which reflected great credit on the staff.

REFUGEE DOCTORS AND EDUCATIONAL EXPANSION

Refugee doctors, numbering several hundred, were another problem. Their degrees, obtained in China, were not recognized in Hong Kong, and although this did not prevent the government from employing them, it precluded them from engaging in private practice. As we were very short of private practitioners, it seemed ridiculous to deny ourselves the services of these men. To enable them to practise privately would have required an amendment to the law. The local medical profession was, however, strongly opposed. Throughout my service in Hong Kong and elsewhere, I have noticed that the medical fraternity is a past master at restrictive practices. In this case, though, there was something to be said on their side; for whilst the standard of some of the medical colleges in China was high, in others it was low. After much argument, a simple form of examination was devised with the assistance of the appropriate medical authority in the United Kingdom, to separate the sheep from the goats, and the former were allowed to practise. These Chinese-degree doctors could always have taken the ordinary examination in Hong Kong, but for men past their first youth, the task was beyond the capabilities of most of them, especially if their knowledge of English was limited.

In the realm of education, the advent of a communist régime in China raised the question of post-secondary and university education in Hong Kong for those Chinese students whose knowledge of English was insufficient for the University of Hong Kong, where English was the medium of instruction. In pre-communist days these students went to colleges in China. Few now wanted to do so, nor did they wish to go to Formosa. To meet their demand, a number of private post-secondary colleges with Chinese as the medium of instruction set themselves up. They were of varying quality, but one and all were anxious to be allowed to use the magic name of 'university', and to have the right to grant university degrees. The University of Hong Kong was jealous of its right as the sole degree-granting authority. On the other hand, the need for university standard—and recognized as such—education in the Chinese language was real. A danger was that communist funds would be forthcoming to set up a rival university to the University of Hong Kong. Starting off with the report of a local committee under the chairmanship of John Keswick (head of the old established China trading firm of Jardine, Matheson & Co.), the matter was argued backwards and forwards at great length. Final agreement, between the University, the post-secondary colleges and the government had not been reached at the time I left. Since then it has been, with the help of the Colonial Office educational advisers, university authorities in the United Kingdom and co-operation all round.

C.N.A.C., 'Yung Hao', and Other Incidents

At intervals the Chinese government conjured up imaginary grievances against Hong Kong, but in the case of the C.N.A.C. and C.A.T.C. aircraft, I think they had grounds for complaint. The China National Aviation Corporation was the B.O.A.C. of China. The Central Air Transport Corporation was also a Chinese concern. Both corporations had substantial American holdings and some of the top management was American. About seventy planes were involved. When the communists overran China, these aircraft came to Hong Kong. I remember well, strongly recommending to two vice-presidents of Pan American, who were on the board of C.N.A.C., that the aircraft should be taken to Formosa, since most probably the British government would soon be giving *de jure* recognition to the Peking régime, and that then we should have no option but to hand over the planes to the Chinese government should they claim them, as they were likely to do. The two vice-presidents would not agree. They said that in the first place the civil airfields in Formosa could not accommodate them—this was nonsense because that is where they finally went—and secondly that if they did take them there, it would be resented by Peking, and Pan American was hoping to recommence flying into China.

A few months later Britain recognized the new government, which duly asked for the planes. The American interests also requested that we release the planes to them. To this we replied that, since there were two claimants, the issue as to ownership would have to be settled in the courts. Action proceeded accordingly: the best counsel being engaged on both sides. In addition, the Americans sent over lawyers from the States, the most prominent of whom was General Donovan, 'Big Bill Donovan', who had been the war-time director of O.S.S. (Office of Strategic Services), the American equivalent of the British S.O.E. (Secret Operations Executive), whose function was to sabotage the enemy's effort. He came to see me, and thumping the table, metaphorically if not physically, insisted that the planes be handed over to him without further ado, for, he said, if it had not been for the United States Britain would have lost the war. Moreover, he added, if I did not do as he demanded he would make it hot for me with the authorities in London. I remained unmoved: the matter must be settled in the courts. Donovan's bullying attitude neither impressed nor offended me. No doubt he had found it successful on other occasions, so thought he might as well try it in this case. He used the same tactics with the Attorney-General with equal lack of success.

I do not recollect all the details of the court case, or rather cases, since it went from court to court on appeal. Finally it became evident that the law was on the side of the Chinese government, and that they would get the planes. The State Department, which by this time was under pressure from the 'China lobby', now took a hand, and represented to London that on no account should the planes be given to the Chinese. The British government was in a dilemma. On the one hand there was the law, and Britain had always upheld the rule of law. On the other, she did not want to offend Washington.

The British have always been realistic, but if they do a thing of which they have reason to be ashamed, they like to wrap it up in a legal covering. So an Order-in-Council was made, which overrode the law as it stood and in effect made a new law, which would inevitably pass the planes to the Americans. And that is what happened. Who was I, a mere governor of a colonial dependency, to complain, and what good would it have done if I had? None the less I felt unhappy: altogether a sorry business.

An incident similar to the aircraft case arose over the oil tanker *Yung Hao*. This vessel had been sunk off Formosa during the war and subsequently salvaged. It was now Chinese-owned, and was being repaired at the Kowloon Dockyard in Hong Kong. One day—this was during the Korean War—the American Consul-General came to me and said the State Department was anxious that the Chinese Government should not get hold of the ship, as it would assist them in their war effort. I told him I would make enquiries and let him know the result. The result of my enquiries was that the vessel was Chinese government property, that even when repaired it was unlikely to be of any use, and that I doubted if I had legal powers enabling me to hold it. Once again the State Department brought pressure to bear on the British government, and an argumentative correspondence ensued between the Colonial Office and myself. I pointed out that if we tried to requisition the ship, those of our officers who attempted to do so would be resisted by force by the communist crew, that serious trouble would result, and that Peking would retaliate against the Colony. But London was adamant; evidently it was more scared of what the United States might do to Britain, than of what China might do to Hong Kong.

We therefore duly requisitioned the *Yung Hao*. I was not so dubious of the legality of this action as I had been in the case of the airplanes. I was more apprehensive of the retaliatory action that the Chinese might take, especially if there were bloodshed during the operation. Fortunately there was none. Steel-helmeted police in overwhelming force swamped any possibility of resistance. As for retaliation, the worst that happened was that the properties of the Shell Company in China were taken over by the Chinese government: and that was no concern of ours. I heaved a sigh of relief when early one morning I saw the *Yung Hao* being towed out of the harbour on her way to Singapore, where she has, so far as I know, remained ever since, beyond repair. No doubt, one day, Peking will present to London a bill for the vessel. The innocent sufferer, apart from the Shell Company, for this misguided proceeding was the Kowloon

Dock Company, which was owed a considerable sum of money for the repairs that it had carried out.

Our basic objection to taking the action that London made us take was that it contravened our principle of avoiding unnecessary provocation of the Chinese. London's retort would probably be that the governing word is 'necessary', and that for reasons of high policy, which were not within the competence of Hong Kong, the requisitioning was necessary.

The C.N.A.C. issue dragged on for three years, with attempts at sabotaging the planes, C.N.A.C. employees barricading themselves on C.N.A.C. property and having to be ejected by force, and a number of similar unpleasant incidents. The *Yung Hao* matter fortunately was of much shorter duration and had few side effects.

In the two instances I have just given, the Chinese had justification for displeasure and even resentment, but in other incidents between Hong Kong and China, they had not; and at times their conduct was inexcusable. One of the most outrageous acts they committed was the shelling, in September 1953, of a Royal Naval launch, engaged on regular anti-smuggling patrol and in international waters at the time. Without any warning, Chinese shore batteries opened up on her, killing seven and wounding five. Strong protests were lodged by the British government, but no apology was ever made nor compensation paid. Less than a year later, a Cathay Pacific Airways plane when on its way to Hong Kong was shot down with the loss of ten lives. In this instance the Chinese paid compensation.

WAR IN KOREA

When the communists launched their attack on South Korea in 1950, I was on leave in England. I thought it would be only a matter of days before all was over, with the hammer and sickle flying from buildings in Seoul and Pusan. True, an emergency meeting of the Security Council of the United Nations had been called, but what did the U.N. do, other than pass resolutions of which the aggressor took not the slightest notice? And was it not less than a year previously that I had asked General MacArthur in Tokyo why the bulk of the American forces had been withdrawn from South Korea, and he had replied: because South Korea was indefensible? The outlook seemed hopeless. I am sure that throughout the world most people were of the same opinion. The communists certainly must have been of this way of thinking, or they would not have launched their attack. But we had reckoned without President Truman, a man of moral courage and resolution. Also the Russians made a tactical error in boycotting the special meeting of the Security Council at which the Korean situation was discussed. In the absence of the U.S.S.R. the Council called on member states to resist by force of arms the aggression of North Korea. This shows what the United Nations could do for the peace of the world, were it not hamstrung by the malevolent tactics of the communist powers. The burdens and sacrifices, which were indeed heavy, fell mainly on the United States. I am, however, not here concerned with the war itself, or the international scene, but with the repercussions on Hong Kong.

In the early stages of the war, before China had entered it with her 'volunteers', the effect on the Colony was slight. A brigade was sent from Hong Kong; troops who had had months of training in terrain not dissimilar from that of Korea. They were, however, regulars from the United Kingdom, and our pride in them was only vicarious. So far as trade was concerned, Hong Kong gained rather than lost, for although exports to North Korea were immediately banned, the demand for supplies of one kind or another, that always occurs in war-time, led to almost boom conditions, since Hong Kong was nearby and was in a position to deliver.

The intervention of China changed the picture completely. The United States government imposed a total embargo on trade between America and China, and much of that trade passed through Hong Kong. Shortly afterwards the United Nations imposed an embargo on the export to China of strategic and semi-strategic goods. Much of that trade too, used to go through the Colony. At the beginning, Hong Kong and the Portuguese colony of Macau were blacklisted along with China by the U.S. authorities, for fear that these two loopholes, if not stopped up, would render the embargo largely ineffective. It was not, however, the intention of the American authorities to strangle Hong Kong and Macau, although sometimes it almost seemed so! They therefore set about devising measures which, whilst maintaining the embargo, would do as little harm as possible to the two colonies, and would specifically make it possible for them to get from the United States such goods as were needed for their own purposes and not for re-export to China. This meant setting up a system of controls that would prevent imports from finding their way across the border.

One of our difficulties was that Hong Kong had always been a free port. Consequently the anti-smuggling staff was small, and although the land frontier with China is only twenty-two miles long, the Colony has 250 miles of irregular sea-coast, with many coves in which junks could be loaded with contraband goods and, within a matter of hours, slip into Chinese waters with small risk of interception by our revenue patrol boats. Profits in smuggling are always high, and the Chinese are as good smugglers as any. In spite of our efforts, a considerable quantity of embargoed goods was undoubtedly smuggled in those early days from Hong Kong into China, but not as much as our detractors made out. General MacArthur, for instance, once accused us of openly selling petroleum products to China, saying he had seen the returns in an official Hong Kong publication. His statement was reported in the American newspapers. Had the General looked more carefully at the return, he would have noticed that the figure inserted against the entry was *nil;* but the elucidation was not reported in the press. The American officials who came out to inspect our controls were in a difficult position. I am sure they wanted to help, but if a leakage from Hong Kong occurred, they would be in trouble at home. By degrees, as we gained more experience, commissioned more patrol craft and recruited more preventive staff, the system was working reasonably well and to the satisfaction of the U.S. authorities.

Controls were also imposed on the export of goods from Hong Kong to America, to prevent products of Chinese origin from finding their way into the States under a Hong Kong label. To begin with evasions took place here too, but gradually a water-tight system was built up. The amount of red tape involved was considerable. The United Kingdom is bad enough, but it is nothing compared to the United States. The classic instance is that of the dried ducks. These ducks were processed in Hong Kong and then exported to America. Many of them came from eggs laid in China and brought to Hong Kong to hatch. Were the ducks from these eggs communist ducks or true-blue British ducks? The correspondence on the subject was voluminous before a solution was finally reached. Provided that an inspector was present when the egg was hatched, that he forthwith rubber-stamped the duckling's foot, and that on reaching maturity a further marking was put on the duck, then the duck might be slaughtered, dried and admitted into the United States. And yet they say that bureaucrats have no sense of humour! However, we had won our point. We could export our ducks.

So far as the U.N. embargo on the export of strategic and semi-strategic goods to China was concerned, it should be noted that this was not a two-way embargo, as in the case of the United States embargo, and that very few of the goods originated in Hong Kong. They came from other countries. The controls were supposed to be exercised at the country of origin. Our complaint was that the controls were not so exercised. Through laxness or connivance, the goods would be shipped to Hong Kong; the owners taking a chance on their being successful in smuggling them through into China. If they did so, then Hong Kong, and not the country from which they came, would get the blame—all very unfair. It is no exaggeration to say that Hong Kong and Macau suffered more from the embargoes than any other country, not excluding China.

Hong Kong had always lived by entrepôt trade. Small in size and with no raw materials to speak of, but with a magnificent harbour situated right on the doorstep of South China, the Colony's existence depended on the flow of goods through its port between China and the rest of the world. Stop that flow, and Hong Kong would die. A certain amount of trade was carried on in which China was not involved, but this was only marginal. Hong Kong also had some local industry; this, however, accounted for only ten per cent of the Colony's exports. The China trade was Hong Kong's life-blood, and now, with the imposition of the embargoes, this was to be cut down to a mere trickle; at a time, too, when the Colony was burdened with a million refugees. One can hardly be surprised that visiting journalists should send home, gloomy despatches predicting the early demise of the Colony.

But they had not reckoned with the resilience and resourcefulness of the Chinese, who turned their attention to industry. Here we benefited in two ways—the only two ways—from the refugee situation. The first was in capital. Capital from China was just as much a refugee as were human beings. In fact it began coming into Hong Kong almost as soon as the Pacific War ended, being discouraged by the near-chaotic conditions in China and attracted by the stability of Hong Kong. For much the same reason, capital had been flowing into the Colony from other countries in South East Asia. Prior to the embargoes, most of it had gone into commerce. Since that was no longer profitable, it now went into industry. A great deal also went into property. The other advantage we got from the refugees was the industrial know-how, both managerial and technical, of those who had come from Shanghai. Shanghai was considerably more advanced industrially than Hong Kong or Canton. So far as unskilled labour was concerned, an adequate supply was available even without the refugees. The government and the banks did all they could to foster the expansion of industry, for they saw that upon its success depended the survival of the Colony. It was successful. Gradually things picked up until a reasonable degree of prosperity had returned.

That the recovery was due almost entirely to industrial expansion is borne out by the trade figures. Today, the products of Hong Kong's factories account for three-quarters of the Colony's exports, as compared with one-tenth previously; surely a remarkable example of self-help, and rightly described as one of the success stories of the post-war era. This very success has, however, brought its own problems, because textiles have been the largest export and Britain the principal market. This has had an adverse effect on the mills of Lancashire. Already, whilst I was still in Hong Kong, the complaints of Lancashire were becoming shrill, but the matter did not come to a head until after I had left. Basically the trouble is that the Hong Kong operative works harder than his English counterpart, and the Hong Kong mill-owner uses his plant more intensively.

In the early days of the embargoes, inevitably some smuggling of contraband goods through Hong Kong into China took place, and it was understandable that this should be resented and criticized by Americans, whose young men were being killed by communists in Korea. The situation was, however, aggravated by the fact that Hong Kong, apart from being the best listening post available, was ideally situated as a base from which to conduct anti-communist activities, such as propaganda, espionage, and even more dubious operations. It was not unlikely that the Americans would be tempted to use the Colony for these purposes. This was at the time when America was imbued with an almost crusading spirit against Chinese communism. Britain, which was just as much opposed to communism as was America, did not believe in 'brinkmanship' or in unnecessary provocation. She opposed the crossing of the Yalu, which was being strongly pressed on Washington by MacArthur. The British government objected and her objections were sustained by Washington, which greatly angered the General, who vented his spleen on the British Ambassador at Tokyo, an entirely innocent party in the matter. He also abused Hong Kong.

MacArthur was an impressive man to meet, which is what one would expect of the general whom Field-Marshal Alan Brooke had described as the greatest commander in the war. The effect was heightened by MacArthur's theatrical manner. At the same time, I felt that here was an example of absolute power corrupting. He successively enjoyed immense power and prestige as Inspector General of the Philippine Army, Supreme Allied Commander in the Pacific and finally, after victory had been won, as the virtual ruler of Japan. Not once during all those years, did he return to his own country when he would have been confronted by at least one, the

President, greater than he, which would have brought him down to earth. It is hardly surprising that he should have come to regard himself as something above ordinary mortals.

MacArthur was not alone among Americans in believing that the reason for Britain's recognition of Peking in January 1950 was to safeguard her commercial interests in China, and to stave off a possible attack on Hong Kong. The fact that this was not so, but was simply because the new régime was in effective control of China, is beside the point: it was believed. Hong Kong, being a dependency of Britain, had of course to follow the policy of H.M.G., whether she agreed with it or not. Everyone in the Colony, except the dyed-in-the-wool pro-Nationalist Chinese, did agree with it. Furthermore, Hong Kong was in a vulnerable position, and if any provocative acts against China had their origin in Hong Kong, Hong Kong would be the first to suffer from Chinese retaliation. As I have already stated, our policy in Hong Kong was neither to provoke nor to appease. The possibilities of disagreement between the Hong Kong authorities and the American Consulate-General, and other American agencies in the Colony, were therefore not inconsiderable. We could not risk the carrying out in, or from, Hong Kong of many of the things that the Americans wished to do.

That we had comparatively few disagreements, and never anything that could be called friction, was due very largely to the successive counsuls-general; men of high calibre. They had to carry out the instructions of their government, but they appreciated the trickiness of Hong Kong's situation. Only occasionally did we have to protest at what they were doing or had done. One of the difficulties they had to contend with—and this is where we on our side had to be understanding—was that although the Consul-General was nominally in control of all the United States government agencies in the Colony, his actual control was often slight, and he did not always know what they were up to. In the early days some of them allowed enthusiasm to outrun discretion.

The American Consulate-General in Hong Kong had, I believe, a larger American staff than any of their consulates anywhere else in the world. Peking constantly used this as a propaganda theme; claiming that it proved that Hong Kong was a base for American imperialism, and that Britain was a stooge of the United States. The staff certainly was very large, and we made more than one request that it be reduced. We should, however, remember that the consulate-general in Hong Kong was the regional headquarters for many of their agencies in the Far East, such as information. Large staffs were also necessary for translations of newspapers and other publications coming out to China—they had a more extensive translation service than we had—and for screening Chinese who wished to go to the United States. Nor should it be overlooked that where a British consulate would employ one man, the Americans would employ two.

I was not particularly pleased when in 1949, or it may have been 1950, the Consul-General advised American women and children to leave the Colony. It was, of course, entirely a matter for him to decide; but I felt he should have given me prior warning of what he intended to do. We could then have prepared in advance a reassuring announcement, say in the form of a reply to an inspired question at a news conference, to lessen the impact on the public. He did not give us advance notice and we were taken completely by surprise. Fortunately public morale was not shaken, and everyone, especially the Americans, thought it rather stupid.

LECTURING IN AMERICA

Hong Kong had, as I have said, a bad name in the United States, principally on account of the smuggling into China. Combined with this was a general misapprehension of our position and a lack of appreciation of what we stood for and were doing. Quite apart from the fact that no one likes to be abused by his friends, the anti-Hong Kong complex in America prejudiced Washington against us, with the result that we frequently had great difficulty in getting the U.S. authorities to permit the export of raw materials required for our factories. Early in 1954 we received a letter from Sir Robert Scott, who was at that time Minister at the British Embassy in Washington, and subsequently the successor to Malcolm MacDonald as Commissioner General in South East Asia at Singapore. The gist of his letter was that whenever he gave a talk in America he would invariably be questioned about Hong Kong, and that he considered the Governor should come to the States on a lecture tour. I demurred, saying I did not consider it to be the function of a colonial governor to go about lecturing in a foreign country, that he should confine himself to providing the ambassador and his staff with ammunition, and that they should do the speaking. Eventually, however, I agreed to go on my way back from England later in the year.

The tour lasted six weeks and covered a dozen cities, in each of which I gave two or more talks, as well as radio and television interviews and discussions with selected groups. I had never done anything of the kind before. It was a new experience and, although strenuous, was stimulating and enjoyable. Since then I have done more lecturing both in America and England, generally finding American audiences more alert than those in England. They like frank speaking, dislike evasions or stalling, and take in good part critical comments on American shibboleths. My main concern was to create a favourable image of the Colony, and to destroy false impressions. I took as my text such themes as 'Hong Kong, the Berlin of the East', 'Hong Kong, bastion of freedom', etc.

How successful I was, even within the limited range I covered, I do not know. What I do know is that once or twice I got into trouble with the home authorities for some indiscreet—yes, they were indiscreet—remarks I made; but apart from a friendly rebuke from the Colonial Office I was nobly defended when questions were asked in the House of Commons. As soon as the tour had ended, I flew back to Hong Kong from San Francisco. In America one has to be hail-fellow-well-met, certainly on a lecture tour. It was quite a contrast getting back on to my pedestal in Hong Kong as 'His Excellency'.

A question frequently put to me in America was: could the Colony successfully resist a military attack by China? Usually the question was formed in a manner that implied that it could not. The questioner would quote, in support of his view, the capture of the Colony by the Japanese in three weeks. I invariably told him that I disagreed with his implication. The conditions of today were different from what they had been in 1941; the enemy then had command of the sea and air, which was not so now. Hong Kong had more trained troops in 1954 than in 1941 and the garrison was quite adequate to resist a sudden onslaught by such forces as the Chinese had in the border areas. If a build-up—indicating an impending large scale attack—was taking place, we should know about it in time for reinforcements to be sent from Singapore and Malaya, where large British forces were available. Finally, I would add, although no military alliance or defence pact between the United States and Britain covered Hong Kong, I was, in my own mind, confident that the powerful U.S. Seventh Fleet and the large U.S. Air forces in Taiwan (Formosa), Clark Field in the Philippines, and Okinawa—which last is no further from Canton than it is from North Korea—would come to Hong Kong's aid, not to defend a British colony *qua* colony, but because the policy of the United States government was to resist the advance of the Chinese communists in South East Asia. My remarks concerning the adequacy of the forces available in Hong Kong and Malaya were not figments of my imagination, but were based on military appreciations made by the Commander British Forces in Hong Kong and the three Commanders-in-Chief at Singapore.

In reply to questions as to how long Hong Kong would continue as a British Colony, I would say that, in my opinion, 1997 will be the fateful year, for in that year the lease of the New Territories runs out, and I could not conceive of any Chinese government of whatever complexion renewing the lease. Nor could I imagine the rump of the Colony—the island of Hong Kong and the tip of Kowloon peninsula—continuing to exist as a viable entity, with the great bulk of the water supplies coming from the New Territories, and the dividing line between the leased and the ceded parts running right through the new runway at Kai Tak, the airport. Looked at from China's viewpoint, it would seem most unlikely that they would launch an attack during the intervening period, for, even supposing they thought the attack would be successful and that they would capture Hong Kong, all they would get would be an empty shell. Hong Kong has no natural resources, it cannot even feed itself, and the British before they withdrew, would assuredly destroy the power stations, the dockyards and so on. Would not the Chinese be better advised—again in their own interest—to wait until 1997, which was not, after all, very far off, when they might expect the British to return Hong Kong to them, complete and intact? Meanwhile they would continue to earn considerable foreign exchange by supplying the Colony's growing population with half its food supplies and other necessities. Here I would throw in a statistic—which I believe is correct—that more hogs are slaughtered in Hong Kong than in any other city in the world except Chicago, and 90% of those pigs come from China.

As a foot-note to my American lecture tour, I shall relate an amusing incident—though it was not amusing at the time—that occurred in Chicago. We were driving in a taxi from the station to our hotel with our suit-cases in the boot. The driver of a passing car shouted to us that one of the cases had fallen out. We stopped the taxi and retraced our route, enquiring at the shops along the street; but no suit-case had been seen. That particular case, as luck would have it, contained my wife's jewels, furs and evening dresses. We reported the matter to the police who were singularly unco-operative. Later they became more so. Present at dinner with the British Consul-General the same night were Colonel and Mrs McCormick of the *Chicago Tribune*, old friends of ours. They put the Tribune sleuths on to it. Evidently there was little news of interest in Chicago just then; at any rate our loss got into the local newspapers with banner headlines, 'Wife of British lord loses jewels' and such like. We were celebrities, a distinction which, in the circumstances, we did not appreciate.

The following evening we received a telephone call from the police: another taxi-driver had picked up the suitcase which he had just brought in; I must come and identify it; so off I went to the police station. An astonishing sight met my eyes. In the midst of a battery of klieg lights, movie cameras and reporters were Detective Sergeant Swee, Tony, the taxi-driver who had rescued the case, and the suit-case. Quite clearly it would be inadequate to the occasion for me simply to identify the case and take it away. So the three of us, Swee, Tony and myself, posed for photographs—myself in the middle with one arm round each of the other two. Naturally I wanted to give Tony a reward. I therefore asked Swee what would be an appropriate amount, $50, $100, $500? He said $100, so I gave that to Tony who was delighted. A reporter standing nearby overheard me asking Swee. In the next morning's paper my question to Swee appeared thus: "I say, old fellah, what should I give this chappie?"! The locked suit-case had not been opened nor the contents disturbed. How fortunate we were.

V.I.P.'s and Other Visitors

With China going communist, the interest of the outside world in Hong Kong increased considerably, and the number of visitors grew correspondingly: newspaper men, politicians, admirals and generals. They came either because they had some definite business to transact or the better to inform themselves, by personal inspection, about a part of the globe of which they knew little. Many were Americans, especially after the outbreak of the Korean War. Tourists also arrived in increasing numbers once they had got over their scare that Hong Kong was going to be attacked by the Chinese. There was a constant to-ing and fro-ing of British ambassadors in the Far East, members of the Commissioner General's staff at Singapore, and ministers and officials from the Colonial Office and other departments in London. Some stayed at Government House, others were entertained at lunch or dinner, or came and saw me in my office.

Visits from officials of the Colonial Office and other Whitehall departments were generally useful, for it enabled them to see our problems at first hand and by on the spot discussions, each of us was able to make plain his point of view. The Colonial Secretary has a number of advisers on education, health, labour, etc., and we found the visits of these advisers or their deputies, particularly the three mentioned, most helpful, for they were men and women of wide experience. The least useful were the visits of the police advisers. Perhaps one reason was that they had never met a situation quite like that in Hong Kong. On one occasion I received word that the Police Adviser was coming out. Just then we happened to be very much occupied with a delicate situation on our hands, so I requested that the visit be not made, giving my reasons. Despite my plea he came, and with a chip on his shoulder, for my telegram had been shown to him at the Colonial Office: a foolish thing to do. However, we managed to soothe him down, but the visit was a waste of time and a distracting nuisance. The visit of the head of M.I.5, on the other hand, was well worth while.

Such visits should not be too frequent, and the visitors should realize, which not all of them do, that the head of the department with whom they are concerned has his ordinary duties to attend to. They should not expect him to dance attendance on them all day long, and to keep him up half the night as well.

Visits of ministers are on a different footing from those of officials. With few exceptions they put heart into the Colony, especially if the minister is the Colonial Secretary himself; for it shows that the high officers of the Crown are genuinely interested in the colony. Why else should these busy men travel 9,000 miles to come out to Hong Kong? During my time we had two visits of Colonial Secretaries: Mr Oliver Lyttelton (now Viscount Chandos) in 1951, and Mr Lennox-Boyd (now Viscount Boyd) in 1955. Both made favourable impressions; Lennox-Boyd the greater because he seemed to be the more humanly interested in Hong Kong and its people. He reminded me very much of Oliver Stanley, a previous Colonial Secretary who had visited us in Nigeria. At first I thought Lennox-Boyd was too kind and nice to be able to be tough if the occasion demanded it. In this I was wrong. Lennox-Boyd was accompanied by his wife which was an advantage. She spent much of her time visiting underprivileged children, and returned the following year to open Tai Lam Chung reservoir at the special request of Hong Kong, which gives the measure of the popularity of the Lennox-Boyds.

Another type of visit that I consider useful, more from the point of view of the Foreign Office than anything else, is that of the Permanent Under-Secretary of State at the Foreign Office to the Far East and Asia generally. Few, if any, of them have ever served in Asia, and now that Asia has become so important in world affairs, they should at least know what it looks like, and have met on their own ground some of the leading personalities there. One such visit took place during my time; that of Sir William (now Lord) Strang in 1949. He had been appointed Permanent Under-Secretary, but had not yet taken up his post. I imagine this is about the only time that a permanent under-secretary can get away from his desk sufficiently long to enable him to visit the capitals of Asia.

We had two small contretemps with Ministers of State. On the first occasion, the Minister was staying at Government House at the same time as Field Marshal Slim, then C.I.G.S., and we had arranged a reception in their honour. When the Minister heard that Slim was to be ahead of him in the receiving line, he was most incensed. I mentioned the matter to Slim who was much amused and said he did not in the least mind where he was in the line. Protocol-wise, the Minister was correct, but the Field-Marshal was a very distinguished general.

A day or two later, the same Minister and I were travelling to Singapore by plane on which the British Ambassador from Tokyo was also travelling. At Singapore airport, Malcolm MacDonald's A.D.C. met us and, since the press wished to interview the Minister, put the Ambassador and myself in a car to go on ahead to Bukit Serene, the residence of the Commissioner General. This seemed a sensible thing to do, but for his pains the A.D.C. was given a dressing-down by the Minister. 'Did he not know that a Minister was more important than an ambassador or a governor?' etc., etc. Of course he did, so did the Ambassador and I. We fully appreciated that outside our own bailiwicks we had no status, but the A.D.C. was merely trying to get us out of the way and to save us from hanging about.

The other Minister of State was also staying at Government House and on his arrival was given a copy of the programme of his engagements. He said that these were agreeable to him. Amongst them was a small stag dinner-party of specially selected local people who, I thought, the Minister would be interested to meet. Early in the evening of the day in question, I noticed a Government House car at the front entrance and, on enquiring of the driver whom he was waiting for, was told that the Minister had ordered the car to take him to a cinema where communist films were shown. He had not mentioned, either to the A.D.C. or myself, that he was not coming down to dinner. Unfortunately, he had made a mistake in the time or the place of the show and he missed both the film and his dinner.

Nehru was a considerate guest. I had always been an admirer of his, regarding him as one of the outstanding men of the century;

apart from which he is one of the few political leaders of Asia and Africa who harbours no resentment for the imprisonment or slights (real or imaginary) that they received in the days of British colonial rule. His affection for Britain and the British was genuine and sincerely felt. Having thus built him up in my mind's eye, I was prepared to be disillusioned. On the contrary, I found that imagination and fact coincided, and that this oriental product of Harrow and Trinity Cambridge, born with a silver spoon in his mouth, had an unaffected simplicity about him. I could, however, well believe that he was capable of losing his temper.

Of the non-official visitors, a few were old friends such as Mr Thomas Dewey, one time Governor of New York State. We had first met him and his wife, Frances, in Bermuda before the war when he was District Attorney in New York, where he became nationally prominent as a courageous and successful prosecutor of New York's vice-kings and gangsters: a nerve-wracking time for Mrs Dewey, as the lives of herself, her husband and children were in constant danger from gunmen and kidnappers. He was now on a self-briefing tour of the Far East and, after he had returned home, wrote a penetrating book of his impressions. He sent me the draft of the chapter on Hong Kong. I thought it good but with a slant I did not much care for. However, this was a matter of opinion and I was prepared to let it go without comment. Casually, I asked Maurine if she would like to have a look at the draft. She said she would. 'I think this gives a wrong impression of Hong Kong. Do you mind if I write to Tom?', she said. 'Not at all', I replied, 'but I don't know what he will think'. There and then, she wrote a long letter to Tom Dewey, in the light of which he revised the draft, even though the book was already in the hands of the printer.

It was my custom, whenever a foreign ambassador or minister was dining at Government House, to propose the health of the president, or whoever it might be, after I had proposed the health of the Queen. On one such occasion I asked the Pakistan Ambassador to China if he would like me to propose the health of the President of Pakistan. 'No thank you', was his reply, 'the Queen is good enough for me'.

Mr Suhrawady, at the time Prime Minister of Pakistan, was staying with us in October 1956. We had just heard that Israel had launched her attack on Egypt. 'It would be a very good thing', he said, 'if the Israelis were to get to the Canal'. Next morning (Hong Kong is eight hours ahead of Greenwich), we learnt of the attack by Britain and France. 'This is going to make it difficult for you, Prime Minister', I said. 'Yes', was his reply, 'but I am not going to make trouble for Britain'. At dinner the previous evening, one of the guests was David Marshall, the Singapore politician. He was holding forth on the iniquities of colonialism. Mr Suhrawady could stand it no longer; so leaning across the table he said to Marshall, 'Do you know, Mr Marshall, that the people of India (meaning India and Pakistan) were happier under the British than they are today?'

Often when we invited to lunch or dinner a visitor to the Colony, we would send a car to fetch him or her. Such a one was the author, Richard Mason, of the book from which the play and film *The World of Susie Wong* was written. A car was duly sent to his hotel. I heard afterwards that some eyebrows were raised at the Governor's car being outside an hotel that was little more than a brothel, for this was the hotel that figures in the play, and at which Mason was staying to get material for his book. We entertained at different times a number of movie stars. On one occasion, when one of the most celebrated of the glamour actors was coming to lunch, an assistant secretary of mine asked if she could take a look at him. 'Certainly', I said. So she managed to be near the entrance as he arrived. Next day I asked her what she thought of her pin-up boy. 'Not at all glamorous—just like any other middle-aged man', she replied in disillusionment.

Mr Nixon, then Vice-President of the United States, came on a visit to Hong Kong. He liked being unconventional and hail-fellow-well-met. During one of his trips round the island, he stopped to pass the time of day with a hawker. After enquiring through an interpreter, about each other's health and families, Mr Nixon asked the hawker if he knew who he, Mr Nixon, was. 'Oh, yes', replied the hawker, 'You're the Governor of Hong Kong'. Mr Nixon also had a habit of going to places not on his programme. A day or two after the hawker incident, he stopped at a school and gave them his autographed photograph. Unluckily he had picked on a school that had been under surveillance for communist activities, and shortly after his visit, some of the teachers were deported to China. I wonder if they took Mr Nixon's photograph with them.

I had an interesting talk with Mr Nixon and not unnaturally the subject of China came up. He said he considered it important that communications should be kept open between the West and China. I enquired what he meant by communications. 'Mental communications', he replied, and went on to say that one of the best ways of doing this was by trade because, before contracts could be made, Chinese and Americans (or Britons or Frenchmen for that matter) would have to meet each other.

HIKING

Whilst we enjoyed our guests and entertaining, we liked to get away on our own for a few hours at week-ends which we did by indulging in our favourite form of relaxation—a walk in the country. On a Sunday morning before daylight, we would set out from Government House to drive to Saiwan, the site of the military cemetery containing the graves of those killed in the defence of Hong Kong. It is situated on a gently sloping hill going down to the sea and looking across Junk Bay to the hills beyond. The cemetery for the civilian internees who had died or been executed during the Japanese occupation is at Stanley on the south side of the island. Here, too, the setting is fine, facing out to the vast expanse of the Pacific and, above the graves, casuarina trees sighing for the souls of the departed. At Saiwan, we would start our walk as the first rays of the morning sun were beginning to lighten the sky. We walked over the hills to Big Wave Bay, the favourite beach of our earlier Hong Kong existence and still the loveliest of all the bays on the island. At this hour the beach would be deserted so we would swim, having the whole bay to ourselves; then home to a well-earned breakfast.

Later on we had the Governor's motor yacht, *The Lady Maurine*. She was most comfortable and attractively decorated. We would board her and proceed to one of the many islands that make Hong Kong waters so delightful. Going ashore we would walk across the island to the other side, where the yacht would be waiting for us. On board again, we donned bathing suits, and went overboard to swim in the deep clear water; completely relaxed, we would cruise gently along to some quiet cove to anchor for the night. After dinner on deck, we lazed in long chairs, marvelling at the serenity of the heavens or a round moon rising over some island peak. On these occasions we took no one with us, not even an A.D.C., for we needed this quiet time alone away from people. We had, of course, the crew and staff, but they appeared only when required.

Our favourite walk, or climb, was to a Buddhist monastery high on a mountain on the island of Lantau. The start was fairly easy, where ancient slabs of granite, worn smooth by centuries of use, paved the path for some way. After this the going became strenuous, with great stone steps cut out of the mountain side; but this was relieved in places by steep or gentle slopes. From time to time we paused to catch our breath, and to admire the glorious view. We could see *The Lady Maurine* far below, a tiny speck on the water. In a narrow defile in the mountain at a certain season—around Christmas I believe—we would stop to gaze at the beauty of an enormous white poinsettia plant that had thrown itself over a rock cliff, where its mass of flowers fell in a fairy cascade. Near the top, Brook Bernacchi, a friend of ours, had a week-end place, and sometimes we would lunch with him. But usually we went on to the monastery to have a word with the friendly monks. From here it was only a short distance to a high ridge, from either side of which the mountains fell away steeply to the sea. It was grand: the top of the world indeed. From this dizzy perch we would enjoy a picnic lunch before starting the descent.

After someone had thrown a grenade, which happily did not explode, at the Governor of Singapore, the Commissioner of Police requested that I always be accompanied by a bodyguard, in the person of a sub-inspector of Police. I told the Commissioner that if anyone wanted to bump me off, he would do so, bodyguard or no bodyguard. Laughingly I twitted him by saying that what he was really after, was to provide himself with an alibi in case anything happened to me. The Commissioner merely smiled. As a matter of fact my 'sleuths' were useful as interpreters whenever I wished to chat with a countryman, or to ask my way during my walks. They were also good company. They carried a revolver which we would use in contests of marksmanship. On the average I was as good as they. One and all were likable fellows. Two of them, alas, subsequently fell by the wayside. One, nicknamed 'Charlie Chan' by his colleagues, was caught smuggling, for which he was prosecuted. He asked me to give him a testimonial as to character, which I did in respect of his service with me. The other, a graduate of a university in China, had charm and intelligence above the average. I thought that he would go far. In due course he gained promotion to commissioned rank. Four years after I had left Hong Kong, he was deported to China as a communist agent.

INCIDENT OF KASHMIR PRINCESS

The attitude of the Chinese authorities towards Hong Kong was a combination of passive hostility with occasional outbursts of active unfriendliness: rather like a pot on the kitchen stove; the pot being Hong Kong. Normally the pot would be kept at the back of the stove gently simmering, but every now and then the cook—the Chinese government—would bring it to the front of the stove when it would boil fiercely. After a while he would move it to the back of the stove again. We never knew when the pot was going to be brought to the boil. There might be an ostensible pretext, there might not. Very occasionally the Chinese had a legitimate ground for complaint, as in the case of the C.N.A.C. aircraft, but we were always careful not to be provocative. We had no intention, however, of not conducting our own affairs in the way we wanted. In the matter of the aircraft, the *Kashmir Princess*, the Chinese government did have reasons to be disturbed, and a protest or enquiry would have been in order by established international practice, but Peking went beyond the bounds of reason: the opportunity to make propaganda and political capital against British Hong Kong was too good to be missed.

The Bandung Conference was held in April 1955. To it was going a party of journalists from China, travelling through Hong Kong. The British *Chargé d'affaires* in Peking was requested to ask the Hong Kong authorities to ensure that the journalists were not attacked or molested whilst in the Colony. This was the usual form, and the *Chargé* transmitted the message to us. The journalists were duly given police protection from the time they arrived by train until they had boarded their plane, a chartered Air India aircraft, on which a guard was placed. The plane took off, and all seemed well; but a few hours later we received word that it had crashed in Indonesian waters with the 'loss of sixteen lives. It soon became evident that sabotage was the cause, and the only place where that could have been done was Hong Kong. Examination of the wreckage revealed that a time-bomb had been placed in one of the wings. The bomb must have been planted there by someone with access to the aircraft while on the ground at Kai Tak. The organizers of the plot most likely thought that Chou En-lai was on the plane, but he travelled by another route.

The whole of the resources of the C.I.D. and the Special Branch of the Police were put on to find the perpetrators, and a reward of HK$100,000 (the highest ever) was offered. After exhaustive enquiries lasting more than a month, the finger of suspicion pointed to one Chou Chu, an employee at Kai Tak whose job it was to service aircraft. A warrant was issued for his arrest, but he must have realized that the police were hot on his trail, for when they went to get him, they found he had bolted. He had, in fact, smuggled himself on to a C.A.T. plane going to Formosa, only a few hours previously. Undoubtedly fellow conspirators had aided him in his flight. The dastardly plot had, investigation revealed, been planned by a Nationalist intelligence organization. Chou Chu himself was probably not a member of the organization, but was bribed to place the bomb on the plane. The British Consul in Formosa requested that Chou Chu be returned to Hong Kong to stand trial. The request was refused and, since Britain did not recognize the Nationalist government, there was no extradition treaty by which this could be insisted on. The members of the intelligence organization found in Hong Kong were deported.

After the crash had occurred the Chinese authorities passed to us certain information, and told us of suspicions they had. Had they given this to us when they informed us about the visit of the journalists—they already had it then—we would have taken the necessary security measures and there would have been no disaster.

It was during the *Kashmir Princess* affair, when feeling in China was high, that Mr Krishna Menon visited Hong Kong and stayed with me a few days. He had just been in Peking endeavouring to secure the release of some captured American airmen, about whose imprisonment by the communists people in the United States and their government felt strongly. He had been unsuccessful, but thought—at any rate that is my estimate of the matter—that if he could produce something which would please Peking, they might agree to release the airmen, and he, Krishna Menon, would be hailed as the great peace-maker. That something was to be the arrest, trial, conviction and execution of the saboteurs of the *Kashmir Princess*. Also, as an Indian, he wanted to see punished those responsible for the deaths of the Indian crew of the plane. At the time of his visit to Hong Kong, the investigations had reached the stage where suspicions, but only suspicions, rested on certain persons. He urged me to have the police use pressure to extract confessions and so secure the vital information we needed. This seemed too much like the third degree and I declined.

Personally, Maurine and I got on well with Krishna Menon and liked him. He is a very sensitive individual which may explain his somewhat arrogant manner. With him as secretary was a youngish fellow who had been a member of the I.C.S. I dropped into his room one day to have a friendly chat, and asked him why he never came down for meals. 'Mr Krishna Menon won't let me', was his reply. Catering for our distinguished guest posed a problem. He is a vegetarian but would not even eat cheese or eggs and seemed to subsist on innumerable cups of tea, into which he would pour a great deal of milk and half a dozen lumps of sugar.

One day when Krishna Menon and I were discussing the future of British colonies in general, and of Hong Kong in particular, I said I knew that eventually Hong Kong would go back to China, and asked him to write a minute in the pertinent file of the Foreign

Ministry when he got back to Delhi, that on the rendition of the colony becoming a live issue, the Indian government of the day would appeal to the Chinese government to treat kindly the people in Hong Kong. The wealthy could afford to go away, the foreigners would do so in any case, whilst the overseas business firms had had their profits. It was the ordinary, humble folk about whom I was concerned. He promised that he would. I made the same appeal to Mr Nehru when he stayed with me a couple of years later, and received the same assurances. India and China were then still good friends.

PEKING REVISITED

As I was due to leave Hong Kong on retirement at the end of the year, 1955, Maurine and I thought we would like to have one more look at Peking before we left the Far East for, possibly, the last time. In point of fact my term as Governor was, shortly after, extended again (I had three extensions in all) until the end of 1957, but that is by the way. For the Governor of Hong Kong to visit the capital of China in pre-communist days raised no difficult political issue, but for him to visit the capital of communist China was a different matter. The Peking government had the habit of making propaganda use of the visits of non-communist V.I.P.'s. If they were to do so in my case, it might have undesirable repercussions in Hong Kong. And even if they did not make propaganda out of the visit, would the mere fact of my going be interpreted in the Colony as an act of appeasement, and possibly even as the first step towards doing a deal about Hong Kong? On the other hand, there was a desire in Hong Kong to be on friendly terms with the government of China, whatever its complexion, and just at that moment our relations were quieter than they had been for some time; the furore over the *Kashmir Princess* having died down. Might not an informal visit by the Governor be regarded by Peking as a friendly gesture that would redound to the benefit of the Colony?

These various considerations had to be carefully weighed and assessed, and I discussed the matter with my advisers. The consensus of opinion was that the visit could do no harm, and might well do some good. The public reaction, as reflected in the local press when the announcement of the impending visit was made, was mixed. I recollect in particular that Harry Ching, the chief editor of the English language *South China Morning Post*, was opposed, and I always had the highest respect for his opinions, for although his editorials were frequently outspoken they were invariably well-balanced and to the point. He liked to pose as a cynic which he was not, being a warm-hearted person who insisted on calling a spade a spade. Why the owners of the *South China Morning Post* let him go I was never able to understand; the paper has not been the same since his departure. Had the campaign of 'sweetness and light'—about which I write below—been in operation at the time of my projected visit, I should not have gone, for a visit at such a time would almost certainly have been misconstrued in the Colony.

Meanwhile I had to obtain the permission of the Foreign and Colonial Offices for the visit, because they might have objections. After a couple of months they replied, and the *Chargé d'affaires* at Peking, who incidentally favoured the visit, was authorized to seek the agreement of the Chinese authorities. This was forthcoming within two or three days, with the understanding that the visit should be entirely private and that I should pay all my own expenses. They scrupulously honoured their undertaking and made no propaganda out of my presence in China. I was treated with the courtesy due to a distinguished visitor, which, as Governor of Hong Kong, I was.

We boarded the train at Lowu for Canton where a young English speaking interpreter-guide from the appropriate government department met us—a not unusual proceeding in the case of visiting foreigners. As the plane for Peking did not leave until the next morning, we had to spend the night at the Oi Kwan hotel. We decided that instead of dining at the hotel restaurant, we would go out to one nearby, which we did. We had heard much about the absence of tipping in the new China, I therefore did not attempt to do so when I came to pay the bill. But I had left over a half-finished bottle of wine. The waiters made a great show of wrapping it up for me to take away. I said it would be troublesome to take with me, would they be kind enough to relieve me of it? They would be only too glad to do so, they said, their faces wreathed in smiles. They had not broken the law against accepting a tip; they had merely accommodated a stranger, and there was no law against that.

At Peking we stayed at the British Embassy with our friends the *Chargé d'affaires*, Con O'Neill, and his wife who had often been our guests in Hong Kong. O'Neill had a very penetrating and critical mind and his despatches were models of lucidity. We had a delightful time and in particular enjoyed a day's outing to the Great Wall and the Ming Tombs. I do not propose to go into a long description of what we saw in China, or whether we thought the people looked happy or harassed. Others have done this frequently enough. Moreover it is eight years now since our visit. Our general impression, though, was of a people throwing out their chests and proud of their country's destiny. As regards the buildings in Peking, the palaces and temples, never had I seen them so well cared for; for instance, when I first saw the Lama Temple in 1915, it was in a dilapidated condition. When we had last been in Peking in 1948, just before the communists came in, the whole temple was in ruins. Now in 1955, it had been completely restored. The same was true of other places we visited in Peking, but the shopkeepers we had previously known, although greeting us warmly, were not the same. They had lost their old air of laughing exuberance; prices were fixed and bargaining was forbidden by law. Considerably cleaner and more orderly than in the past, something of Peking's gaiety had gone. But it had lost the forlorn look of 1948 and was once more the centre of a great empire and still, in my opinion, one of the seven wonders of the world.

My visit being a private one, the only official thing I had to do was to pay a courtesy call on the Vice-Minister for Foreign Affairs, Mr Chang Han-fu, which I did in company with O'Neill. Halfway through the call, whilst we were discussing the weather and other innocuous subjects, Mr Chang said that the Premier, Mr Chou En-lai, would like to see me with O'Neill on such and such a day, at such and such a time, and that he hoped that the ladies, Mrs O'Neill and my wife, would join the party for luncheon. I knew O'Neill had arranged a lunch party that day in our honour, and had invited a number of the diplomatic corps. I could almost hear him thinking what to say in reply to the Vice-Minister. There was of course only one thing to do, and that was to accept, which he did. In due course we went to Chou En-lai's residence. Altogether we had about three hours with him. Taking part in the discussions were Chou En-lai, Chang Han-fu, an interpreter, O'Neill and myself. Chou En-lai greatly impressed me, as he does most people who meet him. Handsome and charming, he can, however, change from charm to toughness in a moment. Before I had ever met either him or Nehru, I asked Mr Dag Hammarskjöld, who was passing through Hong Kong at the time, how he compared the two men. Who was the greater? Hammarskjöld replied that, in his opinion, Chou En-lai was infinitely the greater. My own estimate, based only on three hours with Chou En-lai and a few days with Nehru, was that whilst Chou En-lai was more skilled in *realpolitik*, from the moral point of view Nehru was superior.

My object during the discussions was to keep the talk away from Hong Kong matters, for unpleasantnesses were almost certain to arise. In this I succeeded fairly well. I asked about the expanding population of China. Chou En-lai thought I was implying that because of the pressure of population, China would embark on campaigns of aggression in order to acquire more territory. That was not at the back of my mind when I put the question. I merely sought information. Being reassured, he expounded on the development of Sinkiang and other comparatively empty parts of China. I enquired about the government's policy towards birth control. He said the policy was to encourage it, but not to enforce it. A few months later the policy became one of enforcement, but this did not last long, and, for reasons which have never been adequately explained, the government reversed its policy. I think that sooner or later enforcement will once more become the order of the day. The subject of Taiwan (Formosa) came up. Somewhat to my surprise—considering all the propaganda there had been, and still was, on re-uniting this province to the motherland, and ousting the 'Chiang Kai-shek bandits and the American imperialists'—Chou En-lai was remarkably calm, saying that time was on their side, and that the island would fall into their lap; citing the recent case of the defection of a Nationalist general to the communists. He had much to say on Britain's attitude towards China and her failure to vote for the replacement at the U.N. of Taiwan by Peking. This was not my concern, whatever my views might have been, so I happily left O'Neill to counter the great man's complaints.

I had hoped that the *Kashmir Princess* would not come up, but it did, and although he, Chou, spoke strongly, he did not speak violently, and seemed to accept my explanation of the Hong Kong case. He became somewhat heated on the subject of deportations of communist trouble-makers from Hong Kong. Here I had to dig my toes in, to refuse to budge from our inherent right to deport undesirable aliens, and to say that we were not going to abandon that policy, which applied just as much to pro-Nationalists as it did to pro-communists, mentioning the instance of the *Kashmir Princess* deportations.

Luncheon was a purely social affair, or so I had thought it was going to be. Mrs Chou En-lai, who does not enjoy good health, did not join us. In addition to the wives of O'Neill and myself, Mrs Chang Han-fu, who speaks English fluently, was also of the party. By way of conversation, I asked her how long she had been a member of the Chinese Communist Party. She did not answer my question—I have noticed that communists have a habit of not answering awkward questions, or ones that seem to them awkward. Instead, she countered by asking me how long I had been a member of the Conservative

Party. She obviously did not believe me when I told her that I had never been a member. I suppose it is impossible for a communist to understand the difference between the Communist Party and the political parties of a democratic country.

The lunch was proceeding happily when suddenly Chou En-lai turned to me, and asked if I had heard that the Portuguese in Macau were shortly going to celebrate the four hundredth anniversary of the founding of the Colony. Thinking that my host was still in a light-hearted mood, I replied that I had, that so far as I was concerned it would be a nuisance, as I should have to attend, dressed up in my plumes and feathers. As a matter of fact what I had previously heard about the proposed celebrations had caused me some uneasiness. A minister was coming out from Lisbon, and he was almost sure to talk about the 'sacred soil of Portugal', which would anger Peking. Chou En-lai now adopted a stern mien and said that the Chinese government and the Chinese people did not like these celebrations, nor would the Chinese in Macau and Hong Kong. The last was a thinly veiled threat that the communists would stir up trouble, and probably serious trouble, in the two colonies. I suggested that perhaps it would be all right if the celebrations were limited to one day. No, the whole thing must be called off. I persisted for a little, but saw I could get nowhere, so the subject was dropped, but gloom prevailed for the rest of the meal.

After lunch the men adjourned for further talks and I returned to the charge, being reluctant to leave matters in such an unsatisfactory state. This time Chou En-lai was more conciliatory, and agreed that one day's innocuous celebrations would be unobjectionable. The gist of this was telegraphed that afternoon by O'Neill to the Foreign Office which doubtless passed it on to Lisbon. And when I got back to Hong Kong I told the Governor of Macau of what had passed between Chou En-lai and myself. Very sensibly the Portuguese authorities cancelled the entire programme, including a special issue of postage stamps that had already been prepared; and they pulled down a half completed commemorative monument and no minister came out from Portugal. Apparently the Governor had been opposed to the celebrations all along, but had been overruled by his home government.

The reason given out for the cancellation was that, in the difficult economic times through which Macau was passing, it was wrong to spend a lot of money on celebrations. Considering how far the arrangements had gone, this was pretty thin, and deceived no one. Everyone knew that Chinese pressure was at the back of it. One would have expected this demonstration of the power of Peking in the affairs of Macau to have shaken morale in both Macau and Hong Kong, but it did not.

I always thought that the Macau government, or at any rate some of the personnel, had better liaison or side-door contacts with the Chinese authorities than we had, despite the fact that Portugal did not recognize Peking and that a diplomatic representative of the Nationalist government resided in Macau. In Hong Kong we virtually had none. I think the reason for this was that the Anglo-Saxon is more rigid and aloof and less subtle than is the Latin. The relationship between Macau and Hong Kong was always friendly and cordial; for one thing we were both in much the same boat, and the memory, too, of the assistance during the war that the people of Macau—at no little risk and sacrifice to themselves—had given to those who escaped from Hong Kong to Macau, was ever present in our minds. We had one little contretemps with Macau during my time. It had something to do with rice—I have forgotten the details and even the year; but it was soon straightened out.

One of the places we visited in Peking was Tsinghua University which originally had been an American sponsored institution. The principal was away, so his deputy met us. He was a graduate of Hong Kong University and as the Governor is Chancellor of Hong Kong University, he greeted me like a long lost brother, but we were circumspect in our talk. One of the professors whom we met was the dean of the faculty of architecture. I asked him if, in view of all the new building going on in Peking and elsewhere, they had achieved a synthesis between the beauty of the old Chinese buildings, with their graceful curved roofs, and modern utility buildings. They had not, he said, but hoped in time to do so. The fact is that the old style buildings are costly and wasteful of space, whilst the new ones lack character. Let us forget communism for the moment, and hope that the new China will evolve a style that at least approaches the beauty of the old.

On our return to Hong Kong, the press immediately besieged me and asked if I had met any members of the Chinese government—my visit to Chou En-lai had not been mentioned either by the press or radio in China. On being told that I had met Chou En-lai, the reporters fairly buzzed with questions. Sticking to the truth, but not mentioning Macau, I did my best to satisfy them. Subsequently, at an off-the-record meeting with representatives of the foreign news agencies, I gave a résumé of the Macau discussion with Chou En-lai. These meetings were strictly confidential, and anything I said was not for quotation or even publication, unless specifically authorized. They were to give the representatives the background to whatever was happening, or was about to happen in Hong Kong; all of which was fully understood, and hitherto no breach of confidence had occurred. On this occasion one did. Fortunately, no great harm resulted. I made no complaint to the head office of the agency, but they dismissed the man and were probably right to do so. The other representatives were most incensed that one of their colleagues should have let me down. It never happened again. The representatives of the foreign news agencies in Hong Kong were an intelligent and likable lot of fellows.

Just before my final departure from Hong Kong I received an invitation, through an intermediary, from Chiang Kai-shek to visit Formosa. He even offered to send his own plane for me. I declined with thanks. What a fuss there would have been, had I gone.

'SWEETNESS AND LIGHT'

Not long after my return from Peking, the Chinese government launched their campaign of 'sweetness and light'. This was the time of the Bandung spirit with its *panchila* (the five principles of peaceful coexistence), and when Chou En-lai had presented the face of sweet reasonableness to the delegates at that conference. Hitherto the attitude of the Chinese authorities towards Hong Kong had been one of hostility, with no effort to win over the people or to present China in an especially favourable light. This was now changed. They remained stiff in their attitude to the government, and the guards at the frontier continued to be as stand-offish as ever, but towards the people of Hong Kong a vigorous drive was made to create in their minds a picture of a happy land in which great progress had been made, a picture of a loving and lovable Mother China. Prominent citizens were invited to visit China with all expenses paid. Quite a few went, but the Chinese are not easily fooled. They were impressed with some of the material achievements, but generally they did not like what they saw. The bait was also held out to Europeans, and one university professor made a fool of himself (to the embarrassment of the Vice-Chancellor) by his extravagant praise of things in China. He received a counterblast from another professor who had also made a visit, but who was a more astute observer. The latter came off best in the battle of words that followed.

To counteract an insidious campaign of this nature was not easy. It seemed unreasonable to refuse permission for displays of art or exhibitions from China to be held in the Colony. But we knew what the aim was, to build up the image of Red China and to pull ours down. The displays and exhibitions would no doubt have been excellent, but they would have been used as a weapon of pro-communist and anti-British propaganda. In England little or no risk on this score would arise, but Hong Kong is in a vulnerable position. We rejected the applications on the ground—which was genuine—that they would probably lead to breaches of the peace, for the pro-Nationalist, or at any rate anti-communist, elements in the Colony were numerous, and they would almost certainly have tried to attack the exhibitors. We made one exception in the case of a troupe of Chinese dancers, who had recently returned to China after a consider-able success in London. We imposed restrictions, though, on the movements of the performers outside the theatre—in their own interest—and we forbade any items on the stage that might have a propaganda intent—something that would hardly arise in England. I received an invitation to attend, but declined. I was told that the Queen had attended in London, and that the performers had been presented to her. I replied that Hong Kong was not London, nor was I the Queen of England. Had I gone, political capital would have been made out of it to the detriment of the Colony. I regretted not being able to go, for I believe the performance was very good.

From Peking's point of view I do not think that the campaign was much of a success, so far as the populace of Hong Kong was concerned. Perhaps it might have been, if we had not taken measures to counter it. I do not know. At any rate the campaign gradually died out, and in a few years, with the rape of Tibet, which greatly shocked Asian opinion, Peking had evidently decided that public opinion could be ignored, and that fear was a more potent force than love.

During the phase of 'sweetness and light', a strong local demand arose for the frontier to be reopened, it being claimed that conditions in South China were now normal, and that if the frontier were opened, no more people would come into Hong Kong than would go out. This we doubted, but not much harm would be done by putting it to the test, for we could always close it again. Arrangements were accordingly made to admit freely Chinese from China, provided they possessed a re-entry permit back into China from the authorities there. At the end of seven months, from February to September 1956, 60,000 of the entrants had not gone back but had melted into the rest of the population. We therefore closed the frontier again; the Chinese authorities having declined to control entry into Hong Kong from their side. Negotiations were also held between the Hong Kong and

Chinese railway administrations, with the intention of recommencing
the through running of passenger trains. Agreement was reached on
the technical details, but broke down on the question of each side
having the right to return to the other, within a period of seven days,
persons whom they considered to be undesirable. This the Chinese
would not accept.

A Nationalist Air Force Plane Lands

Coinciding with the campaign of 'sweetness and light', but in
no way connected with it, was the incident of the Nationalist Air
Force plane that, without warning, landed at Kai Tak one day in
January 1956. It had been engaged on photographic reconnaisance
along the China coast, been chased by communist planes and, in order
to escape its pursuers, had come down in Hong Kong. We put the
plane under guard and the pilot under detention. The question now
was what to do with the plane and pilot. Apparently the Chinese
authorities were not yet aware that the plane had landed at Kai Tak,
but they would very soon learn of it; for its arrival had been seen,
and this would quickly be reported to Canton by communist agents
in Hong Kong. We decided the best thing to do would be to let the
pilot fly the plane away to Formosa at first light the next morning;
which is what the pilot wanted to do. It was only a short distance,
and the chance of it being intercepted by communist aircraft was small.

Here I made a mistake. What I should have done was to have
sent the plane off, and then reported the incident to London. London
would have been glad to have been relieved of the responsibility.
Instead I telegraphed to the Colonial Office, telling them what
I proposed to do. In the normal course of events, the telegram would
not have been dealt with until after the plane had gone. But luck was
against me. In the middle of the night I received a telegram, telling
me not to let the plane go pending further instructions, as the matter
was being referred to ministers. I knew what that meant; an interminable delay. All hope of flying the plane to Formosa without a
storm of protest from Peking was gone. Moreover, the Chinese air
force would be on the alert to shoot it down the moment it was outside
Hong Kong jurisdiction. Meanwhile, Peking delivered a series of
violently worded protests through the British *Chargé d'affaires*,
demanding the surrender of the plane and the pilot, and alleging that
it had been engaged in attacks on the Chinese mainland. These
allegations were false, because the plane was unarmed. It was pointed
out to the Chinese government that according to established inter-

national practice, the aircraft and pilot were permitted to leave. This made no impression on Peking whatever.

After a lapse of several weeks, we were told we could release the plane. By now the morale of the pilot, who had been detained at the airport, was so low that, when informed that he could go, was physically sick and refused. I do not blame him. He said, with some justification, that the aircraft which had been out in the open all this time was not flight-worthy. This meant further complications. How to get the plane and pilot safely away? Eventually, we unobtrusively put the pilot on to a coastal steamer going to a port in Formosa. I do not recollect the name of the ship, but I remember that she sailed at five o'clock one Saturday afternoon, for I saw her leave. Metaphorically speaking, I waved good-bye to the pilot. Shortly after, and without further incident, a Nationalist merchant vessel came and collected the plane. All very humdrum no doubt, but worrying at the time for those on the spot.

THE RIOTS OF OCTOBER 1956

More serious than the riot of March 1952 were the riots of October 1956, when more than sixty persons were killed. These riots were not communist inspired. October First is the national day of the communist régime in China, and October Tenth, the day of the Nationalists. On these two days the Colony is plastered with flags; communist sympathizers flying the five-star flag of communist China; Nationalist sympathizers flying the Nationalist flag, the latter greatly outnumbering the former, especially in the squatter and resettlement estates, since most of the people living there are refugees from Red China. The police were always on the alert during these days to prevent the two sets of protagonists from getting at each other's throats. Hitherto, no serious clashes had occurred.

The spark that started the blaze in October 1956 was the removal of a Nationalist flag from the verandah of a resettlement block on the orders of a government officer. In the light of subsequent events his action was possibly misguided, but tension was already so high and tempers so violent, that there would probably have been an explosion in any case. At any rate, rioting broke out and spread like wildfire; gangsters and hooligans joining in. Kowloon was the storm centre, in and around the resettlement estates principally. One of the worst areas, though, was at the New Territories town of Tsuen Wan which contained several factories, with the labour unions divided into pro-Nationalist and pro-communist groups, the former being much stronger numerically. The police lost control here before the arrival of troops who had been called out. For a time the mob raged unrestrained, and many communist-union workers were savagely beaten up and some killed before order was restored. No rioting occurred on Hong Kong island.

I was already on my way back from leave when the trouble started, and by the time I arrived the worst was over. As was to be expected Peking reacted strongly and, protesting at the alleged failure of the Hong Kong authorities to protect innocent Chinese citizens, threatened to send troops into the Colony to do so. The communist press also waged a campaign against the amounts of compensation paid to pro-communist victims. In point of fact compensation was paid, after careful assessment by a tribunal appointed for the purpose, to all non-rioters who had suffered in life, limb or property, without regard to the political sympathies of the claimants.

The October riots brought to a head the question of deportation. I have already mentioned that in pre-communist days Chinese aliens of certain categories of convicted criminals and other undesirables were regularly deported, and that this practice was accepted by the Chinese authorities. When the communists came into power, it became more and more difficult to deport to China, for the deportees were refused admission. The only exception made by the Chinese authorities was in the case of political deportees, those being deported for subversive activities, who were always accepted. The result was that we were saddled with thousands of the worst criminal elements.

This was particularly serious in the case of triad or secret society members, since it was well-nigh impossible to secure a conviction against them in the courts, because their victims, whilst willing to complain to the police, were intimidated from testifying in court. The triads took full advantage of the situation. The position had been getting worse and the riots were the last straw. Legislation was therefore passed giving Executive Council power to order the detention of any person against whom a deportation order had been made and who could not be deported. A special detention centre was set up on the island of Lantau. The setting was lovely and the buildings did not in the least look like a prison. Every six months the cases were reviewed by a tribunal, consisting of qualified lawyers and justices of the peace. Their recommendations, as to whether or not the detention of the persons concerned should be continued, were submitted to Executive Council, whose decision was final. The system proved effective in curbing the power of the triads and was welcomed by the public.

THE NAVAL DOCKYARD CLOSES

The Royal Naval Dockyard had been in existence almost as long as had the Colony. It was the symbol of Britain's presence in Hong Kong and, until the construction of the naval base at Singapore in the thirties, was the Navy's only base of any size in the Far East. Since then it had taken second place, and soon after the end of the Pacific War the Commander-in-Chief had moved his headquarters from Hong Kong to Singapore. Although the Hong Kong yard was efficient, to have two dockyards within the same area was clearly uneconomic. Moreover, the Singapore yard was both larger and more modern. Consequently the Treasury in London was constantly pressing for the closure of the Hong Kong yard. Just as constantly, I resisted the pressure with all my might and main. In this I had the firm support of successive commanders-in-chief and the Admiralty. The reasons for my resistance were twofold. In the first place, the dockyard was a large employer of labour, and if it were closed the unemployment situation would be aggravated, at a time too, when it was already serious because of the influx of refugees. In the second place—and this was a more fundamental objection—the hauling down of the white ensign would be taken by the people of the Colony as a sign that Britain was going to withdraw altogether from Hong Kong. That this was not so, but was solely for financial reasons, was beside the point. It just would not have been believed, and confidence would have been severely shaken.

When, however, in 1957 the British government published a White Paper which stated that a number of other dockyards, including some in the United Kingdom, were going to be closed down, my objection to the closure fell to the ground, for it would now be seen that the closure of the Hong Kong yard was part of an overall policy, and had nothing to do with the question of Britain remaining in the Colony. Furthermore, the Navy was not going to withdraw completely. Certain shore establishments and a basin for small craft would continue to be maintained. The fact, too, that the Colony would on the closure of the yard get back a large piece of valuable land, whose tenure by the Navy was hindering the development of the centre of Victoria, sweetened the pill. But the Treasury demanded and got a large pound of flesh in the way of payment from Hong Kong for the land that the Navy gave up.

The difficulty of the dockyard employees, some few thousand, who would lose their jobs remained. The Commodore and the Commissioner of Labour collaborated closely on this problem, and a special committee to deal with it was set up. Chambers of commerce and similar bodies urged their members to offer employment to the displaced workers. The response was good. Not ungenerous, but also in the circumstances not over-generous, severance pay was given by the Admiralty. We urged them to be more liberal, but they refused, on the ground that it would create an awkward precedent elsewhere, e.g. Malta. That a precedent would be created is the excuse that governments often advance for refusing to do what they know they ought to do. The dismissal of so many workers was too good an opportunity for the communists to miss, and they made the most of it. But the committee did its work so effectively that the Dockyard workers were, on the whole, well enough content not to let themselves be greatly stirred by the agitators. A number, too, found employment in China which was in need of skilled men. We had far less trouble than we had feared. Another hurdle had been surmounted.

In September 1957, the Minister of Defence, Mr Duncan Sandys, visited the Colony. On the last visit of a Minister of Defence in 1949, the Minister, Mr Alexander, had come to see what reinforcements were needed in Hong Kong. Such was not the object of Mr Sandys' visit. His object was to see what reductions could be made, for at that time the British government was seeking to reduce its commitments. This was unpalatable both to the service chiefs and myself. I remember saying to Mr Sandys, 'Very well, if you reduce the size of the garrison, we'll reduce the size of our military contribution'. To which he replied that he would not be blackmailed. The issue was not settled until after I had left. Hong Kong lost on both counts; the garrison was reduced, and the military contribution was increased.

CHAPTER EIGHT

RETROSPECT

APART from the difficulty over the closure of the Naval Dockyard, 1957 was a relatively quiet year. It was also my last in Hong Kong: a good point, therefore, from which to look back in retrospect at the ten years since I had arrived as Governor; at what had been achieved, at what had not been achieved, and at the change in our relationship with China. So far as purely internal affairs were concerned, the rehabilitation had been completed, and there had been noticeable progress beyond. We had more schools and more hospitals than ever before. Nearly finished was a brand new airport, capable of taking the world's largest aircraft; good progress was being made in slum clearance; a ten-million pound reservoir had been put into service; another, even more costly, was under construction. All this could be termed normal progress for a growing and progressive city such as Hong Kong. The harbour was full of ships and the economy in a flourishing state. The Colony had developed a social-welfare consciousness as never before; the kaifongs had become firmly established; constitutional reform had been put into cold storage, not because the Hong Kong administration or the Colonial Office were reactionary, but because of the realization of the grave risks that such reform would entail in Hong Kong's unique situation.

New problems unforeseen in 1947 had also arisen. These stemmed from the communist victory in China. Of basic importance was the fact that a strong government had come into power, rather than that it was a communist one. The new régime was consistently unfriendly, but by 1957 we had become used to this as part of our normal existence; just as we accepted as a fact of life that every so often the Chinese government would make difficulties for us, creating incidents out of nothing, if they felt so inclined. The most conspicuous problem arising out of the communist victory was the influx of refugees. At first we had groped our way, but eventually evolved a new policy which was proving successful. The problem is likely to continue for many years, but the method of dealing with it had become routine, albeit a routine that is a heavy drain on the Colony's resources.

Then, for a time it looked as though the United States and the United Nations embargoes on trade with China would result in the economic ruin of the Colony. But they did not. Hong Kong turned to industry, which became a much more important part of the Colony's economic life than the traditional entrepôt trade. This new development brought its own problems which continue. We had had disagreements with the United States administration over their China-trade embargoes, but these had been smoothed out.

I had observed a gradual easing of the rigidity of American policy. Even before the death of Foster Dulles, brinkmanship and threats of massive retaliation had ceased to be the order of the day. 'The wraps had been put back on Chiang.' Neutralism was no longer immoral. This mellowing of American policy in the Far East was interesting to watch. It also affected—for the better—Hong Kong. The fact that it narrowed the gap between the policies of Britain and the United States was also a matter of relief to us in Hong Kong.

CHINA AND HER NEIGHBOURS

Here I shall permit myself to digress for a moment, and to speculate as to the probable, or at any rate the possible, development of the power situation in the Far East. It seems to me natural that China, whether communist or not, but a strong China, is bound to become the predominant power in that part of the world, particularly in relation to her weak neighbours and near neighbours. Chiang Kai-shek had the same ideas as the present rulers: to restore the ancient power and grandeur of China, and to reassert her suzerainty over former vassal states. Was it not the Nationalist government that in 1961 opposed the admission of Outer Mongolia to the United Nations, on the ground that it was part of China? Chiang Kai-shek would have subjugated Tibet, just as Mao Tse-tung has done; the only difference being that the Nationalists did not have the strength to carry out their aims. Also is it not understandable that China should resent the presence of American forces on an island, Taiwan (Formosa), which she regards as part of her territory? Americans, with their natural sensitivity over Cuba should appreciate this point of view; and Cuba was never a part of the United States as Taiwan was of China. The one thing on which Chiang Kai-shek and Mao Tse-tung agree is that mainland China and Taiwan are one. What a Moscow-controlled Cuba would be to Washington, so a Washington-controlled Taiwan would be to China. Would America like to have Russian or Chinese troops stationed in neighbouring Mexico? If the answer to these questions is *no*, as clearly it is, is it unreasonable for China to object to the presence of foreign soldiers in neighbouring

Laos? It may be said that the West has no aggressive intentions against China. We know that to be so, but do the Chinese? Their ignorance and lack of understanding of the outside world is abysmal.

If the Monroe Doctrine is all right for the Americas, why should it be wrong to have a similar doctrine for Asia? None has been proposed, but Asians want to settle their affairs themselves. The alliance between the Nationalists of Formosa and the United States is a marriage of convenience and not a love match. The same is true of the arrangements between the United States government and those of Thailand and South Vietnam. An intriguing speculation is what the reaction of the Western powers would have been if Nationalist China, and not communist China, had been exerting pressure on Laos and the other countries of South East Asia. The threat to the independence of these countries would have been the same, but would the Western powers have intervened as they are now doing?

We do not know if China will attempt to swallow up her weaker neighbours, or if she will be content to let them remain as independent, but non-communist neutral states with no foreign forces stationed on them. Finland is in just that position *vis-à-vis* Russia. She would never venture to do anything that would be displeasing to Moscow. It is not unlikely that this will become the relationship between China and the countries of South East Asia. Cambodia sees it that way, and even Malaysia, which is staunchly anti-communist, will not join the South East Asia Treaty Organization (SEATO), lest it be regarded by China as too hostile an act. Thailand is at present in the pro-Western camp, but how long will she remain there? May she not come to the same conclusion as Cambodia, that she would be safer as a non-communist neutralist, than as an anti-communist, i.e. anti-Chinese, member of SEATO? South Vietnam follows the same line as Thailand in being pro-Western, but the position here is complicated by the fact that the country is divided into two at the 17th parallel; North Vietnam being communist and South Vietnam anti-communist.

Neutralism is the best we can hope for; but we should remember that China is closer to South East Asia than is any Western power. China's influence will therefore inevitably be the greater for that reason alone. China has always been feared by her weaker neighbours. It is the same today as it was yesterday. Communism, as such, is secondary.

Of more immediate concern to Hong Kong is the future of Formosa. The Generalissimo has no natural successor and no one in Formosa has his prestige. What will happen when he disappears from the scene? Peking anticipates that the island will fall into its lap like a ripe plum, and that the military and civil leaders will defect. If they do, or if a large number do, how will America react? Will she intervene militarily? I doubt it. The commitment of the American people—as distinct from the government—to Chiang Kai-shek is largely emotional. He was a gallant war-time ally who should not be let down. From the military aspect, can it be said that Formosa is essential to the defence of the United States? In 1949, the U.S. administration did not consider it so, according to a White Paper issued by the State Department in August of that year. The outbreak of the Korean War in 1950 altered this view, for the communist attack in Korea posed a threat from the north to an American interest, Japan. If Formosa were taken by the communists, a simultaneous threat would appear from the south, and this was regarded as un-acceptable. Hence the military necessity of denying Formosa to the communists. But now that the threat from the north (Korea) has ceased to exist, or at any rate is reduced to what it was before the White Paper, the military argument for holding on to Formosa would seem to fall to the ground. In any event is it not likely that, on the disappearance of Chiang Kai-shek, there would be an 'agonizing re-appraisal' in Washington and that whilst this was going on the Chinese themselves would solve the problem? The re-absorption of Formosa into mainland China and the liquidation of the Nationalist régime would be a bitter pill for the United States, but in the long run would help to ease tension, because a major source of conflict between the two countries would have been removed.

If Formosa is absorbed into the Chinese empire, the American air-base at present there will no longer be available for the defence of Hong Kong, but those at Okinawa and Clark Field will still be, so will the U.S. Seventh Fleet. Of greater importance to Hong Kong, though, than the fate of Formosa, is the overall relationship between China and the United States.

FAREWELL

All this, however, is looking into the future. My story in these last chapters is concerned with the years 1947 to 1957, and I have now come to the end of it. A story is supposed to have a hero. In my story of Hong Kong I have no one hero, but a multitude, Chinese and non-Chinese: the social worker, the resourceful businessman, the farmer and the fisherman, the government official, the British serviceman, the doctor, the teacher, the patient refugee. There were villains too: the drug trafficker, the gangster, the smuggler. Hong Kong, generally speaking, was a happy place, despite the desperate poverty of many. Hong Kong was not a paradise on earth, but what place is? Certainly not communist China, whence a million people had abandoned their homes to seek sanctuary in British Hong Kong. By 1957 the Colony was on an even keel. Long may it remain so. No doubt as in the past, storms will assail it from time to time, and the boat will rock. But that is what life is in this tempestuous world of ours.

The time had come for us to say good-bye. Our innumerable friends of all walks of life gave us farewells that were both heart-warming and heart-rending. On 31st December 1957 we sailed out of Hong Kong harbour for the last time. Were we going home or were we leaving home?

INDEX